HOW TO
STOP
A STALKER

"At last, a book about a tough topic that will make a difference . . . because the author knows whence he speaks; meaning to say, he takes the subject seriously and is more experienced than anyone I know . . . which of course accounts for his success with countless cases! *How to Stop a Stalker* therefore works as a self-help handbook and/or as a classroom text. And yet it's an easy read, given Detective Proctor's informal approach. . . . It's as though he were talking to you!

"The author's use of actual case histories to illustrate stalking's causes and cures further serves to make the book both interesting and informative. The reader can quickly recognize Mike Proctor's expertise as one of the pioneers in this field, and why stalking is sometimes not taken seriously by one's friends, family, and/or the officials . . . unfortunately. His success stories, however, can serve to give a victim hope.

"In sum, I recommend without reservation. . . . Definitely a thumbs up!"

W. Garrett Capune, Ph.D.
Director of Criminal Justice for University of Southern California,
and Professor and Coordinator for the Department of Criminal Justice,
California State University at Fullerton

"[Proctor] demonstrates a vast knowledge of his subject. He presents his upfront and personal information in an open forum in a very concise and professional manner."

David Coupland
National Security Operations Branch,
Royal Canadian Mounted Police

"This book is a great guide for stalking victims to learn how to protect themselves and build confidence, while assisting investigators with collection of evidence for prosecution."

Earl Carpenter
Director of Public Safety,
Pepperdine University

HOW TO
STOP
A STALKER

DETECTIVE MIKE PROCTOR

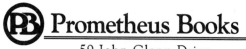 Prometheus Books

59 John Glenn Drive
Amherst, New York 14228-2197

Published 2003 by Prometheus Books

Inquiries should be addressed to
Prometheus Books
59 John Glenn Drive
Amherst, New York 14228–2197
VOICE: 716–691–0133, ext. 207
FAX: 716–564–2711
WWW.PROMETHEUSBOOKS.COM

07 06 05 04 03   5 4 3 2 1

Library of Congress Cataloging-in-Publication Data

Proctor, Mike, 1948–
    How to stop a stalker / by Mike Proctor.
        p. cm.
    Includes bibliographical references and index.
    ISBN 1–59102–091–3 (pbk. : alk. paper)
    1. Stalking. 2. Stalking—Prevention. 3. Stalkers. I. Title.
HV6594.P76 2003
362.88—dc21

2003010858

Printed in the United States of America on acid-free paper

CONTENTS

ACKNOWLEDGMENTS

This work could not have been completed were it not for the love and support of my wife, Brenda. She was the one that stood by me during all the 1 or 2 A.M. robbery, homicide, or stalking call-outs. She basically raised our kids as a single parent for over eleven years. She understood why I spent more time with my partner and with victims—often females—than I did with her. And she still had time to listen to me when I eventually dragged myself through the door.

I also want to dedicate this book to all the stalking victims out there in the trenches. I hope this guide helps to answer some of the questions you might have and assist you in putting the power of self-confidence back into your life.

INTRODUCTION

Depending on your circumstances, you probably picked up this book and started thumbing through its pages for any one of a variety of reasons. Maybe it was the catchy title or the interesting cover. Possibly you have a burning curiosity to learn about stalking, or you have to review this work as part of a class project. Or perhaps there is another more ominous reason: *you or a loved one is currently being stalked, and you are hoping this book may assist in some way.* Whatever the reason, I'm glad you've decided to peruse the pages of this guide because no matter what, I strongly believe that you're going to get something out of it. So if you can pull up a comfortable chair and grab some good reading light, let's begin to get into the subject of stalking. Remember, it's like going into a Starbucks Coffee house for the first time: you've got to learn the language before you can order. But before we do that, let me first take care of a couple of housekeeping chores.

First, I think it is very important that you get to know me a little better and find out where I am coming from with regard to the stalking phenomenon. When I take a class or attend a seminar, I like to know something about the horsepower of the instructor presenting before I can take that intellectual leap of faith. Assuming you're the same way, let's put my background briefly under the microscope.

After graduating from California State College at Long Beach in 1970, I entered the honorable profession of teaching. I had a degree in geography and could coach, so naturally I taught drivers' education and physical education. (It should be noted that teaching young, oftentimes uncoordinated youth how to operate a three-thousand-pound death machine on wheels is what turned my hair white.) While teaching, I was required to take a ride-along in a police car. I chose to ride with an officer who worked for the City of El Segundo, a small beach community located right next to Los Angeles International Airport. That experience dramatically changed my life.

One day I was teaching high school, the next I was driving around in a black-and-white, what we call our patrol cars. Like a priest to the cloth, my calling was to the badge. For the next twenty-five years I worked as a police officer with the Westminster Police Department, a medium-size agency located in the western half of Orange County, California (near Disneyland). During the last eleven of those twenty-five years I worked as a robbery/homicide detective. Due to the crime rate the city suffers from, my partner, Terry Selinske, and I had no problems finding a great deal of work in either category. For the last six of those years, I was heavily involved in working not only homicides but other predator-class criminals, specifically stalkers.

My work in the stalking field began in May of 1991, when I got a call from the security department of a major life insurance company. The agent was concerned because he had just received a call from someone claiming to be a hit man for hire. This individual had told the agent that he had just been hired to kill a subject by the name of Ronol Potter. The caller told the agent that the person who had hired him was Ronol's wife, Sandra Potter. When I started checking into the matter I found that Sandra had been stalked by the caller for nine years at that point, and claiming to be a hit man was just another one of the many harassment tactics he used to upset her. Sandra, a young, well-manicured business executive, was at her wit's end with her stalker. My investigation cut deeply into an ever-festering wound.

Shortly after I closed out my initial investigation into the insurance matter, Sandra came to our police department to plead her case, having found no satisfaction from other police departments or relevant agencies. She came to us in the hopes of finally getting someone to help her with the stalker who had followed, harassed, robbed, and beaten her, making her life a living hell for the past several years. Sandra told us the stress from the stalking had gotten so bad, she was at the point of contacting her stalker and letting him beat her once more so that she could at least get the police to arrest him for assault. As Sandra sat on a chair between Terry's desk and mine—both of which were stacked high with cases from an average weekend: two shootings, one stabbing, and one gang-related homicide—she began to tell her story.

Her hands clenched a thick wad of diary logs, legal paperwork, and newspaper articles that she then dropped on my desktop. This collection of items was well worn from being carried from one agency to the next with little or no results. Tears streamed down her face and she began to shudder. After listening to Sandra's unimaginable stalking epic, it was obvious that this woman, and now her husband, had gone through untold terror at the hands of this maniacal stalker. There sat two seasoned robbery/homicide detectives with reputations for putting away the bad guys, but between us we couldn't think of a thing to do for this poor woman. After a couple of days of mental meltdowns, we turned to Detective Laurie Clemons, our sex crimes investigator at the time, who suggested that we learn about some of the new laws that had just been enacted, one of which was the new California antistalking law. (Unfortunately, when an investigator specializes in one particular area and has a heavy caseload, he is often guilty of not keeping up with every piece of legislation that comes along.) After one read of the new stalking law—which was the first of its kind in the nation—I knew Sandra's case fit, and so began the long road to solving her biggest problem in life.

At the time, I wasn't aware that Sandra would in fact become a repeat client. (This, as we will discuss later, is often the case with stalking victims because the stalker is for the most part a repeat offender.)

This is probably as good a time as any to discuss my outlook on law enforcement, which, by the way, is shared by many of the men and women in blue with whom I associate. I am not a preacher, but I am a believer. I believe I was meant to become a cop. I believe that once you take the oath, you live it. I feel that we are a warrior breed assigned to help and protect the victims in our society. Many of us seem to have been directed to this line of work.

Sandra calls me her "guardian angel"; I call it being open to possibilities. Shortly after that initial in-depth conversation, I arrested her stalker, Jake Simpleton,* for stalking. However, because there was no restraining order in place, the offense was only a misdemeanor. When Jake completed his initial jail sentence of about six months, he was released and was then served with a restraining order that would not allow him to be *within ten miles of Sandra*. (This was how concerned the issuing judge was with Jake's violent potential. Keep in mind, most distances on a restraining order are set at one hundred yards.)

It should be noted that when we first arrested Jake, the stalking law was in its infancy; it has been amended several times since its inception. One of these additions makes arresting a first-time stalker what we call a "wobbler"—a felony or a misdemeanor, depending on the severity of the offenses leading up to the charge of stalking. Now in California a felony arrest can be made without a restraining order being in place.

I knew that Jake would not cooperate with his probation officer, and in fact he did abscond, which was predictable. Given his history, Jake was then profiled on *America's Most Wanted*, on a program in which Sandra and I participated. The program was dedicated to the issue of stalking.

Throughout our careers in law enforcement, both Terry and I had attended several profiling schools and seminars primarily hosted by members of the FBI's Behavioral Science Unit. One such class, taught by Mary Ellen O'Toole Ph.D., greatly assisted us in developing several of our profiling techniques. These methods have not only assisted us in the profiling of stalkers, but also in developing homicide and other types of unusual cases that are serial in nature.

When I become involved in a stalking investigation, either as the

---

* Jake Simpleton is a pseudonym for Sandra Potter's stalker. We don't want to empower these individuals, and putting their name in print might just do that.

lead investigator or as a consultant, one of the first things I do is prepare a historical documentation of the stalker. This allows me access to the stalker's world and helps me to analyze his stalking behavior with past victims. It also enables those of us participating in the investigation to better track and control the stalker.

Let me illustrate by discussing the profile I developed on Jake. I composed Jake's stalking profile by conducting a series of interviews with known relatives, social contacts, previous law enforcement contacts, and other victims. I found in the early stages of investigating stalkers that unless we had encountered them during the course of their first stalking, most go on to stalk others. It becomes imperative that we locate these other victims in order to find out more about their behavior patterns. My inquiries proved very interesting and damning at the same time. I was able to find out the following concerning Jake:

- His father had died at an early age.
- His mother developed a great fear of him, since he was a large, unruly child. She also had a physical disorder—deafness—which hindered her in providing guidance in his upbringing.
- Jake had sustained a head injury in his youth that might have contributed to some of his antisocial behavior.
- Jake was starved for male companionship.
- He was molested as a child by one of his (male) neighbors.
- He was then befriended by another male. This male was reported to be a homosexual and probably a pedophile. Jake moved into this individual's house during his late preteen years.
- While in the state of Alabama he dated a young counter waitress. (Jake would later stalk another young waitress in California—Sandra Potter.) When he got too possessive, she broke off the relationship. He began to stalk her. He kidnapped her, took her to a friend's fishing shack, and sexually assaulted her. During the course of stalking this female, Jake ran her new boyfriend off the road. On another occasion, he drove up next to her, pulled a gun, and kidnapped her for a second time. He was

finally arrested when he broke a window in the victim's house, entered, and then chased her with a large Bowie-type knife. Even though he was taken into custody for burglary, police records show that he spent very little time in jail. The records gave no reason for this.

- I was able to determine that Jake had a photographic memory. He ate white bread from the inside out. He would quote Bible scripture as well as read it sometimes with a blanket over his head. He claimed to be a card-carrying member of the Ku Klux Klan. (We could never prove his affiliation with the Klan.) He liked to start fires, and probably burned down a group of apartment building garages in Anaheim, California. He was then reported to have burned "KKK" and racial epithets into freshly mowed grass in the areas near where he would start fires.

- Jake was very strong. On one occasion while in a rage, he grabbed his aunt's head and face in a crushing grip. Once he had injured her face, he then squeezed her chest so hard that it caused her to be hospitalized with cracked ribs and a damaged diaphragm. This same relative told me that when she was finally able to look into a mirror, she was horrified because the damage Jake had done to her face was so bad she could not recognize herself. It was reported that Jake stuck a crowbar through the hand of a man that had made a remark he didn't like. The victim was so terrified of Jake that he never reported who had assaulted him. During one of my stalking victim interviews, I was able to find out that Jake had stalked another female he had lived with in Riverside County. On more than one occasion, when he believed she was looking at other men, he would place her in a closet and feed her tuna and water while he read Bible verses to her from outside the closet door. When this same victim attempted to finally flee from Jake, he found her, beat her so badly he thought she was dead, and then dumped her in the desert. (This victim said she did not report this incident to the police because she had had him arrested before, and he always came back. She wanted him to believe she was dead so he would never come looking for her again. It should be noted that this victim was so terrified of Jake, she became severly agitated that we could even locate her for the witness interview.)

- Jake had an obsessive-compulsive disorder. He was obsessed with being clean. Even if he was homeless and on the streets, he would keep very clean. Jake would wrap each article of clothing as well as his toothbrush and soap in separate pieces of service station hand towels.

- Jake would frequent churches on the days they offered free meals to the homeless. This would also give him the opportunity to befriend the elderly. He would con them into allowing him to come and live with them. Once in the home, he would take over their lives. He sucked off of them like a huge human tick, telling them what they could do, where they could go, and what he wanted them to do for him. He took money from them and had them ferry him around. When they did not comply, he verbally threatened or beat them. (Unfortunately, I have encountered this type of stalker all too often; Jake's is not an isolated case.)

- Jake's other haunts consisted of any coffee shops or libraries close to where he had his life-support victim housed. He was an avid reader and liked to discuss/argue about any topic while sitting for hours in these places.

Because of the profile we had composed on Jake, we felt he would be living with someone, probably an elderly female, and taking advantage of her financially. Suspecting Jake might frequent restaurants and coffee shops within certain areas of Orange County, Terry and I began to canvass these locations. Within a couple of weeks I received a call from security personnel at the Crystal Cathedral in the city of Garden Grove. We weren't far off—one of the church's parishioners, an elderly disabled woman, had been allowing Jake to live with her until he got too demanding and possessive. (Among other things, Jake demanded money from the woman, and forced her to take him places and pick him up whenever he called.)

She believed he might be frequenting a theater that was located in the middle of our search area. When we contacted theater employees and showed them Jake's photo, they advised us they had allowed him to come into the theater at no charge (stalkers can be very charming and persuasive) and watch one particular movie for the past three days. We finally arrested Jake as he sat in the last row of the theater, watching *Basic Instinct*.

It gets better. In 1995, Jake was resentenced and did a couple of months in jail for his probation violation. But being very intelligent, he got out and talked the Probation Department into sending him to Alabama to serve out his remaining couple of years on probation. (At that time, Alabama didn't have a stalking law. I later assisted them with information when they were developing their stalking statute.) We found it ironic that Jake was transferred back to Alabama where, if you will remember our profile had revealed, he started his initial stalking behavior. That profile investigation also showed that after he finished with that stalking victim, he moved to California and began stalking Sandra Potter. Sandra was elated to get rid of him, as was I along with his other California victims. Jake was transferred and would cause no more trouble—we thought. But about four or five months later, as I was driving in the city of Garden Grove with my two young sons, I passed by a familiar park. In unison the boys began chanting, "We want to go to this park! We want to go to this park!" I wasn't in the mood to take them to that specific park, because I had some errands to run near another park we normally visited in an adjacent city. As little ones do, though, they still clamored for me to go to this particular park. I gave in and pulled into a church parking lot adjacent to the park's playground area.

The play area inside that particular park has a fence with dense growth around it, making it impossible to see in or out. After the boys played for a while, one of them told me he had to use the bathroom. As we walked hand-in-hand out of the enclosure into the heart of the park, Jake walked directly in front of us carrying a duffel bag. Unbeknownst to me or Sandra, he had gotten into a verbal fight with his

Alabama probation officer and fled Alabama's jurisdiction. (I was later told that Jake felt the probation officer was too strict with him, so he decided to leave.) I secured the boys, who were both anxious to tell me they would help dad take down Jake. I then called the Garden Grove Police Department, which assisted me in taking Jake into custody once again. The *Orange County Register* had a good time with the story: "Stalker Has a Surprise Run-in with Detective." Perhaps Sandra or I should have played the lottery that day; do you care to make a guess on what the odds are of this situation occurring?

(Recent update on Jake's continuing criminal activity: On October 10, 2000, we began assisting the Tuscaloosa, Alabama, Sheriff's Office in a case involving the savage beating death of a sixty-two-year-old male city employee. Our boy, Jake, who is 6'4" tall and weighs 230 pounds, and his 6'3", 260-pound, thirty-year-old cohort had been staying with this man in the Tuscaloosa area. They reportedly tied the man to a chair and began using him as a human punching and kicking bag. When they were done, they left him in a bloody heap to die. This murder victim was Jake's life-long friend. In fact, he was the individual whose fishing shack Jake had used to sexually assault his first stalking victim back in the 1970s. One can see why it is not a good thing to be a so-called friend of Jake's.)*

As I said earlier, I always seem to be placed in a position to best assist those I am supposed to be protecting. My wife has always said she believes that "God watches out for fools and cops"; she keeps reminding me I easily fit into both categories. To prove that point, here's another example that you might find interesting; I know I did. In May of 1994, I was investigating a strong-arm robbery case involving a Los Angeles-based gangster. The only person other than me who knew what the suspect looked like was my police intern, Darin Upstill, now a Westminster Police detective. He had compiled a photo line-up that included the white supremacist gangster's mug (i.e., arrest photo) so that he could show it to the robbery victims. I was working at my desk when the intern called me excitedly from his

---

* On July 3, 2002, I flew to Tuscaloosa, Alabama, and testified as an expert in Jake's sentencing hearing. He received two consecutive life sentences for his crimes in that jurisdiction. Sandra Potter also testified at that hearing.

home. He had just finished working out and had sat down in front of his television to take a break. During the course of his channel surfing, he came to the talk show *Geraldo*. Immediately he recognized one of the gangster panelists on the show as the guy we were looking for. I got on the phone to CBS, and upon discovering the show was broadcast live in Los Angeles, sent the members of the Los Angeles Police Department down to arrest panelist number 3. Again the newspapers had a field day: "Bit of TV Fame Leads to Arrest"; "On the Next 'Geraldo': Suspects Caught When Appearing on TV." This is how my life seems to unfold. But I would not have it any other way.

In November of 1996, I retired from full-time duty in the police department for medical reasons. Diabetes and injuries to both knees, my arms, and my back had finally taken their toll. (Falling off a building, being run over in a pursuit, breaking both feet, and being rear-ended three times [once by one of our own patrol guys]—along with the continual 2 A.M. call-outs and sixty-hour-plus workweeks—tend to cut down on your longevity! But then, it goes with the job—a job that I truly loved.) Just as I was about finished cleaning out my desk, the captains and the chief of the department powwowed and came up with an idea. You see, they knew that I wasn't quite ready to quit cold turkey. They also were aware that Terry and I had made some promises to the relatives of a couple of homicide victims about not wanting to leave until we had more of a chance to solve the murders of their loved ones. (You develop a bond with the surviving relatives of a murder victim. They look to you to solve the case so that they might have closure.)

I also knew there was still a great deal left for me to learn about stalkers. The administration was able to convince the city to rehire me under a separate contract, which enabled me to consult on stalking cases as well as work on a limited basis on old homicides. I was reassigned to the police department's newly formed Family Protection Unit as the consulting detective in charge of stalking investigations. Terry and I are also involved in investigating some of our old unsolved homicides.

Over the years, my exposure to the stalking phenomenon has grown. I have been able to share this expertise throughout the state via a continuing series of seminars offered to district attorneys, investigators, probation officers, and correctional personnel, in addition to several victim advocacy groups. I have also returned to teaching, this time at the college level. Through all of these venues, I have been able to shed some light on the nature of the stalking predator. As I mentioned, the stalking issue has been picked up by the ever-vigilant eyes of the national media. In the past several years I've made appearances on such programs as *20/20*, *America's Most Wanted*, *Case Closed*, and the *Maury Povich Show*, to name a few, and most recently on an episode of *Unsolved Mysteries*, concerning an old homicide Terry and I are currently investigating. My work has been referred to in magazines, books, and newspaper articles analyzing stalkers. I have published material in a professional law enforcement journal on the subject of stalking case management. I was also honored to be one of the consultants on a two-hour law enforcement training video on stalking produced by the Commission of Police Officers Standards and Training (POST) for the State of California. (I should mention that same commission has recently produced another training video and workbook package for law enforcement due to the ever-changing dynamics of stalking.) I have also developed a protocol for the investigation of stalking that has been adopted by other law enforcement agencies.

Now that you know a bit about my background, you might be saying to yourself, "So this guy's been involved in the unusual atmosphere of the stalker. Does he think he knows everything about the subject?" The answer is, absolutely not. Anyone who represents himself as knowing everything about any subject needs the microscope kicked up a couple of powers. Working on investigating well over one hundred or so suspected stalkers, both as a lead investigator and a consultant, I encounter something new every day. It is my hope this accumulated data will help me as well as other investigators in solving the next stalking case encountered.

The next question you might have is, "Are there other stalking experts or groups heavily involved in the stalking issue?" Yes, but not in great numbers. These groups include but are not limited to the Los

Angeles Police Department's Threat Management Unit (TMU), San Diego's Stalking Strike Force, and the San Francisco Police Department's Domestic Violence Unit. In conjunction with these law enforcement groups are the growing number of domestic violence special prosecution units throughout the nation. Good examples of these also include the Sacramento County District Attorney's Domestic Violence Unit and the Los Angeles Stalking and Threat Task Force, which was put together by Los Angeles County Deputy District Attorney Rhonda Saunders in 2000. Other agencies outside of California include the Cook County Domestic Violence Task Force and the Colorado Springs Domestic Violence Unit, to name a few. Countries like Great Britain, Australia, Canada, and Japan are also becoming more and more involved in the issue of stalking; in fact, Japan recently passed a national antistalking law.

I have recently conducted a nationwide survey on stalking laws and the existence of antistalking units. Of the many states that responded, I have found that there does not appear to be a great many specialty antistalking units, but there are a large number of domestic violence units within police departments that specifically handle the stalker whenever the need arises, especially the larger ones like the New York Police Department. (In 2002 while in New York City, I had the opportunity to talk to some of the investigators there. They informed me that their individual divisions' domestic violence units would handle stalking cases. They also said their special operations division would probably handle any unusual or high-profile stalking cases.) Unfortunately, there aren't as many law enforcement agencies knowledgeable about the crime of stalking as we would like. Our numbers are growing, however, due in part to the intense media coverage on the subject, as well as stalking victims' demands for a more thorough investigation of their cases.

Those of us who actively investigate stalkers make it our mission to educate others and work toward maintaining, improving, and promoting the current antistalking legislation now in effect throughout the United States, including new federal antistalking laws. (It should be noted that there is a growing number of private threat management consulting firms coming on-line with protection from stalkers as part of their portfolios. These groups' main thrust is that of consulting for large corporations, media conglomerates, and individual stage and screen personalities. These corporate consultants specialize in the ongoing threat of workplace violence, which often involves a stalking situation. We will discuss that issue in a later chapter.)

Interestingly, the primary reason the American public—and most likely the world—is now being educated on stalking is because of threats and vicious attacks on celebrities such as Rebecca Shaeffer, who met her death on July 18, 1989, as a result of gunshot wounds delivered by her deranged nineteen-year-old stalker. He executed Rebecca on the front doorstep of her Los Angeles apartment. In 1982, actress and victims' advocate Theresa Saldana was viciously attacked by a knife-wielding stalker on the streets of her neighborhood. The stalker stabbed her repeatedly and would have killed her if not for the actions of a brave delivery man who intervened. Stalkers of stars are drawn like a moth to a bright flame fanned by the media personality's larger-than-life presence. That same flame caught the attention of lawmakers like Congressman Ed Royce and Orange County Judge John Watson, who were both instrumental in drafting the first antistalking legislation in California and the nation. They both worked on the language while then California State Senator Ed Royce pushed through the legislation. As a U.S. congressman, Royce then crafted the federal antistalking legislation we now have today. He is continuing to spearhead the fight against the stalker and stand up for victims' rights throughout the country. It is this type of legislation that we hope will generate a groundswell of national support on behalf of stalking intervention and legislation.

I should also explain how this guide is going to be laid out and why. My mission in writing this short work is both to enlighten the reader about the stalking phenomenon and to give her a framework with which to handle a possible stalking situation. The structure is designed to be simple in presentation. Remember, this writing falls into the category of self-help, not the works of Homer. Therefore I want you to learn the basics and enjoy the book as much as possible despite some of the disturbing subject matter that will be presented.

You should also be aware that I get a little "soapboxy" from time to time. That's one of the reasons my colleagues refer to me as the "Duck": I am always in and out of hot water, and all the inherent garbage that comes with the job seems to roll off my back. Terry Selinske, my partner, is referred to as the DCO—damage control officer. He smoothes out the feathers of those I might ruffle during the course of an investigation. So don't mind me if I get a little passionate about this topic, or anything else that has to do with the rights of victims. I am extremely tired of stalking victims getting the short end of the stick. I promise I will do my best not to sound like a zealot, stumping for victims' rights, but after all, these are the people I work for—the victims of the crimes I investigate.

Additionally, I tend to write in terms of "we," because I personally get tired of reading how an author did this or did that. (I did enough of that here in the introduction.) So when you read *we*, it often means me. Depending on the context of the sentence, it can also refer to those who help me investigate these stalking cases.

I should add, of course, a word about the names used in this book: all the persons discussed as victims in this book are real persons in cases I have worked or consulted on; however, all but two of their names have been disguised to protect their identities. *Any names associated with a stalker are also fictitious.* Finally, I have to include the following disclaimer: even though the suggestions we give on how to defend against a stalker have worked in the past, *they aren't always going to work every time in every scenario.* There are always variables in any life situation. If you find yourself faced with a stalker, you should contact the law enforcement entity in your jurisdiction and attempt to work with it concerning your circumstance. When following some of the procedures discussed in this book, be sure to check with that same law enforcement body to verify that your actions meet the legal requirements of your particular region.

In closing, it is my hope and desire that this book can, in some small way, assist you in whatever quest you are on in dealing with the serious issue of stalking.*

---

* If, after reading this book, you look in the mirror and see a stalker staring back at you, please stop what you are doing and immediately seek professional help. (Of course, most people we've encountered who exhibit stalking behavior seem to be in denial and they *just don't get it*. Thus self-realization rarely, if ever, takes place. To date, I have met several stalkers who know full well that their behavior is that of a stalker but who always justify their behavior in their own mind.)

CHAPTER I

STALKER IDENTIFICATION

DEFINITION OF A STALKER

Before we can discuss stalking in greater detail, we first need to define this phenomenon. The first few pages of this chapter will discuss the legal aspects of the crime of stalking. We will then go into the symptomatology of what takes place when a stalking occurs. It is our goal in this chapter to construct a sound informational foundation from which to understand the full meaning of stalking. We feel a short review of a few states' existing stalking laws will help the reader better understand what criminal statutes on stalking exist and how some are more encompassing than others.

Stalking can be defined in a number of ways. *Webster's New Collegiate Dictionary* defines *stalk* in the following manner: "to pursue quarry or prey stealthily." The California Penal Code offers the following definition of the stalker and the crime of stalking: "Every person who willfully, maliciously, and repeatedly follows or harasses another person and who makes a credible threat with the intent to place that person in reasonable fear for his or her safety or the safety of his or her immediate family, is guilty of the crime of stalking" (California Penal Code, sec. 646.9[a]).

A SAMPLING OF OTHER STATES' DEFINITIONS OF STALKING

Through our recent survey of several states' stalking laws, we have found that many states' definitions of the crime of stalking are very similar to California's, but there are some differences.* For example, The Minnesota antistalking law is presented as follows: "[Minnesota Criminal Code section 609.749] prohibits harassing another person by engaging in intentional conduct in a manner which would cause a reasonable person under the circumstances to feel oppressed, persecuted or intimidated, and which causes this reaction on the part of the victim." Ohio's equivalent law—Menacing by Stalking—states: "No person by engaging in a pattern of conduct shall knowingly cause another to believe that the offender will cause physical harm to the other person or cause mental distress to the other person" (Ohio Code Annotated, secs. 2903.21.1 and 2903.211). The state of Hawaii says: "A person commits the offense of harassment by stalking if, with intent to harass, annoy, or alarm another person, or in reckless disregard of risk thereof, that person pursues or conducts surveillance upon the other person: (a) Without legitimate purpose; and (b) Under circumstances which would cause the other person to reasonably believe that the actor intends to cause bodily injury to the other person or another, or damage to the property of the other person or another" (Hawaii Code, sec. 711-1106.5).

Our review of these laws also turned up distinctions in wording concerning the elements that have to be committed for the crime to be charged. Let us first look at the differences and the commonalities of these laws. In Oklahoma a person is considered to have been stalked if he or she exhibits "emotional distress" defined as "significant mental suffering or distresses that may, but does not necessarily require, medical or other professional treatment or counseling" (Oklahoma Session Law, sec. 21-1173 F-3). This has to be coupled with a

---

* The "Stalking and Domestic Violence" section of the OJP Violence Against Women Grants Office, Third Annual Report to Congress published in 1998, has a model antistalking law that is designed to assist states in developing their laws. You can find it on the Web at www.ojp.usdoj.gov/vawo/grants/stalk98/.

course of conduct also defined in their stalking statute, under section 21-1173 F-2, as "a pattern of conduct composed of a series of two (2) or more separate acts over a period of time, however short, evidencing a continuity of purpose." North Carolina also delineates "emotional distress" in their stalking law by stating that a stalker can "cause [a victim] to suffer substantial emotional distress by placing that person in fear of death, bodily injury, or continued harassment, and that in fact causes that person substantial emotional distress" (North Carolina General Statute 14-277.3, subsec. 2). In examining the antistalking laws in many of our states, we were able to see that several of these states' laws have been modified to include such things as "emotional distress," a broader definition of "harassment," which includes things like annoying and threatening via computers or other electronic devices. Other areas that were added or enhanced revolved around striking and/or unwanted touching, as well as a greater inclusion of what constitutes an "immediate family member" or "significant other."

While examining the various penal code sections for antistalking legislation in many of our states, we would like to take this opportunity to survey the types of punishment that stalking poses to the stalker. Our review showed that in most states a first-time stalking offense is considered to be a misdemeanor punishable by imprisonment in a county jail—usually up to a year—or by a fine and county jail time. It has been our experience that the first-time, misdemeanor stalking offender will get some jail time. However, there is always a possibility that the sentencing judge will suspend the sentence and place the stalker on formal or informal probation with the threat of a year hanging over the head of the stalker, if he offends again. (Formal probation means the subject is assigned a probation officer he must report to during the course of probation. This individual is usually subject to submitting his person, vehicle, and/or dwelling to a warrantless search by the probation officer or other law enforcement personnel during the probationary period. "Informal" or "summary" probation means the subject does not have to report but is admonished not to violate any laws and in most cases is also subject to warrantless search and seizure.) In Nevada we found that the first offense of generalized stalking without placing that person "in reasonable fear of death or substantial bodily harm" is a misdemeanor. The law also stated that "for any subsequent offense," it was a "gross misdemeanor."* However, if the stalker did cause reasonable fear of death or substantial bodily harm, the crime was upgraded to "aggravated stalking," which is a felony (Nevada Revised Statutes 200.575, sec. "Stalking: Definitions; penalties").**

According to the "Guide for Stalking Victims" that I obtained from the Minnesota's Attorney General's office, stalking was construed as a "gross misdemeanor" but could be a felony punishable by up to ten years in prison under the following circumstances: (1) if the perpetrator possesses a dangerous weapon; (2) if the perpetrator targets a victim because of the victim's race, color, religion, sex, sexual orientation, disability, age, or national origin (this portion of the statute is unusual in regard to stalking, but in our opinion a well-thought-out addition); or (3) if the perpetrator commits a second or subsequent offense within 10 years. (It should be noted that in many states surveyed, the second time a stalker was taken into custody for stalking the same individual within a set time frame, for example 5 years in North Carolina and Virginia, or 7 years in Mississippi and South Dakota, the stalker was then charged with a felony.) We also learned that in some other states, such as Kentucky, stalking was considered a felony as a first-time offense only if a protective or restraining order was in place before the offender was charged. Kentucky has a stalking in the first degree charging section (Kentucky Revised Statutes, sec. 508.140) that allows a first-time stalking offender to be charged with a felony if certain types of sexual contact occur, serious physical injury occurs, there is already a current criminal complaint or litigation against the stalker, or an act is committed while the defendant had a deadly weapon on or about his person. (It should also be noted that California

---

* We have found that a "gross misdemeanor" is a charging section, used by many states, that lies between a simple misdemeanor and the lowest-grade felony. The length of jail time can be longer, and the fine is usually greater than that of the simple misdemeanor.

** If you are interested in what states have what charging sections—misdemeanor or felony— for stalking, look on the Internet at www.ojp.usdoj.gov/vawo/grants/stalk98/appendb.htm.

is one of those states in which a first-time stalker can be charged with a felony, even if a protective order is not in place, depending on the circumstances of the stalking, such as how aggravated the stalking behavior was [i.e., was there a violent and direct threat, was a sexual assault threatened or attempted, etc.].)

We encountered states such as Arizona, Alabama, and Kansas, where stalking is an initial felony charge. Many states such as Kansas have degrees of felonies in their charging structure. Some charges carry more prison time than others. For further information check with your state's penal code, easily obtained at your local library in the legal research section or on the Internet by simply logging on and using key words such as "Arizona Revised Statutes" or "state stalking laws."* We also found it of interest that in Utah's stalking punishment section, there is a clause that allows other similar crimes outside of the state to be entered into its charging section (Utah Code Annotated, Criminal Code, sec. 76-5-106.5). In layman's terms what the statute means is if the stalker in Utah has been convicted of other felony crimes in another state that meet Utah's definition of the same crime in their state—e.g., stalking in Wisconsin has the same elements as it does in Utah—then Utah can use that felony conviction from Wisconsin to enhance their sentencing against the stalker. Many jurisdictions have a similar statute. When I recently went to Alabama to testify as a homicide/stalking expert, one of the primary reasons I testified was so that the district attorney in Alabama could use my testimony to show previous criminal history. He did this by having me testify to the twenty years of criminal activity I had documented on the defendant, whom I had investigated off and on over the previous ten years. The district attorney was also able to get certified copies of felony convictions the defendant had in California and was able to use them to demonstrate that the suspect was in fact a career criminal.

One of the other interesting things we uncovered during our research on the code sections concerning stalking is that many of the

---

* You can research all fifty states' stalking laws by visiting the Angels in Blue Web site at http://members.aol.com/lrfuzz1/StalkingLaws/StateLaws.html.

states surveyed also had penal code sections on harassment statutes situated in or around the stalking section. In fact, in many cases the harassment sections, most frequently charged as misdemeanors—at least upon the first conviction—are worded very similarly to those of the stalking section. For example, under Nevada's harassment section it is stated:

> 1. A person is guilty of harassment if: (a) Without lawful authority, the person knowingly threatens: (1) To cause bodily injury in the future to the person threatened or to any other person; (2) To cause physical damage to the property of another person; (3) To the person threatened or any other person to physical confinement or restraint; or (4) To do any act which intended to substantially harm the person threatened or any other person with respect to his physical or mental health or safety; and (b) The person by words or conduct places the person receiving the threat in reasonable fear that the threat will be carried out.* (Nevada Revised Statutes, sec. 200.571)

In California, harassment is known as "criminal threats"—section 422 of the penal code—and is often a section that prosecutors and we use in conjunction with a charge of stalking, because it can constitute another felony charge against the stalker. In California, the criminal threats statute can also be used as a "strike" count against the defendant upon conviction of a felony.** We feel that the criminal threats charge is also easier to prove than stalking because of the statutes' conduct requirements. If it is more difficult to prove the extended course of conduct required for stalking on a particular case, we can use the criminal threat charge, if the corpus (the elements of the crime) exists, to take the potential stalker into custody, put him in jail for a period of time, and get him on some type of probation, thus allowing us more case management options. According to the Orange County district attorney

---

* For more information on state stalking laws, see "Harassment and Threats by Level of Offense," available on-line at www.ojp.usdoj.gov/vawo/grants/stalk98/appendc.htm.

** A "strike" refers to a category assigned to a group of violent crimes. When an individual is convicted of three crimes from this group, he is then considered to have "three strikes" and can be sentenced to very long sentences, such as twenty-five years to life in California and other states.

we spoke with, we can obtain a warrant for someone making these threats in another state and arrest that person under sections 778 and 778a of the California Penal Code, bringing the individual back to California for trial. We were also told that one of the determining factors for extradition on the charge of criminal threats was the severity and extent of the threat(s) along with the cost of picking up the suspect. We had a case in which we drove to Arizona to pick up a potential stalker on this charge and were told that the primary reason we were allowed to extradite him on the warrant was because he was within driving distance. Funding, unfortunately, is a concern for any state or municipality involved in the law enforcement process.

One of the factors expressed in some of these harassment sections is a kind of third-party transference of threat. In other words, if suspect A relates to subject B that he wants to kill or do bodily injury to victim C, and C is then told of the threat from A by B, the threat is just as valid as if made by the stalker himself. The question one might ask is, Does it matter where the stalker is when he makes this threat for it to be construed as a crime? Can the stalker be in another state and still be at risk for making the threat? I put that question to Orange County Assistant District Attorney Jane Shade (refer to her biography in the resource section). Jane said that in her opinion, in California it would fall under penal code sections 778 and 778a. Jane also said she believed it was the same in many other states.

As in Minnesota, we again see a section of Colorado's harassment code lending itself to stopping or thwarting the ever-increasing "hate crime." Colorado Revised Statutes, Criminal Code section 18-9-111 (h)(2) states, "If the offender commits harassment pursuant to subsection (1) of this section with the intent to intimidate or harass another person because of that person's actual or perceived race, color, religion, ancestry, or national origin," the crime will be charged as a Class 1 misdemeanor.

ELEMENTS OF THE CRIME OF STALKING

Now that you have some idea of the legal or penal code definition of stalking, let's break stalking behavior down into its basic components. We think that most jurists involved in stalking litigation would agree that the following elements have to be present for a crime to be considered stalking: some sort of harassment, a credible threat, and a course of conduct that leads to physical or emotional damage. Before we can go any further we need to define each one of these elements.

Harassment

We would define harassment as repetitive annoying and disturbing behavior directed toward a person or a person's family members or significant others over a period of time, which has no positive or legitimate reason for taking place other than to harm the victim. Oklahoma defines harassment in regard to stalking as "a pattern or *course of conduct* directed toward another individual that includes, but is not limited to, repeated or continuing *unconsented* contact, that would cause a *reasonable person* to suffer emotional distress, and actually causes distress to the victim" (Oklahoma Session Law, sec. 21-1173 F-1). (I have emphasized "course of conduct," "unconsented," and "reasonable person" in this definition because they will come up in many other states' definition of harassment.) The types of harassment generated by the stalker will discussed in greater detail in chapter 3, "Tools of the Stalker"; they include verbal; telephonic; Internet; written or any other annoying, threatening communications; vandalism; unwarranted surveillance; and sexual and physical assault, among others.

Credible Threat

Our definition of "credible threat" for the purposes of stalking is a direct or indirect threat generated toward the victim through a series of acts that causes that victim to become fearful of death, personal safety, or great bodily injury, or to exhibit a great deal of emotional distress. The perpetrator of the threat must at least appear to have the present ability to—i.e., be able to—carry out the threat. Mississippi defines a "credible threat" as "a threat made with the intent and the apparent ability to carry out the threat so as to cause the person who is the target of the threat to reasonably fear for his or her safety" (Mississippi Penal Code, sec. 97-3-107[5]). (Our definition of credible threat may not match that of your state, so check the Internet or go to your local library for a definition.) When some states initially introduced their antistalking legislation, they required any threat to be a direct or specific threat such as, "I am going to kill you, bitch!" Over the years, though, the language has changed to the usage of the "course of conduct" understanding of threat, much to the annoyance of many a defense attorney. In the course of conduct scenario, the threat does not have to be direct or specific. (Refer below to the definition of "course of conduct" for further information.)

Course of Conduct

Our definition of course of conduct is a series of acts directed against the victim that, in its entirety, would cause a reasonable person to perceive a threat to the person's personal safety or to suffer great emotional distress for the well-being of the victim herself, the victim's family, or a significant other. Kansas defines course of conduct as "a pattern of conduct composed of *a series of acts over a period of time*, however short, evidencing a continuity of purpose and which would cause a reasonable person to suffer substantial emotional distress to the person" (Kansas Statutes Annotated, sec. 21-3438 [d][1]). (We have emphasized "a series of acts over a period of time" because many states require some amount of time to elapse between acts of harassment before they will construe a course of conduct to have taken place.) Many states like North Dakota and South Carolina require a minimum of two incidents in order to invoke course of conduct. South Carolina further defines the "pattern" of stalking not only to consist of at least two incidents, but they must also occur within a ninety-day period. We found one of the most delineated time measures placed on course of conduct in the Arkansas definition of course of conduct: "a pattern of conduct composed of two or more acts separated by at least thirty-six (36) hours, but occurring within one (1) year" (Arkansas Code, sec. 5-71-229 [1][A]). Now, don't forget that all this rests on what we call the "reasonable man's doctrine." That simply means what a reasonable person would perceive. Some states rely on that doctrine when determining when or how long a course of conduct has taken place.

Now that I have discussed the elements required for stalking, I should tell you that I use California's statute as the basis for the definition of stalking when I lecture. I do this not because it was the first stalking law enacted, or because it has been modeled by many other states, but because I find it to be simple and straightforward.

That being said, I believe we need to take a little time to discuss two other points concerning the investigation of stalking in your particular state. First, the detective assigned to your case is the one in the trenches who should be fighting for you. Second, that investigator must continually fight against having the following issue ever coming to fruition: a problem I refer to as "poor prosecutorial aggressiveness." This is a phenomenon we as detectives seem to encounter all too often. It is an age-old problem and is not reserved for prosecuting the crime of stalking. I have experienced this problem, as have many of the investigators I counsel and consult with. Even though the stalking statutes are on the books, they are not, in my opinion, always properly enforced. The biggest problem seems to be in the way some prosecutors as well as some judges view "course of conduct." As we have mentioned, course of conduct is a series of acts perpetrated by the stalker that causes the victim to exhibit fear or emotional distress. A direct threat does *not ever* have to be expressed by the stalker, only a credible one. It has been my experience, as well as that of other detectives involved in stalking cases, that prosecutors continually tell them, "Well, the guy never made a direct threat," or, "I really don't think because he followed her for two months, left several unwanted love notes at her home and office, as well as poured paint on her car when she didn't return the multitude of unsolicited phone calls, is enough for a credible threat." It is our hope that your detective's persistence and additional education on the subject of stalking will put these prosecutors on the right track.

There are always two sides to every coin. I have had the pleasure of dealing with judges and prosecutors from a variety of jurisdictions who understand the plight of the stalking victim and hold their office to a higher standard by vigorously prosecuting these cases. We still have a great deal of work to do when it comes to getting all prosecutors to file legitimate criminal cases. I offer this as an example of what we as detectives face concerning certain aspects of our judicial system. I had a stalking case in which one judge had issued a no-bail felony warrant on this particular stalker, who had a perceived propensity for violence. The mere fact that the warrant was issued with a no-bail attachment should have clued any other magistrate in to the distinct possibility that this stalker was a danger to others or, at the very least, maybe a flight risk (i.e., he might flee the jurisdiction). When the stalker learned that we had a warrant for his arrest, he got his attorney and appeared before a different judge from the one who had issued the warrant. The stalker's attorney told the presiding judge that his client was just having domestic problems with his estranged wife and that he would be a good boy. The judge dismissed the warrant, which he knew little about, gave the stalker a new court date, and allowed him to be out on his own recognizance (i.e., without any bail being set). This type of judicial decision-making adds a tremendous burden on not only the detective assigned to the case but also the victim the detective is attempting to protect.

Stalking is pretty straightforward. The person who decides to stalk you is basically a domestic urban terrorist that has established a clear-cut goal in life: to make your life a living hell for as long as he deems necessary. Later we will analyze why stalkers stalk, the different types of stalkers, and the tools and mechanisms applied by stalkers to further their trade. But for now we just want to elucidate the simple symptoms of stalking.

BASIC STALKING SYMPTOMATOLOGY

Generally speaking, it has been our experience that for a stalking to occur, the following symptoms are commonly manifested:

(1) *The stalker fixates on his victim for reasons initially known only to him.** The victim may be an ex-girlfriend, an acquaintance, someone that the stalker has encountered through a business situation, or merely someone seen in an area that the stalker frequents. For example, in August 1986, a white male stalker who worked as a pool cleaner walked into a well-known California bank with a friend. His friend was waited on by an attractive, raven-haired teller named Carmen. The next day that stalker walked up to Carmen's teller window with a bottle of chocolate syrup and a bag full of Hershey brand candy kisses. According to Carmen, the note accompanying these items read, "I want to pour this syrup all over your body and then lick it off." Then the stalker tried to get Carmen's attention by coming into her bank wearing t-shirts or sweatshirts with her name on them. When it became obvious that Carmen was in no way interested in the stalker's advances, he came into the bank wearing a T-shirt with "window 2" circled, with a line through it (Figure 1). This unnerved Carmen since teller window 2 was normally the teller window she was assigned to in the bank. She had never dated or even acknowledged this individual in any way. When Carmen came to us with her problem, she had already had the stalker arrested once in a neighboring Orange County city for other charges stemming from the ongoing stalking and was still looking for relief.

The ensuing eleven-year period of stalking caused Carmen to lose jobs, pay out hundreds of dollars for damages done to her personal property, and eventually be forced into mental health rehabilitation. Even though the majority of Carmen's stalking took place outside our city, we took on the case. It is our policy to take the *entire* case in order to assist the victim. In Carmen's situation, we generated a 760-page

---

* Since most stalkers are male and most victims are female, we will be referring to stalkers throughout this book as "he" and most of the victims as "she," except in the case of female stalkers.

Figure 1. T-shirt worn by stalker inside victim's bank.
(Courtesy of the Westminster Police Department)

crime report. During the course of our investigation we profiled the stalker, who was on the run from another charge. Our profile revealed several interesting things about him.

- Carmen's stalker was very religious. That does not mean he practiced the true path of Christianity; that means he could quote chapters and verses of the Bible. When we conducted a search warrant on his storage facility, we found that he had numerous spiral notebooks where he would write scripture over and over again, and then add little sayings concerning not only Carmen but other victims that he had stalked as well.

- He had rubber stamps made with the names of the women he had stalked in various cities. He would use these stamps to endorse letters and poems that he wrote to the victims.

- He had an extensive collection of pornographic movies that were predominantly about multiple sexual partners, bondage, and rape.

- He had photographs of his victims taken without their knowledge. Some of the photos seemed to be directed around the victim's buttock area.

- The stalker kept ledgers where he chronicled his contacts with persons that he felt were either out to get him or were in some way important to him.

- We found several photographs of pools that our stalker was resurfacing. The photos showed that he would etch the name of his victims in the pool along with sayings about love or hate. He would then photograph the pool's etchings before he resurfaced them. He would also have T-shirts made with the first name of the victim followed by the word "pools" in big, bold letters; an example would be "Carmen's Pools." He would wear this into the bank where the victim worked.

- We located large quantities of Hershey brand candies and found that the stalker would take trips to the northern California Hershey plant to purchase the candies that he would initially give as gifts to his stalking victims.

- We also conducted a second search warrant on his motel room. There we found detailed notes on stalking, along with videotapes where he had recorded programs concerning stalking from the motel room's television. We also located a set of files that contained newspaper and magazine articles on stalking. He had other articles that discussed police misconduct cases and curiously enough a series of articles on ethnic churches being burned. (We knew that our stalker felt that the police were persecuting him. These files reinforced our observation that our stalker was experiencing paranoia.)

Because we suspected via our profile that this particular stalker would probably be stalking other unsuspecting young female bank tellers, we canvassed businesses in the area where the stalker had last resided. We were able to find one of the stalker's canceled checks at a local merchant's store. Because the check had been drawn on a bank other than the one Carmen had been working for, we decided to run down the information on this branch. This ultimately led us to a bank branch located in a northwestern Orange County city. When we interviewed tellers at that bank, we learned that the stalker was currently doing business at that branch, and had been giving large Hershey candy bars to two of the tellers. We notified the law enforcement in that jurisdiction, who later arrested the stalker on our warrant when he came back into that bank branch to harass the tellers. When we searched his car, we found that he had all the court paperwork, including a copy of the restraining order Carmen had served him a year or so before. (Keep in mind that even though this stalking had taken place over a period of years, this victim had obtained a series of restraining orders against this stalker. When the original workplace restraining order obtained by her bank expired, she applied for and got another. If this had been a domestic violence stalking case, Carmen could have applied for and probably received an order with a ten-year life span. [At the time this case took place, stalking restraining orders were not available.] We will discuss restraining orders further in chapter 7, "Legal Remedies.") This paperwork had notes concerning our investigation and Carmen's comings and goings.

During the course of our videotaped interview—we videotape all of our stalker and homicide interviews because it assists the district attorney and ultimately the jury in seeing how the suspect's body language plays out when responding to certain questions—we verified some other items we had developed in our profile. We had a suspicion that Carmen's stalker was extremely annoyed with her over the death of another teller that used to work in the same branch as Carmen did for a period of time. This particular woman had killed her young child and then placed herself in front of oncoming traffic on a major freeway while holding her dead child, killing herself. (We found newspaper clippings concerning this incident when we conducted our searches of the stalker's effects.) When we questioned the stalker about how he felt, he became somewhat agitated. He said in essence that when he entered a bank, he began a "relationship" with a teller. These contacts consisted of two- to five-minute encounters while he was obtaining change for a few dollars, or cashing a check of minor importance. The stalker said that none of the tellers agreed to go out with him but that he still felt a great connection to them.

The stalker told us that during the course of his "relationship" with the teller that ultimately killed herself, he felt that he had become her friend and counselor. The stalker continued, saying that they talked about her son, God, and her frustration with her family. The stalker said that he felt he was about to make a breakthrough with this woman just before she committed suicide, but due to his problems with Carmen was not allowed to re-enter the bank and continue his liaisons with this women. The stalker disclosed that *he personally held Carmen responsible for the death of this woman.*

It should be noted that after this interview, we were able to better understand some of the photos that we had collected at the stalker's storage locker. One set of photos were of headstones photographed in a cemetery. When we found out the name of the female teller who had killed herself, we realized those photos were of her headstone.

Another group of photos that we couldn't understand while conducting our search were two or three photos of a large commercial site that looked like an area under demolition. During our background investigation we uncovered yet another stalking victim, you guessed it, another bank teller, with whom our stalker was so enamored that he wanted to marry her. The investigation showed that she had at one time worked as a clerk in a card store in the mall that used to be in the location where the photos were taken. When we showed the photos to the victim, she told us that the building under demolition in the photos was the building she used to work in. It appeared as though the stalker was reminiscing about the contacts he had with this poor stalking victim. (As the book progresses, you will continue to see more examples of this type of bizarre behavior—stalkers that fixate on unassuming victims for reasons known only to them.)

On the day of the trial, we got a call from the district attorney handling this case. She informed us that after all the pretrial motions were heard, the stalker told the judge something to the effect of, "Well, Your Honor, if I were a jury and heard all the evidence against me, I guess I would convict me, too." This stalker showed a very keen insight into the obvious and pled guilty to felony stalking.

(2) *The stalker begins a campaign of terror.* Because the majority of stalkers are known to their victim(s), we are going to explain this part of their symptomatology—a campaign of terror—within the framework of stalkers who make themselves known. Stalkers usually begin their overtures to the victim with presents, cards, notes, and letters. As they perceive it in their own twisted way, they believe they are the right person for the victim or must have the victim for whatever reason they deem appropriate. (We should mention that many times a dating relationship has occurred prior to the stalking.) As a result of this, the state of Texas has recently enacted a new criminal code under section 71.0021 of their Family Code, entitled Dating Violence. The section is defined as "an act by an individual that is against another individual with whom that person has or has had a dating relationship and that is intended to result in physical harm, bodily injury, assault, or sexual assault or that is a threat that reasonably places the individual in fear of imminent physical harm, bodily injury, assault, or sexual assault (but does not include defensive measures to protect oneself)." (We believe the term "defensive measures" used in the Texas statute would be when a person is in the act of fending off an assault in a lawful manner.) The section goes on to describe a dating relationship as a "continuing relationship of a romantic or intimate nature."

Law enforcement has made leaps and bounds in its fight against domestic violence; this law appears to be another good piece of legislation that has begun to plug up some of the holes in the campaign to further combat domestic violence. It also represents another tool that Texas can use to short-circuit a potential stalking scenario. (In California, battery in a dating relationship has been included under the domestic violence umbrella, in California Penal Code, section 243 [e][1].)

When rebuked by the victim (stalkers are usually clueless as to the meaning of the word "no"), the stalker will then begin to follow, harass, or repeatedly call the victim, damage the victim's property, and in many cases threaten her. For example, Jill, a 22-year-old white female, had dated Ben for only about two months when she perceived him as becoming too possessive. Shortly after their breakup, Ben called Jill's work number over one hundred times in less than an hour. On two occasions he told her he was going to blow up the sports bar where she worked. He continued to call her at that location for four consecutive nights, causing her to lose her job. Ben threatened Jill with a gun and on one occasion attempted to stab her with a knife. He even jumped atop her car once, blocking her view and causing her to crash into a parked vehicle. Ben was eventually arrested, sentenced, and placed on probation.

(3) *The stalker may also target family members in the course of the stalking*. It has been our experience that members of the victim's family become potential targets when a stalker is attempting to gather information on his prey. When initial stalking legislation was introduced in several states, family members and/or significant others were not included. When more was learned about the pathology of stalking, many states amended their stalking legislation to include sections on family members and others in a close relationship with the primary stalking victim. For example, under the Colorado Harassment—Stalking Statute 18-9-111, section 35818 (III), a person who "repeatedly follows, approaches, contacts, places under surveillance, or makes any form of communication with another person, a member of that person's immediate family, or someone with whom that person

has or has had a continuing relationship in a manner that would cause a reasonable person to suffer serious emotional distress and does cause that person, a member of that person's immediate family, or someone with whom that person has or has had a continuing relationship to suffer serious emotional distress" is guilty of stalking.

The Colorado code further defines "immediate family," under section 35818 (C) subsection (4) (III), as the victim's "spouse, parent, grandparent, sibling, or child." We find it encouraging that this statute also specifically names the grandparents as a class of victims that can be stalked. Many of the stalking cases that we've investigated do involve the grandparents. They are harassed and threatened when they are babysitting the children or end up having the estranged stalking victim living with them.

We have found the stalker will also attempt to frustrate or harass the victim's family in an attempt to elicit a response from the victim. For instance, the father of a female victim had his sports car's tires slashed so many times by his daughter's stalker, he had a contract with a local tire store to replace the tires. During the course of the stalking, this man spent well over $2,500 on tires.

This type of harassment can also be transferred to the victim's pets, as the stalker may kidnap and then injure the animal. We have reports of dog poisoning as well as other animals being hurt or killed. We know of a case of a female victim from out of state who had a pet parrot. During the course of her stalking, her male stalker would call her and threaten to kidnap the bird and then break its neck as she listened over the telephone. On occasion she would receive phone calls with a parrot squawking on the other end of the phone, followed by what appeared to be the sickening sound of a bird's neck being snapped. If you think this is unusual, you should read one of the many newspaper articles regarding divorce proceedings in which the only unresolved item in the custody order doesn't revolve around the children but who gets visitation and custody of the pets.

(4) *Stalking can and often does lead to physical abuse, sexual assault, and even death.* Let us begin by saying that not all stalkers kill

their victims, but unfortunately a certain percentage try and sometimes succeed. It is reported that 90 percent of all domestic violence victims killed by their spouses or significant others are stalked prior to being killed. Unfortunately my partner and I have investigated so-called murder-suicides that could have been prevented if we or some other professional organization had been allowed to intervene. We present the following examples to show that death makes no distinction as to age and wisdom amid the plague of stalking. We also want to present these three examples because at the time they took place, my partner and I were not yet well versed in the dynamics of stalking. We were interpreting these homicides as "crimes of passion" or "love/hate relationships." In hindsight, we realized we were wrong. Although certain facts have been changed in order to better disguise identities and dates of occurrence, all of these incidents took place and are true.

Example 1: My partner and I responded at around 6 P.M. to a middle-class neighborhood in the central portion of our city on a call of a double homicide. When we got to the location, we found an older woman lying dead in the kitchen of her residence with a gunshot wound to her torso. We then encountered a middle-aged male lying in a pool of blood with what appeared to be a single self-inflicted through-and-through gunshot wound to the head. Lying next to the male, who was later pronounced dead at the hospital, was a .38 caliber revolver. We were told that the male and female were not living together but had a dating relationship. We conducted our preliminary investigation, set up forensic exams of both subjects, and processed the house, all of which was our standard operating procedure. We began developing information for our homicide book and producing our initial write-up as a "normal" murder-suicide. (When you are working robbery/homicide cases, which include all attempted murders as well as those that are actually committed in an active city like ours, what appears to be a clear-cut domestic violence murder-suicide, although tragic, is far less labor-intensive than an active, ongoing investigation. The reason for this is that the murder-suicide generates no prosecution at the end of the investigation, because the assailant is dead.)

Our outlook on this case changed when we learned that there had been extensive verbal exchanges between the couple as well as a fair amount of what we would now classify as stalking behavior occurring within the relationship. We learned from relatives that the deceased female had complained about the suspect becoming more and more possessive. The female had broken off her relationship with the male just a few days before the murder-suicide occurred. We also learned that the male suspect had threatened or attempted suicide in the past. (This is something we would later discover is one of the behaviors we see exhibited in many of our domestic violence stalking investigations. It is not uncommon for the male or female stalker to attempt, have attempted, or threaten to attempt suicide during the course of the stalking. Obviously, this becomes something we now look at very closely when conducting our Threat Assessment Interview.)

The regrettable thing that stands out about this couple's problem was that it was grossly underreported due to many factors, including the couple's ages and extended-family ties, as well as the female victim's reluctance to complain due to cultural and environmental elements in her upbringing. Many people of this age group and older were trained and /or schooled by parents not to air or express their personal problems. With the advent of a greater flow of information to both those potential victims of middle age and older, domestic violence and stalking problems are starting to diminish, but we still encounter it, even in the over-fifty age group. The fact that this woman had no knowledge, as did we, of what stalking was, or at least no label for the problem she was experiencing, was a contributing factor to her brutal death.

Example 2: A young, vibrant female athlete with a promising career got out of a friend's car on a hot summer day in an upscale residential area. Approximately thirty yards from her car sat her estranged boyfriend—a bright, compulsive youth who had followed her to that quiet street. Earlier in the day he had gone to a local gun shop, purchased a 12-gauge pump shotgun, and a box of double-aught buck 12-gauge shells. The male exited his vehicle yelling at his victim, who was still in her sports uniform. As she turned to confront her assailant, he pulled the trigger, sending thirteen .32-caliber-size projectiles into her body and killing her instantly. While several residents stood frozen in disbelief, the killer placed the barrel of the shotgun to his chest and blasted himself into the ranks of mounting numbers of murder-suicides this country experiences each year. Newspapers have a field day with these types of killings, calling them a "love gone bad" or a "romantic tragedy." Not so in this case. Our investigation into this homicide revealed nothing romantic about this sad scenario; rather, it was another stalking that proceeded to the point of death. We would also like to point out that this murder-suicide, along with others in California, was one of the factors that led to new state legislation requiring a waiting, or, in this case, a cooling-off period before one can purchase a rifle or shotgun.* Prior to these incidents, there was a waiting period only on handguns.

I am a gun owner; I believe in the right to bear arms and greatly enjoy recreational shooting, but I do believe in a background check and a waiting period on the purchase of handguns and rifles. I know of at least two separate cases that I've recently worked where this so-called cooling-off period prevented or helped in preventing potential murder-suicides.

Example 3: During the course of my career as both a homicide and predator crimes detective, I have had the opportunity to investigate many strange and unusual cases. ("Predator crimes" refer to stalkers and those criminals that commit serial-type crimes, such as serial rape, home invasion robberies, etc.) Due to my background in the occult (not as a practitioner but as an investigator), I get most of the "X-File"–type cases as well as the stalkers. You know, the body taken from the crypt, or the cross found wrapped in a freshly cut dog's heart found under a headstone, or the crate full of chickens and goats found dumped along the freeway with all their heads cut off and blood drained. I got used to hearing other investigators saying, "No way am I working that case; that's a Mulder case, give it to Proctor—he'll work it."

---

* A "cooling-off period" refers to the time provided to a person to calm down prior to obtaining a handgun or rifle.

But one of the most unusual domestic violence murder-suicide cases with overtones of stalking I ever worked occurred late one night on the 405 freeway, which runs south to Orange County and north to the San Fernando Valley. The 405 has four lanes going either direction and is jammed with high-speed traffic at most hours of the day or night. It was Sunday, and I had already investigated two shootings and a suicide that weekend. When I arrived on the scene, I couldn't believe what I was told. The male suspect, who had been driving the vehicle, had shot the female victim in the head, killing her instantly. He then turned the gun on himself, delivering a fatal gunshot wound to the head while still driving at over sixty-five miles per hour southbound in the diamond lane (the car pool lane next to the center divider). Now that would have been unusual enough if it hadn't been for the fact that the woman's three-year-old boy had been sitting in the back seat of this compact car when both the boy's mother and her estranged boyfriend were killed. Unbelievably, the vehicle had continued down the freeway until it careened into the cement center divider and somehow came to a stop with only minor damage done to the car. When other motorists stopped in an attempt to give aide to the couple involved in what looked to be only a minor traffic accident, they found the three-year-old still sitting in the back seat, patiently waiting for someone to help him. When units from the California Highway Patrol arrived on the scene, they took custody of the boy until he could be released to relatives.

Due to the location of the crime scene—where drivers moved past us at high rates of speed, some veering as if intoxicated or uncon-scious—I called for a flatbed tow truck, which hauled the car, bodies and all, to the Orange County crime lab garage to complete our forensic examination.

When I began contacting friends and family members of the female victim I found that a pattern of stalking had started and had been getting worse. First, I was told that the male suspect could not stand not knowing where the female victim was at all times. He was reported to be so clingy that he would often not allow her to take a shower without him being in the shower along with her. He had remarked he was very fearful of the victim leaving him. He read scripture from the Bible continually and made several attempts at "forcing" the victim into a "religious" state. (We will touch on the reading and quoting of scripture when we discuss personality disorders in chapter 2, "Types of Stalkers and Why They Stalk.")

On one occasion, the subject was reported to have sustained a large gash on his leg after the victim went out without him. I was told that it was believed that the subject cut himself to try and gain sympathy from the victim. There were two things that I felt were obvious danger signals, which for whatever reason no one acted on or even took heed of. The male suspect drank heavily, became angry when drunk, and had at least one handgun in his car or on his person at all times.

With the knowledge my partner and I have developed over the years, we can now look back at not only these cases but others and see what our mistakes were. Armed with the information we now have, we can greatly reduce the chances of the stalking homicide taking place again. There is one caveat to this kind of thinking. We have to be made aware of the stalking before we can act. We don't want to do any more behavioral postmortems.

CHAPTER ONE SUMMARY

- In California, a stalker is defined as someone who "willfully, maliciously, and repeatedly follows or harasses another person and who makes a credible threat with the intent to place that person in reasonable fear for his or her safety or the safety of his or her immediate family." As we have shown, many other states have similar definitions. Most states' stalking statutes have definitions for "credible threat," "course of conduct," "emotional distress," and "immediate family." Many states also have harassment laws that can be used as an added charge to the stalking or as another tool to get a potential stalker into custody.

- A common scenario perpetrated by the stalker follows: The stalker attempts to make contact with the victim through letters, cards, and/or gifts. A dating period may then ensue. When rebuked, he then begins a pattern of monitoring the victim, which can lead to harassment and vandalism of the victim's property as well as threatening behavior toward other family members and possible injury to family pets. In some cases, the victim experiences physical trauma, which sometimes ends in death. However, not all stalkers express a direct threat of violence toward their victim, nor do most exhibit an overwhelming propensity for killing their victims, at least not in the initial periods of the stalking.

CHAPTER 2

TYPES OF STALKERS AND WHY THEY STALK

W hen giving lectures, I usually begin my presentation with the question "How many persons in this room have been stalked?" Most of the time the response is varied, because some people do not want to admit that they have been stalked, and others have been but don't realize it until after the class has concluded. Still, many do raise their hands and later express their grief and outrage over a variety of issues. During the production of one of the law enforcement tele-courses on stalking that I was involved in, one of the producers told me at the end of our time together, "I was followed and harassed by an individual who initially saw me in the supermarket. Now I know I was being stalked." This same person said she had recently gone to see a production of *Phantom of the Opera* and realized the story was in fact a tale of a violent stalking. Although as a musical I hold *Phantom of the Opera* in the highest regard, this producer had made a very cogent observation concerning how a great deal of our society (and the world) views stalking. Too often it is dismissed as a romantic compulsion, when as a matter of fact we now know it is not.

When I was interviewed by the Japanese media concerning stalking, the producers of the news group I was dealing with echoed these same sentiments. According to these journalists, in their society, stalking—which is a problem in almost all human communities—is treated as a romantic interlude, not the criminal problem that it is.

One of the first things I am asked when instructing classes on stalkers, along with, "Why do stalkers stalk?" is the question "Are there different types of stalkers?" Before answering that question, we have to look at the overall stalking picture. Stalking has probably been with us since the dawn of mankind, at least the dawn of "intelligent" mankind, and likely before. The history of early mankind has shown that some men followed, monitered, raped, and in fact killed early women. This is definitely not a new behavior in our or any other society. Until recently, not much empirical data have been compiled on the subject.

Let us look at a few harrowing statistics that we do have available. Some of the most telling figures on the stalking issue have come out of a study from the Violence Against Women Grants Office. We find it very disturbing that their report shows that stalking is both more of a problem than first suspected, and much more widespread than originally estimated. They estimate that 8.1 percent of all women and 2.2 percent of all men of the population they queried had in fact been stalked at one point in their lives. Furthermore, they were able to estimate, based on population figures supplied by the U.S. Census Bureau on the number of adult men and women in America, that one out every twelve women in America, or 8.2 million women, have been stalked at some time in their lifetime. The report also indicated that one out of every forty-five men in America, or 2.0 million men, have also been stalked during their lifetime. The researchers of this study went on to say that 1,006,970 women are stalked annually in the United States. They also estimated that around 370,992 men are stalked annually. Finally, according to the study, approximately 59 percent of all the women stalked were stalked by some type of "intimate partner."[1]

Another study we want to address briefly that might be of great interest to college students and their parents, The National College Women Sexual Victimization Study (NCWSV),[2] was conducted from February through May of 1997. The study sampled female students from 223 colleges and universities. Although the study deals with a different sector of our society from that at the Violence Against Women Grants study, it provides us with another view of the stalking equation. The study states that 13 percent of the college women surveyed said they had been stalked from the fall of 1996 until the survey was conducted. Of those who claimed to have been stalked, 80.3 percent knew their stalker. About 15.3 percent said their stalkers had attempted to harm them, and only about 3.9 percent had obtained a restraining order. These are only a few of the findings of the study. We bring them to you to illustrate that our college campuses mirror what is taking place in the rest of our society.*

We are not the only country researching the stalking phenomenon; for instance, in October 2002, I contacted Tracey Budd, one of the researchers in the 1998 British Crime Survey (BCS), which covered stalking in England and Wales. Budd sent me the following information concerning their findings: "It is accurate to say 2.9 percent of adults (ages sixteen to fifty-nine) interviewed in the 1998 BCS said they had experienced stalking (defined as persistent and unwanted attention) in the twelve months prior to interview. The best estimate of the number of victims using the most inclusive definition is 0.88 million." Budd went on to say, "Restricting the definition to incidents that result in violence or fear of violence gives a best estimate of 0.55 million victims."[3]

Given the prevalence of stalking, it should be noted that more mental health professionals, such as J. Reid Meloy, Ph.D., formerly chief of the Forensic Mental Health Division of San Diego County, a true pioneer in stalking research and now a highly sought-after speaker, consultant, and author; Michael A. Zona, M.D., educator and consultant, a principal of the Omega Threat Management Group, Inc.; and Park Dietz, M.D., Ph.D., well-known forensic psychiatrist, have compiled and are continuing to compile data on the stalking phenomenon. This is partly because law enforcement has seen an increased need to bring these professionals in as partners in the threat assessment process, thus enhancing our overall work product.

---

* For additional on-line information on this study, see www.ncvc.org/src/statistics/ncwsv.html.

Dr. Zona and John Lane—formerly the lieutenant in charge of the Los Angeles Police Department's Threat Management Unit—have compiled and published statistical information on stalking and its components. During the course of Lt. Lane's tenure as head of the Threat Management Unit, he founded and developed an organization known as ATAP (Association of Threat Assessment Professionals), of which I am currently a member. He brought together threat management professionals from the law enforcement, medical, and private sectors. Lane, now retired and a partner in the Omega Threat Management Group, Inc., a company designed to assist business and media personnel in the threat management process, recently co-authored a chapter with Dr. Zona in *The Psychology of Stalking* titled "Psychiatric Diagnosis and the Offender-Victim Typology of Stalking." In this chapter, they outlined the types of behavior exhibited by several of the stalkers they have investigated over the years and then classified them into four specific categories or types:

Simple Obsessional: "These are cases wherein the victim and suspect (perpetrator) have some prior knowledge of one another." Zona and Lane believe as we do, that many of these stalkers began their stalking behavior in a domestic situation, but of course not all. They also advise that their research shows that this type of individual is probably the most dangerous of all the stalkers.[4]

Love Obsessional: Zona asserts, "These cases are characterized by the absence of an existing relationship between the perpetrator and the victim." Lane and Zona inform us that this group of stalker often goes after the celebrity or media personality, but they caution that this individual can also stalk the ordinary citizen as well. Zona goes on to state, "A large number of these stalkers suffer from schizophrenia or bipolar disorders. . . . Many are socially maladjusted and have seldom, if ever, been involved in a meaningful intimate relationship."[5] (We have run across a few of these types, an example of which is included in our section on the Acquaintance stalker. The Love Obsessional stalker can also be applied to our "stranger" category of stalker. The key here is that there has been no prior *intimate* contact between the victim and the stalker.)

The *Erotomanic* stalker is another type that Zona describes: "The suspect delusionally believes that he/she is loved by the victim." Their research showed in these cases that the suspect was usually female, and that the victims were usually "older men of higher socioeconomic status."[6]

The last example of stalker types and victomology they describe is what is commonly referred to as the *False Victimization Syndrome*. We have experienced this type of syndrome on only two occasions out of the more than one hundred cases we have worked or consulted on. According to Zona and Lane's research, it is not a very common occurrence. Zona comments, "Cases develop when an individual constructs an elaborate scenario to falsely support the position that he or she is being stalked."[7] Their research has revealed that most of the individuals claiming to be stalked are women, who usually have developed this ruse to try to regain control of a failing relationship.*

Both of my supposed victims were females claiming to be stalked by men. They both had failing marriages and were trying to elicit support from their estranged spouses. The support these women seemed to crave was emotional caring or compassion from their husbands. In one example, we had a middle-aged white female come into the police department with claims of being stalked by a black male. When we interviewed her, she gave us a graphic description of the supposed stalker not only as to height and weight but as to other physical characteristics such as the cut of his hair and how he wore his clothes. The woman said she would often be followed and on one occasion harassed by this individual, whom she said she did not know. Our subsequent investigation showed that the woman was currently estranged from her husband and was hoping by our contacting him for further information about the nonexistent stalker, he would get back together with her.

These women have been known to go to great lengths to develop these false scenarios, such as striking themselves with objects to feign

---

* Kris Mohandie, Chris Hatcher, and Douglas Raymond, "False Victimization Syndromes in Stalkings," chap. 12 in *The Psychology of Stalking: Clinical and Forensic Perspectives*, ed. J. Reid Meloy (San Diego, Calif.: Academic Press, 1998).

being beaten, cutting themselves, and tearing and soiling their clothes in an attempt to show they were attacked. I recently watched a movie concerning this issue in which the woman was quite ingenious in her efforts to show that she was sexually attacked. She found a large male, convinced him to have rough sex with her that included being sodomized. She had earlier found a motel room and put her own bed sheets on the motel room bed. Once she had sex with the male, she removed the bed sheets and took them home. She then hung a bunch of baseballs in a pillow case, and struck herself about the head and torso with the balls. She then rolled in the sheets that already had the semen, body hair, and sweat from the male she had sex with, thus mingling her blood with his left-behind biological traces. At that point, she called the police, claiming to have been raped by a stalker.

A related example involved my wife, then a nurse, who was taking care of a young patient in her twenties, who had been hospitalized with a large number of unexplained bruises. One day while conducting her patient rounds she came into this female's room and found her striking herself with the phone receiver in the face and head area. This woman was not married and did not claim to have been assaulted by anyone, but she kept seeking treatment for these recurring self-inflicted injuries. It was felt that she was injuring herself to generate sympathy and attention, more than likely from family members. Again, these kind of feigned cases are rare.

In August 2002 I attended the Threat Management Conference in Anaheim, where Kris Mohandie, Ph.D., a well-known Los Angeles-based psychologist, was a presenter. A few days later, I had an opportunity to interview him. Dr. Mohandie has been involved in the research and behavior of stalkers over several years. (Refer to his résumé, listed in appendix A.) Mohandie, who has been involved with many high-profile cases such as that of O. J. Simpson and has interviewed both Madonna's and Steven Spielberg's stalkers, said that there are at least twelve different stalking perpetrator typologies described and published in research journals, papers, and books. Mohandie said that he has developed another typology, Context- and Relationship-

Based Stalking Typology (CARBST), which he has incorporated into a work he has just completed for the California District Attorneys' Association titled "Stalking: A Twenty-First-Century Perspective."

Lane and Zona's stalking classifications are used by many of us involved in the field of stalking. Because I like to simplify terminology, and make categories easier to remember, I prefer to use three more general classifications. Given the research I have reviewed, coupled with my own experiences, I estimate that about two-thirds of all stalking is related to domestic violence, so for the purpose of this book we will refer to the stalker born out of a known or "intimate" relationship simply as a *domestic violence stalker*. Then there are those persons who stalk coworkers or other acquaintances; we'll call them *acquaintance stalkers*. The last group comprises the stalkers who are complete strangers to their victims; let's refer to them as *stranger stalkers*. Even though I have used these classifications for years, I should tell you that I don't claim to have coined them. In fact, these terms are pretty much freely traded throughout the industry. My partners and I like these classifications, and we feel they fit the stalkers we encounter the best.

Nearly all the stalkers we have investigated or experienced or consulted on have one thing in common: they are serial in nature. For our purposes this means they all (with two exceptions) had stalked before. Our investigations have turned up one or more additional stalking victims in the stalker's past. Does this mean that all stalkers will *definitely* stalk more than one victim? We don't feel we have gathered enough data to conclude that, but there appears to be enough information to show there is definitely a common behavioral thread among most of the stalkers we have investigated or consulted on. (Much of the research studies done on the domestic violence stalker bears this out.) Most stalkers do in fact have multiple victims and will offend again. One stalker for whom we could not identify previous victims was a seventeen-year-old male. Is it possible that the stalking incident that brought him to our attention was the first of many for this young man? (The other case involved a fifty-year-old male who began stalking a male who was dating a woman the stalker felt very attracted to. Our research showed no prior history of stalking.)

Even though we have found that stalkers may perpetrate multiple victimizations over the course of their lives, we have observed another, even more profound stalking behavior emerging from a review of all our cases. Many stalkers seem to have a primary or significant victim that we refer to as the *genesis victim*. The genesis victim (GV) is the one victim that the stalker either returns to or obsesses over more than all his other victims. To illustrate this finding, let us give you some examples that have led us to this conclusion.

- We recently investigated a stalker who had a relationship with one woman whom he sodomized on a regular basis. He coerced her to have other women and/or men present when they had sex. Our investigation showed that he stalked at least three other women in his life, including two ex-wives. During the course of his relationship with these women he would continually talk about his genesis female to them as well as other persons he had any type of personal relationship with. Once he was stopped from stalking the other women, usually via law enforcement intervention, he would once again try to find and stalk the genesis female. We also found that he would always try and promote sodomy and multiple sex partners with the women he was currently dating and would then ultimately stalk. We found that for the stalker in general, the genesis female is almost like a drug or comfort food for their psyche.
- Another example of this was the Sandra Potter case, which we discussed earlier. No matter how many other victims Jake would stalk and in one case marry and subsequently stalk, he would still come back after Sandra. Our investigation showed that he felt that somehow Sandra and he were married, were life partners, and would never be separated.

An interesting feature of stalking patterns that we found is that the activity of many stalkers is triggered by dates or times of the year. One of our victims receives fruits, vegetables, and a Christmas card from her stalker around Christmastime. Another gets her tires slashed and notes left around the time of her birthday. Believe it or not, some of our victims complain about the stalking becoming more intense during a full moon. A victim may experience a lull in the stalking, and then on her birthday (or some other type of anniversary that means something to both the stalker and the victim), the stalking will begin all over again. We were told by one victim that no matter where she moved or who she was living with, she would always be fearful of her birthday. She would always get a card, a letter, or even a phone call from her long-time stalker. The lull, as we mentioned, may be the result of a number of reasons, such as incarceration on related or unrelated charges; the stalker maybe stalking someone else for a time; or he may become incapacitated due to illness or injury.

DOMESTIC VIOLENCE STALKERS

By the very nature of stalking behavior, any stalker at any time, given the right set of circumstances, can express violence that could lead to bodily injury, sexual violation, or death. Domestic violence stalkers (DVSs) seem to exhibit a greater propensity toward violence, because, we believe, they have already been in an intimate relationship with their victims. This history of relationship usually allows stalkers to exert a great deal of control over their victims, and stalkers can become extremely agitated when victims try to flee the relationship. Dr. J. Reid Meloy, along with Beth Davis, Ph.D., and Jon Lovette, Ph.D., recently conducted a study on the behavior of stalkers that indicated stalkers who have had a previous sexually intimate relationship with their victims are much more prone to violence against those victims as well as the victims' property.[8] I discussed this research with Dr. Meloy before the study was published.

Bear in mind that a relationship doesn't have to take place over a span of years for it to be classified as a DVS scenario—we have had stalkers begin their control/ pursuit games after a few weeks, and, on one occasion, only days after a relationship began.

Examples of violent DVSs

It's 2:00 in the morning. A thirty-year-old female is startled in her sleep by the pounding at her bedroom window of a thirty-five-year-old biker, her estranged boyfriend, with whom she had a sexual relationship. She opens the window and tells him to leave. The biker tells her to come with him or else he is going to kill her young son asleep in the next room. The woman knows this 6'2", 280-pound drug enforcer is capable of doing what he says, because she has seen him beat those who didn't take care of their drug tabs to a bloody pulp. Fearing for her son's safety she leaves with her ex. He has her drive to a "low-life" part of town to what she calls a "dirtbag" motel. The woman is then told to pay for the room. Once in the room our "hero" throws the victim on the bed, strips her, ties her hands and legs to the bed posts, and then proceeds to repeatedly rape and sodomize her. A few years later, we ended up arresting and successfully prosecuting this individual for felony stalking and burglary charges stemming from the prolonged stalking of another female whom he dated, married, and then later divorced. While in prison on those charges, my partner and I interviewed him concerning the shotgun execution-style murder of another of his ex-girlfriends, for which he is considered a suspect.

During the course of that interview, we were contacted by prison officials who took us into a private room and disclosed the following: apparently, our boy had been housed in a cell with another inmate who had drawn attention to himself by tearing up or attempting to destroy something belonging to our subject. When prison officials intervened, they found a notebook and diary that our heavily "inked"—i.e., tattooed—stalker had been keeping in his cell. The log had a series of articles on me! Due to the nature of my job, I've appeared on local television on a regular basis, and am even in the national media from time to time. I was also quoted in a number of newspapers due to the type of crimes my partner and I investigated. My partner would never talk to the press, so I was always the one nominated to handle the telephone interview and/or go before the camera.

This stalker had been cutting out the newspaper articles and making comments on or around them. Once we had this information, it explained why at the conclusion of our homicide interview with him, the stalker had said, "Hey Proctor, you had better stop watching *Star Trek!*" The *Orange County Register* had done a full-page spread with photos on me a year or so before this interview. The article had not been about police work directly but was rather more about the fact that a local homicide detective writes children's books and articles in his spare time. In the article I talked about how I enjoyed fantasy, science fiction, and *Star Trek*. Obviously, our stalker was able to read and wanted to convey in an indirect way that he was keeping an eye on me.

The incident with this stalker still had one more remarkable turn. The other inmate that was housed with our log-keeping stalker just happened to be a recently convicted murderer. Not just any murderer, but one that my partner and I had just put away for committing a stabbing death that had taken place some thirteen years earlier—it had remained unsolved for that period of time. Needless to say, he wasn't very happy with me. Again, what do you think the chances are that out of the hundreds of inmates in that prison those two would be housed together?

Keeping tabs on select law enforcement personnel is not unusual behavior for a stalker, since that officer has intervened between the stalker and his victim. Stalkers try to gather as much information as possible on those in the judicial system they encounter, such as judges and probation and parole officers. It is actually not uncommon for some of them to begin stalking these individuals.

When we conduct search warrants or arrest stalkers, we will often find notes and/or logs describing contacts with police. These include dates, times, and what interactions they felt took place during these contacts. Some stalkers will also come in and talk to us after their convictions and try to justify their behavior, even though we could care less. Some even begin their stalking campaign by sending letters to us, many written in such a fashion to manipulate us into conveying what is said to the victims. In some cases that information has to be shared for safety purposes or in order to gather more information from the victim; however we try to keep that to a minimum.

Domestic violence stalkers exhibit a variety of characteristics. Many are parasitic in nature: they tend to dominate and live off of their victim(s). For example, one of the stalkers we investigated would "collect" victims by meeting them in coffee shops, where he'd charm and befriend them in order to move in with them. For this particular stalker, it made no difference whether the victim was male or female, because he was bisexual. After a short period of time he would slowly begin to take over and control his victims to the point that they would be forced to spend their money only on what he wanted. They would go only where he wanted to go. If he wanted to be taken to a certain location and dropped off, they would then have to stay home so he could call them in order to be picked up—this often meant late in the evening or early morning hours. If they failed to comply they would be severely verbally abused. If that didn't elicit compliance, they would be brutally beaten. Domestic violence stalkers we have encountered, including the one just described, look for their victim's primary weaknesses, be they emotional or physical. They then feed off these deficiencies to build their span of control over the lives of these victims.

Another example of this behavior is that of a thirty-five-year-old male who became involved with a forty-eight-year-old divorced female. When he moved in with her, he convinced her to leave the apartment she had lived in for several years. He persuaded her to move into a more expensive two-bedroom apartment, just so that he could turn the spare bedroom into a shrine for all of the fishing gear that he had acquired over the years. Of course he lived off her, beating her when she did not work as hard as he thought she should or wouldn't comply with the sex act he wanted, which was usually oral copulation on an on-demand basis. When his meal ticket vacated the apartment to live with another man, he began to stalk her.

Our investigation revealed that he had stalked other women, on one occasion beating and throwing one of them down a flight of stairs. As we do with all stalkers, we profiled this particular individual so that we knew the best way to approach him when it came time to serve both an arrest warrant and a search warrant simultaneously. From the data we had gathered, we knew that this suspect probably had an obsessive-compulsive disorder. From this we expected to find his apartment to be in immaculate condition, with everything put away and having its own place. We were also told that he was an avid bike rider and that he held his fishing gear collection—much of it shoplifted from various discount houses—out to be among his most prized possessions. These factors gave us a formula to follow when we arrested and searched. Since we knew this individual was going to be particularly possessive about his property, we took the following actions:

1. We selected members of our narcotics detail to perform the search. These detectives are trained to do a combination of searches, and do them well. The kind of search we wanted to employ is what we call the "center dump search." This search technique is simple: we take all the items in each room out of the drawers, cabinets, and closets. After we search the areas, the items are placed in a pile in the middle of the room.

2. We wanted to hit the stalker's apartment when he was home. We chose to make contact and entry around 5:00 P.M. When we arrived, we found the stalker coming out of his apartment wearing his bike shorts and T-shirt. He had his custom-made cross-country mountain bike with him. We escorted him back into the apartment and assigned one detective to look over his bike while he sat handcuffed in his living room. We found his place to be just as we suspected—incredibly neat, clean, and organized.

3. We could tell by the look on the stalker's face that he was surprised and agitated with the investigator who was playing with the controls on his bike. Seeing this, I instructed the other detectives to conduct their searches in the rest of the rooms, and to make sure that the stalker knew they were actively searching each of the rooms in his apartment. We could see that the

stalker's demeanor was starting to change from an expression of surprise to one of frustration and mental anguish. We knew we had struck a nerve when he began whining, saying, "Do you guys have to touch all my stuff?"

4. The last room to search was the stalker's second bedroom, which he had in fact turned into a fisherman's shrine. He had hung all of his poles, lures, and other fishing gear neatly on the walls along with fishing posters. Because I was going to be the person to eventually interview this stalker, I took the lead on searching this room. I also made sure the stalker was in the room as I conducted this search, which totally devastated him. While conducting the search, I would pull all of his gear off the walls, making sure I worked all the mechanisms on his poles. I went through all of his tackle boxes, emptying out their contents on the floor so I could get a better look at what was in the boxes. In one box I located a hypodermic syringe, which in California is a misdemeanor to possess, unless it is for prescribed medical purposes. Even though possession of a syringe is illegal, fishermen commonly use them to blow up their worms so that they look more appealing to fish. I held it up to the stalker and told him that I was going to have to add an additional charge of needle possession to his booking slip.

Once we were done with the search, the stalker was escorted out of his apartment and was poured into the back of a police unit. When he was interviewed, he admitted to all the stalking behavior he was charged with, was convicted, and was placed on formal probation. Because we had done our homework on our stalker's background, we knew that touching his personal effects would cause him a great deal of stress and would break down his emotional resistance to what we were trying to accomplish, making him more inclined to tell the truth when we interviewed him. Remember, we have to be in control in the interview process, not the stalker. This is yet another reason why we find profiling such a critical tool when working with these individuals.

Hopefully, this example gives you a little insight into how we approach these people.

Many of our female DVS victims mention that their stalkers are heavy users of pornography. This pornography can range in content, depending on what type of sexual proclivities the stalker may exhibit. We have encountered the entire gamut of pornography, from straight sex to gang rape to bestiality. Many victims complain about control tactics being used in the sexual relationship, such as being handcuffed, tied up with cords, or sodomized. The stalker may refer to their victim as a "whore," "slut," or another person during sex. They may even demand that they dress in a certain fashion prior to or during sex. We had one stalker who would demand his former girlfriend dress as a "whore" prior to their having sex. Then during sex he would refer to her as a "slut" or "bitch," along with the names of women other than herself. We later found out via an interview that this stalker felt he needed to demean his victims in order to obtain a sexual climax. He also indicated that he felt all women were "whores."

Many victims complain that their stalker* caused them to lose friends, because he did not want them to associate with anyone but him. Most of them said that their stalker demanded to know exactly where they were at any given moment. Stalkers always seem to keep their victims on a mental time clock. Obviously, if you are beginning to experience some of these problems in a relationship, you might want to step back and take a good look at what is going on.

Another thing that we see quite often with the DVS is the threat of or an actual attempt of suicide. The stalker will threaten to commit suicide if the victim doesn't stay with him or her. We had a female stalker lie down by the side of her bed with a loaded handgun placed in her mouth staged in such a way as to shock her male victim—her boyfriend—when he entered her house to check on her welfare. We have had one male stalker try to poison himself in his parents' garage

---

* Though we would prefer to say "the man" or "the woman" stalking the victim, we use the phrase "their" stalker for the sake of simplicity, not connoting possession. Nor do we want to imply the victim wants any relationship with any stalker.

with carbon monoxide, knowing full well—or we guess, in his case, hoping—that he'd be saved before it was too late.

From time to time, I am called into the police department by social workers or detectives we work with concerning a female who they feel is in need of a stalking intervention interview. Even if the cases end up being handled by an agency other than ours due to jurisdictional lines, I still make an appointment to evaluate the potential stalking victim. I do this on a fairly regular basis to assist victims, no matter what jurisdiction they are going to end up in. I then document my findings and ship the report off to the handling agency. One of the social workers I work with had been told about a case that had been worked by another police department in another state. She wanted to tell me about the case because she thought it was somewhat unusual, and she believed I would find it interesting enough to use in my lectures.*

I offer this case from an out-of-state agency for examination, because it incorporates some of the methods of control we have alluded to that are used by the DVS but also to illustrate, for lack of a better term, a "unique" way this stalker chose to virtually control his victim. Now before we get into this particular scenario, I want you to keep an open mind—listen to all the facts and don't prejudge. We have found some unbelievable behavioral anomalies take place when a stalker enters a person's life, especially with a victim that may not know how to or cannot fight off the control the stalker imposes on her. Here are the facts of the case as given to me by the social worker as they were related to her:

- This older woman was reported to be an intelligent, caring individual that was at the end of her rope concerning the control the stalker had used on her over the years.
- The victim met the stalker in a workplace environment. (Not an uncommon location for a stalker to meet his prey.) A "normal" dating relationship ensued, with the victim and stalker moving in together after a few months of dating.

---

* As we have said before, to protect the victims described in this book, we must at times heavily disguise certain facts concerning the case to provide anonymity for the victims and any close associates. The stalking we describe in these cases did take place. We have left out certain identifiers that could lead to the discovery of these victims.

- Shortly after the stalker moved in with the victim, he began demanding sex on a repetitive basis. When his demands were not met, he would harass and browbeat the victim into submitting. During at least one of his outbursts the stalker had forcibly thrown the victim around the room.

- The victim was eventually able to get the stalker to move out of her residence, and she obtained a three-year restraining order. The stalker violated the order throughout this three-year period. The police were called, but to the best of the victim's knowledge, no arrests were made. It is unclear at this point whether that was due to lack of a more sustained action on her part or the police dropping the ball.

- Over a period of years, the victim received several phone calls a day from the stalker, most of which she perceived as threats. During these calls, the stalker threatened primarily to do three things. First, he said that he would contact the victim's ex-husband and tell him—as well as describe by example—how crazy and "psychotic" the stalker was. He then said he would tell the victim's ex-husband that even though she knew he was a mentally troubled individual, she allowed him not only to live with her and to sleep with her but also to have control over the ex-husband's and the victim's children. The victim related that the thought of her losing custody of or visitation rights to her children scared her so much it would kill her if it came to fruition. The stalker also threatened to show up at her home, her church, and her place of business to harass her as well as the people she dealt with in any capacity. The victim said he had already harassed her at her home, causing her untold embarrassment and mental anguish. The victim said that the stalker continually called her and repeated these threats as well as others over and over again. (We have seen these types of threats in more than one of our cases.)

- The stalker made the following demands on the victim or else he would carry out his threats: she would have to call him every morning when she arrived at work, when she arrived home from work, and before she went to bed. She also had to agree to see him on certain occasions no matter what other plans she had.

We were told that during the course of the victim's evaluation process, the out-of-state investigators began to feel that there was something else she wasn't telling them, which was causing her a great deal of pain. They felt there was a secret commitment that she did not want to discuss. Unfortunately, they were right. We were told that she broke down and admitted that a marriage had taken place. The victim said that after an intense three- to four-week campaign of continual calls and other harassing techniques generated by her stalker, she gave in and secretly married him. We were told the victim had been very close to committing suicide at that point in the stalking, and she felt there was nothing else she could do. Apparently the woman said the intimidation was so intense she felt she was going to lose what was left of her mind if she didn't somehow stop the stalker's relentless day-and-night harassment. The stalker kept telling her that if she would only marry him, he would stop harassing her. Our social worker was told by the investigators handling this case that it is crystal clear to their victim that this marriage was just another major control lock on her and her life.

Even if you, the reader, don't understand or agree with how this woman has handled her problem, keep in mind that she is still very much a victim, needs help, and is definitely being stalked.

The social worker told us she was informed by investigators that this poor woman felt that no one would believe that anyone could be controlled like this. We were told that the experienced investigators handling her case explained to her they had seen this type of control exerted on women over and over again. We would have told the victim the same thing. When we asked the social worker if she had heard anything about what had happened to the women in this case, she said she had not heard what the outcome was.

Another very important point we would like to make here concerning the DVS is the use of their own children as a tool against the victim. We usually see this with male stalkers and on occasion with estranged female stalkers. This is the primary reason we really dislike dealing with this type of stalker. The DVS will use his children, or in some cases her children from another marriage that have cohabitated with him (prior to the stalking taking place), as information gatherers on the victim's daily activities. He will then attempt to brainwash the children against the victim, telling them things like, "Your mother caused all this. She is a no-good whore and an adulterer," or "She brought people to court to testify against your daddy; what do you think about that?" The additional tragedy is that this stalker gets visitation rights at least until the victim can get either law enforcement or civil representation to assist her. (We will often work with the victim's civil attorney as experts or witnesses in their cases against the parent-turned-stalker.) When the stalker has the children on a visit, he or she works over the children, often causing them extreme mental anguish. This trauma is then brought home to the victim when the children act out, creating more stress on the victim.

For example, we investigated a DVS who had recently been estranged from his wife after fifteen years of marriage. At every opportunity he would get hold of his young children and begin grilling them about what their mother was doing, where she was going, and whom she might be seeing. (These interrogations were so forceful that persons who did not know the victim personally would take the time to find out who she was and write her letters expressing their concern for what the children's father was doing to them.) He told the children to call him at any time and give him reports about what she was doing. He would then contact neighbors in front of his children and refer to his ex-wife as a "slut" or a "whore." He then told the children that he was the only person they had to listen to and not to do anything their mother, who had physical custody, told them to do.

The besieged children were in crisis. The continual mental stress was manifested in repeated complaints of upset stomachs, headaches, and other stress-related symptoms. It was also reported that this stalker also instructed his young son to leave the side garage door of the victim's residence open, so that he could gain entrance and snoop around while she and the children were gone. He would contact the victim's babysitter and attempt to pump her for any information he could get on the victim's whereabouts or other activities.

My partner and I have experienced all these things nearly every time we deal with a DVS who has had children with the victim. On one occasion, the stalker took his twelve-year-old son to his ex-wife's house and had him watch while he broke into the house and turned on all the gas in the residence while vandalizing much of the victim's property. This stalker's intent was to have the victim's residence fill with gas and blow up when she flicked on a light switch or some other ignition source. Fortunately for the victim, there was enough ventilation for the gas not to cluster in any one portion of the house. This same stalker went into the victim's garage and modified her exercise bike. Being a semiskilled engineer-type, he was able to remove the victim's bicycle seat, adjusting it in such a fashion that when she began to ride the bike, the pedals would fail and cause the seat to fall away from the buttocks and pelvis of the victim, which would then expose the stainless steel seat post to the same areas of the rider. Remember, these individuals often are very intelligent and just as devious. They spend hours upon hours figuring out ways to cause the victim grief.

Another problem we experience with the DVS who has had children with the victim is involvement with the family court system. Now, we realize each state may have a different setup for complainants to battle out their differences when it comes to custody issues. Unfortunately, we have found ourselves at odds with many of the decisions of commissioners or judges involved in these custody battles. We have had cases in which the child has a separate, court-ordered attorney with a different agenda than what we in law enforcement have. Then other child welfare agencies get into the mix without knowing all the facts, which exacerbates the problem.

For example, we recently had a case in which we obtained a restraining order from the superior court against the estranged stalker boyfriend. The order prohibited him from bothering or harassing the victim and her two children, one of which was theirs out of wedlock. The stalker had been previously using visitation as a way of continuing to harass the victim and others with whom she was associating. Because the stalker's parents wanted to have visitation rights for the one child that belonged to both the victim and the stalker, his parents had another attorney go before a family court commissioner and get an order allowing the stalker limited visitation. This plan succeeded even though our investigation had uncovered that the stalker was probably molesting or had molested both young children! As you can see this is not only a nightmare for the children and the mother/victim but also for those of us in law enforcement who are trying to protect the innocents in these cases. We often feel that the left hand not only doesn't know what the right hand is doing but doesn't always seem to care, either.

While we are on the subject of stalkers and children, we feel the need to discuss another very unfortunate problem we have encountered during some of our investigations, so that the investigator or mental health professional reading this book might be alerted to some serious problems. One of the reasons we conduct background checks on our stalkers is to gather data that will allow us to better predict behavior. When we use the term *background check*, we are not only talking about finding out about the stalkers' previous criminal history but their emotional and environmental history as well. We have found that if stalkers were molested during their adolescence, they may well pose a significant threat to young children who are secondary to the primary stalking victim. This can and does often include their children.

A recent example of this was a stalker who had reportedly been molested in his youth by a babysitter's boyfriend on more than one occasion. Hearing this information, we contacted the female victim being stalked by this individual and warned her of the possibility of his molesting their young daughter. I was very concerned about this victim's daughter, because we knew that the stalker was still very fixated on the victim, specifically continually wanting to have sex with her. He had repeatedly expressed not only a desire but a "need" to have additional sexual relations with her. Therefore I felt strongly that in this particular case he might try to molest their daughter as a form of sexual transference. In other words he would fantasize that he was having sex with this female while actually sexually assaulting their daughter. We have seen cases in which the stalker also molests out of anger and as a form of retribution toward the stalking victim, knowing that the victim would be devastated when the molestation was found out. After I expressed my concerns to this young mother of two small children, I got a phone call that I didn't want to get. The mother/victim was in tears when she told me that her pre-adolescent daughter was trying to orally copulate with her young son in the bathtub, saying things that would indicate that "daddy," the stalker, was having her do the same to him. What the woman was telling me was that her daughter had been molested and was acting out what had occurred to her. This type of behavior is not unusual after a child has been molested.

Trust me, I don't always like to be right in situations like this, but unfortunately a psychiatric and forensic examination conducted on the victim's daughter showed that I was. Some of the things the stalker did and said while molesting his daughter also bore out my fantasy theory. Later reports also indicated that the stalker had also sexually molested the victim's pre-adolescent son. That stalker was eventually convicted of stalking and is at the time of writing on formal probation. The molestations took place in another jurisdiction, which complicates matters. It is still in the investigative stages at that agency. We have consulted on the case with the other agency's sex crimes detective and offered to assist in the investigation.

That brings us to another problem for those of us conducting stalking investigations, that of jurisdiction. When we begin a stalking investigation, we determine under which jurisdiction most of the stalking has occurred, and will notify the appropriate authority. If that law enforcement entity decides for whatever reason not to take the case, we will take the entire case, even if we have had limited numbers of stalking episodes take place in our city.

Once law enforcement personnel have taken care of the victim's needs and obtained satisfaction and relief through successful prosecution, the victim will continually come back to those personnel for every aspect of what is transpiring in their life in regard to this stalker, even when that victim has moved out of the jurisdiction. This is something we explain to the law enforcement personnel whom we instruct through our seminars; they need to know this so they are ready for it. I still have victims whose cases I completed working on years ago page me concerning questions or issues they have concerning their stalker or other current law enforcement problems. It could be visitation or molestation of a child that took place somewhere else. These victims trust the people they work with; they don't want to explain their case to several other people. They want the same people to handle the case or, at the very least, coordinate with the other detectives involved. We do our best to coordinate with other law enforcement agencies (most of which are very responsive to the plight of victims), and in some cases we actually do take over that department's case, if it can be cleared through the division supervisors of our respective agencies. For the most part, if a crime occurs within the boundaries of one city or county, that agency will investigate that crime. Most victims understand that I work for one city and cannot just come into another city and take over a case, but it is still hard on them if they feel they are not getting the same cooperation from the new agency. They don't care about politics or jurisdictions; all they care about are results. I can't say that I blame them. Because of this, we have somewhat of a reputation for not completely following all of the policies that are in place, thus stepping on a few toes to get some cases filed out of our jurisdiction. That is one of the reasons why I have a partner nicknamed the DCO (damage control officer) as well as a very understanding division commander.

We can best describe how sometimes even our best efforts are thwarted by an outside agency that just doesn't understand the stalker mentality by relating the following story. We were contacted by a woman who found out that the individual she had married was in fact a stalker that we had arrested on a few occasions prior to his becoming involved with her. This woman was in the process of divorcing this individual at the time and was also being stalked and threatened by him. She complained that his threats of violence were causing her to have a nervous breakdown as well as destroying a successful business she owned. She asked for our assistance. We contacted the "handling" police department, which was outside of our county. We informed them of the violence this stalker was capable of and sent them a great deal of background information on him. After obtaining the facts of their investigation, we knew they had a very good felony case against the stalker. I talked to their district attorney and offered to testify as a stalking expert for them. We even had our vertical-prosecution* domestic violence prosecutor call and talk to their district attorney in order to offer her assistance in regard to prosecuting this stalker. The next thing we knew, the stalker had pled guilty to a misdemeanor and was placed on probation with minimal terms.

In another case, we convicted an individual for felony stalking whom we are still investigating for possibly molesting his daughter. What brought this girl to our attention was again the fact that the stalker had been molested as a child, this time by his alcoholic father. The other thing that disturbed us was the fact that the daughter had recently begun to mutilate herself. She had been cutting her arms and other body parts, showed marked signs of depression, and discussed committing suicide. Her father, who was convicted of stalking another female, had reportedly dressed his daughter in provocative clothing and told her how nice her legs and body looked. This girl was at the time in her early teens.

While we are still in the DVS section of this book, we need to address the youthful offender class of stalker. It has been our experience that this category of stalker usually offends in intimate partner relationships that usually entail dating or even some type of cohabitation. This is not to say that there are not youthful stalkers whose

---

* Vertical prosecution is when a case is handled by the same district attorney from the preliminary hearing until it is completed at trial and sentencing. It eliminates confusion and other problems that can occur when a case is passed from one district attorney or prosecutor to the next.

actions fit in the acquaintance or stranger category, but we have not encountered them in the course of our investigations. We have found that the youthful offenders we have investigated resort to violence a great deal of the time.

We would like to take some time here to discuss a trend we are starting to see when it comes to youthful offenders, not only in the area of stalking, but in all areas of violent crime, especially major assault and homicide. We would first like to bring to your attention some very sobering statistics concerning these problems, compiled in *Trends in Juvenile Violence: A Report to the United States Attorney General on Current and Future Rates of Juvenile Offending.*[9]

- From a period of 1990 to 1994 the rate of killing by adults aged twenty-five and over declined 18 percent. Young adults ages eighteen to twenty-four gained only 2 percent, but homicides committed by youths fourteen to seventeen years dramatically increased by 22 percent. This surge in youth crime was found to have actually increased at the same time that there is a decline in teenage populations in the country. But as the youth of this nation grows, the crime rate still may rise.
- The report said that from 1985 to 1994, the rate of murder committed by teens, ages fourteen to seventeen, increased 172 percent. This increase took place among both white and black males but not in the female side of the equation.
- As a result of the offspring of baby boomers having babies, there are now over thirty-nine million children in this country under the age of ten. The report, published in 1996, further notes that "millions" of them live in poverty and lack the proper support groups necessary to foster positive goals and direction. The study states that "57 percent of the children in America do not have full-time parental supervision and that by the year 2005, the number of teens, ages fourteen to seventeen, will increase by 20 percent." This is very important because most of the published statistical studies show that this age grouping is where

most of the high-risk criminal behavior takes place. If you have raised kids in this age group, you know many of the reasons this is so: peer, cultural, and environmental challenges and influences, biological and hormonal changes, and what we refer to as "media corruption." (We feel that the continual onslaught of video and computer games that promote violence, especially hate-crime–type violence, causes a modern teenager to express a greater degree of violence to solve a perceived problem than teenagers of previous generations did.)

- "The largest increase in juvenile homicide involves offenders who are friends and acquaintances of their victims." This factor holds true for juvenile stalkers as well. For the most part, they stalk friends or known acquaintances. It would then stand to reason that there would be a certain number of juvenile stalkers who end up killing their victims.
- From 1989 to 1994, the arrest rate for violent crimes (murder, rape, robbery, and aggravated assault) rose over 46 percent among teenagers but only about 12 percent for adults. Even though this portion of the study was derived from information ending in 1994, we are still seeing an increase in juvenile crime.

We are fully aware that the country as a whole has experienced a drop in the overall violent crime picture. We are also aware that crime, like life, runs in cycles, and history does repeat itself. Over the past year, however, our law enforcement criminal planning and forecasting division has been advising us that we are currently gearing up for a criminal onslaught the likes of which we have not yet seen. They believe it will hit us around 2010. This coincides with our community's youth reaching the age of the highest-risk crime offenders, coupled with our demographics—a large grouping of low-income persons viewing themselves as disenfranchised, living in disrupted nuclear family units, etc.

If you are a parent and start to see the symptoms of stalking occurring in one of your children's lives, take heed. Our findings show that young people often let their emotions rule them, leading to disastrous results. This trend, like the ones we have just discussed, have not gone unnoticed by researchers; a study presented in the U.S. Bureau of Justice Statistics (BJS) advised, "Vulnerability to violent crime victimization varies across the age spectrum." The researchers went on to say that the age of twenty seems to be where the greatest number of victims fall, and the numbers slowly decrease from that age onward. The report also said that teenagers tend to experience the highest rates of criminal victimization.[10]

These same studies also tend to back up what we in the field of stalking are finding—that the greatest risk of violence seems to occur when the victim tries to leave the relationship. The youths who become stalkers don't seem to develop the coping mechanisms needed to make rational decisions, so they seem to go "over the top" quicker than perhaps an older stalker would. Some of these youths reach the point of desperation in a very short period of time. They don't contemplate the meaning and essence of life and end up following the stalking credo to its fullest: *"If I can't have you, no one else will."* As many are aware, youth suicide is not an uncommon occurrence, nor is the act of juvenile or teenage murder/suicide. Of all the behavior discussed in this section, the likelihood of violence seems to be greatly enhanced when the stalker falls into the ranks of counterculture entities and fringe groups such as skinheads, Satanists, cultists, etc. These over-the-edge belief systems can often help to ignite the loose cannon's behavioral fuse much quicker than would otherwise happen.

Due to the recent outbreaks of youth violent behavior toward others in school environments, the FBI, through the National Center for the Analysis of Violent Crime (NCAVC) and the Critical Incident Response Group (CIRG), under the tutelage of Supervisory Special Agent (SSA) Mary Ellen O'Toole, Ph.D., has launched a several studies on how and why this type of deadly behavior occurs. Even though this particular group of studies has nothing to do directly with the teenage stalker, reviewing the information and conclusions from these projects can many times assist us when we begin to evaluate the threat potential of not only this type of youth but that of the youthful stalker.

We have seen youthful offenders beat both male and female targets during the course of the stalking. Others sexually assault their victims. For example, we arrested a seventeen-year-old Asian youth who had been stalking his estranged girlfriend for some months. He came into our purview when he kidnapped her from her high school campus and took her to a relative's house a few cities to the east. There he took her into an upstairs bedroom, secured the room by nailing the bedroom door shut, and began sexually assaulting her. During the course of our interview, we asked him why he had raped his captive. He responded that he wanted to possess and control his victim and that if he could impregnate her, she would have to stay with him forever. (Unfortunately, due to some elements in that victim's culture, she did not fully cooperate during the time of trial; we were only able to convict the subject on lesser charges.)

ACQUAINTANCE STALKERS

The acquaintance stalker (AS) is not as common as the DVS but is more prevalent than the stranger stalker. These stalkers encounter their victims in a variety of ways, from an initial chance encounter in a supermarket to meeting them in the workplace, at church, or in some other public location. In each one of these cases the victim knows that the stalker exists but has never had any kind of intimate or sexual relationship with that individual. They may have a casual, noncommittal relationship, but nothing that has led to anything significant, at least not in the mind of the victim.

We investigated the stalking case of a nineteen-year-old, blonde-haired, blue-eyed male with a model's physique and classic boyish good looks, who lived with his parents in our city but was a member of a church in a neighboring town. One day a very attractive twenty-two-year-old female exotic dancer came to the church, saw our male victim, and got someone in the church to arrange an introduction between the two. Shortly after the introduction, the stalker told several of her associates that the victim was "Jesus" and she wanted to "fornicate" with him forever and have his children. In the beginning, our victim did not feel threatened by the stalker, even though she wore skimpy clothes, dyed her hair multiple colors, and was a smooth talker. On one occasion, she was able to gain entry into his house without him being there by claiming to his father that she was one of his girlfriends. While in the victim's house the female began to circulate throughout its interior, looking for his room. We believe she was not only canvassing the interior of the house, getting the layout, but was also looking for "trophies." The stalker was short-circuited when the victim's mother came home from shopping. Mom took one look at our stalker, kicked on her intuition radar, and sent her out of her house.

One night the victim's fear quotient dramatically changed. Around 2 or 3 A.M. the well-endowed stalker came to the young victim's open bedroom window wearing what could only be described as the bare minimum. She began dragging her nails across the window screen, demanding in a low, sexy voice to come in. The stalker continued to plead with the youth, telling him she needed to make love with him. Though she had appeared this way before him on other occasions and had sent him nude photos of herself, this night was different. When she continued with her urgings to gain entry, he told her that he thought she was "crazy" and asked her to go away. The stalker then pressed her face up against the screen of the victim's open window and in the words of the victim, "morphed into a demon bitch from hell." Then this transformed hellion said, "Don't you ever call me crazy again! I don't want to hurt you like I did the others!" The victim said he was so terrified, he fell off his bed, rolled underneath the box springs, and hid there until he could no longer hear her haggard breathing at his open window.

Further investigation showed that on one occasion our female stalker had become so enraged with her current boyfriend that she had taken two butcher knives, stuck them into the mattress on the side her boyfriend normally slept, and pulled down both knives through a good deal of the mattress. That takes a tremendous amount of strength, especially for a petite female. When we finally were able to take the stalker into custody, she was attempting to get a plane ticket out of the state. When we interviewed her, she admitted to believing that our victim was in fact Jesus Christ. She admitted to us that she did want to have his children and that she felt he had the most beautiful eyes she had ever seen.

This stalker pled guilty to felony stalking and was supposed to report for a psychiatric evaluation before sentencing. Before that could take place, however, she was bailed out of custody by a relative and fled the state. A warrant has been issued for her arrest. We have been told she may be living in Hawaii.

We should tell you that when we conducted a search warrant on this stalker's apartment, we found diary notes she had kept on our victim. The notes revealed that our stalker had already picked out names for the children she was planning to have with the victim and discussed sexual feelings she had for him (Figures 2 and 3).

Even though we know that domestic violence and intimate relationship stalkers have a higher propensity for violence in general, that doesn't mean acquaintance or stranger stalkers cannot commit their share of violence. For example, I consulted on another Orange County case involving a young female victim in her twenties, whom we will call Wilma. The investigator who handled the case is a seasoned homicide detective who had attended one of my stalking seminars held by the Orange County District Attorney's office. While investigating a series of contacts the stalker had had with Wilma, the detective had researched the stalker and had found out that he had done time in northern California for stalking another female. During the course of that stalking, he had put a loaded shotgun in that victim's mouth and poured gasoline on her, threatening to burn her to death. He was subsequently arrested and convicted. While in prison this stalker became a prison inmate firefighter who put out forest fires. He traveled throughout the state working in this capacity and stayed in halfway houses while assigned to the firefighting detail. Once on parole, this stalker began a casual relationship with Wilma, telling her he was a firefighter. He just didn't happen to mention that he fought fires during

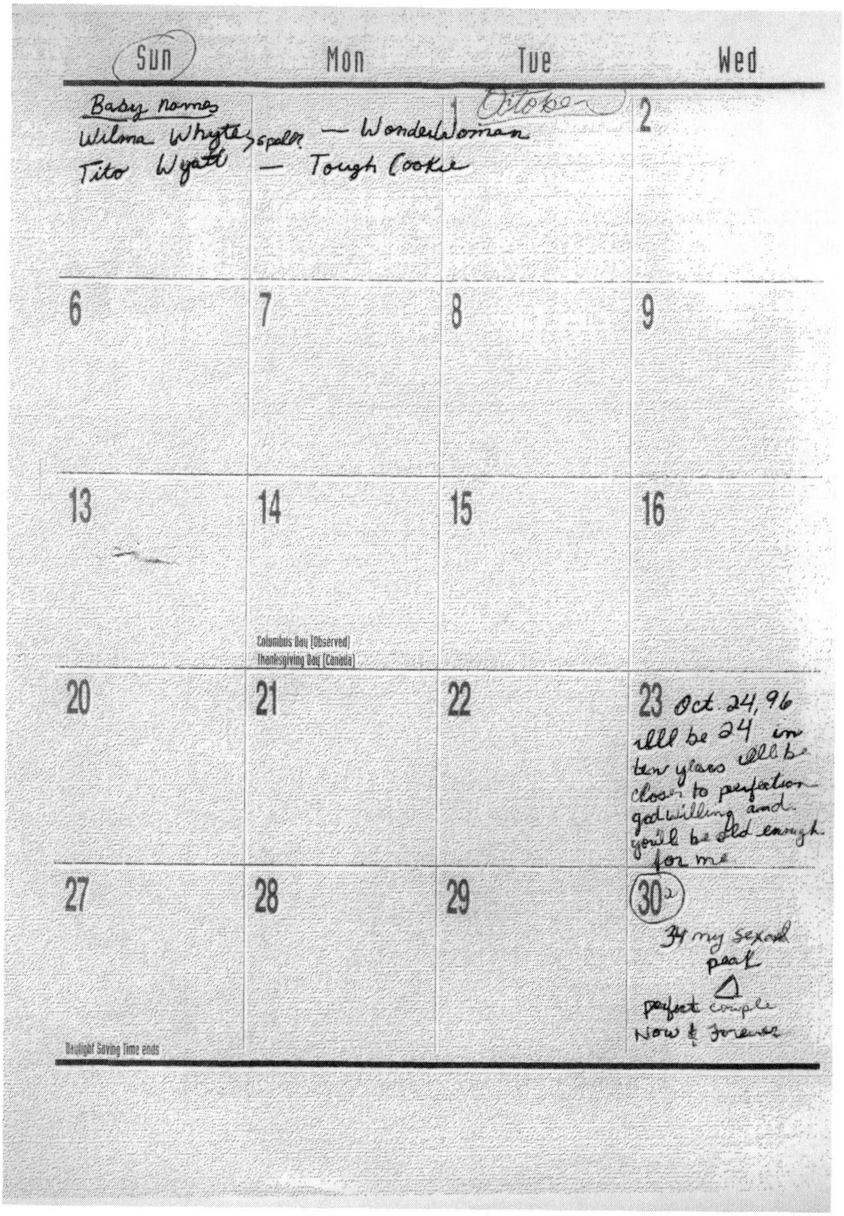

Figure 2. Female stalker maps out her sex life for herself
and her intended victim.
(Courtesy of the Westminster Police Department)

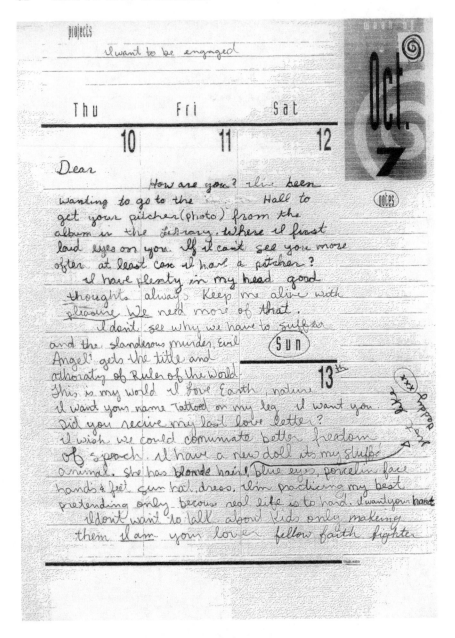

Figure 3. Female stalker's love letter to unwilling victim.
(Courtesy of the Westminster Police Department)

the day and slept in a custodial environment at night. (Remember, we told you these individuals are charming and resourceful.) According to the detective, Wilma never had a relationship with the stalker other than a casual, nonsexual type. While dating or associating with another northern California female, the stalker would travel to Orange County to harass Wilma. One of the things he did to let Wilma know when he had been in her neighborhood was to leave an unusual calling card: a live 12-gauge shotgun shell on the windshield of her car.

Due to the stalker's violent past, coupled with the fact that the contacts and threats were getting more frequent, the detective set up surveillance on Wilma's residence. As it turns out, his quick thinking saved Wilma's life. The stalker arrived in a stolen car and was immediately taken into custody. When the vehicle was searched they found duct tape, a ski mask, gloves, and a loaded shotgun and handgun, which had both been stolen. The stalker later told the detective that he was going to kidnap the victim, turn her into his sex slave, sexually assault her for a while, and then kill her.

It should be noted that the detective recently related to me that after he had put the stalker away on these charges he began to get regular letters from the stalker. The stalker wrote the letters in such a fashion that it appeared as if he were writing to an old friend. The detective advised the prison officials to discourage any further communication being transmitted to him by the stalker.

Also under the AS category is the stalker encountered at the workplace. Of course, all stalkers are problems, but these stalkers are real pains. They create a whole new set of problems for the victim as well as his employer. The stalker usually works in the same building or an adjoining complex. This means he has regular, seemingly legal access to the victim for the purpose of work. It is especially difficult when the stalker is the victim's superior.

Unfortunately, gender still seems to bias the chance of resolving this type of stalking in too many of these cases. (Of course, not all employers are ignorant, but many still lack the insight or training to handle these situations.) If the victim is female, and the stalker is male (as is the case more often than not), the victim may have an uphill battle. For instance, we counseled an intelligent thirtyish female who worked for a public entity. She had been stalked for several years by a male fellow employee whom she had never dated. During that time she had gone on several occasions to her male superiors with this problem. Initially, they told her not to worry about it; they said the stalker was just infatuated with her. When the stalker persisted, so did she in pressing the issue. The superiors finally contacted the individual and told him to keep clear of her. This worked for a few weeks, but then he started again. The superiors' disregard for the victim's plight became even more apparent when the stalker got into a minor problem with the law (unrelated to the stalking) and was given community service as a punishment. So what did the stalker do? He put in for community service in the same department as the victim's—in a desk right next to hers. This request was granted by—you guessed it—her superior. The victim told us that it had now gotten so bad that she had been told by her supervisor that if she still had a problem, she should think about quitting. (Folks, this type of posture should probably have been rethought by this woman's superior. Failure to provide for a safe working environment is becoming a growing area of civil litigation among wily attorneys.)

We should also mention that stalking can also occur on the premises of the workplace by a stalker who doesn't work there.

The following is an example of how a callous and cavalier attitude by management can backfire when it fails to deal properly with a workplace stalking issue. I assisted in writing a civil brief in what is believed to be the first stalking tort case in California and probably the United States. At issue was a female employee of a large supermarket chain. Over a period of time, a male customer had fixated on her; this unsolicited infatuation led to stalking. The female complained and asked for relief from store management on several different occasions, but she received none. The stalking behavior increased until an encounter in the store parking lot between the victim and the stalker, along with other associated threatening behavior generated by the stalker, finally led to the victim's bringing an action against both the store for failure to provide a safe working environment and the stalker for the emotional damages that he had caused. The victim prevailed. Needless to say, if the store administration had just taken a few simple steps to assist the victim/employee, this could have been remedied without any type of civil litigation.

STRANGER STALKERS

All stalkers create their own brand of terror. In the case of the stranger stalker (SS), however, the unknown adds an additional element of fear to the mix. The SS is someone who fixates on a particular victim but is unknown (at least consciously) to that victim in any way, shape, or form. This person then begins to make contact with the victim in a variety of ways that initially may seem harmless. When continued over a period of time, this contact mounts and generates fear and terror for the victim. Some clarification is in order here. Many of us have sent flowers or other gifts to someone we would like to meet and eventually date. At times we have sent these gifts in the name of a secret admirer, or something to that effect. The difference between us and the stalker is that we have let the person of our desires know who we are a short time later, usually in an attempt to progress in that relationship. It has been our experience that the SS does not make himself known for a much longer period of time and continues with the stalking behavior.

We were contacted by a young aerobics instructor who worked for a chain of workout studios in the area. The instructor said that someone unknown to her had been leaving notes of a sexual nature on her car at work. She mentioned that was a common occurrence and didn't think much of it until she came home one day and found that someone had entered her apartment and had written the words "I am watching you" in the dust on her television with something, possibly a finger. She told us that she was moving because of this incident; we have had no further contact with her.

Another example: we are currently monitoring a case in which several incidents have occurred over the past $1\frac{1}{2}$ years. A nice-looking, well-kept, divorced woman about forty-five years old lives in a middle-income residential neighborhood. She owns her house and keeps it and her grounds immaculate. The woman works days, lives alone, and keeps to herself. Over the observed time period she has been finding things in her yard, usually in the back yard, stacked in threes: trash cans arranged in threes, small pieces of folded paper arranged in threes on her rear window sill, and so on. Just recently things took a more unusual slant when she found three large butcher knives stuck into the ground in her garden. That caused some concern, so we canvassed the neighborhood and came up with two possible suspects—one being a retarded youth, and the other being a forty-year-old male that prowls the neighborhood at night. Her most recent contact was when someone had left a piece of paper laying next to her furnace pilot in her outside furnace box. The paper had been rolled in such a fashion as to indicate to us that someone was going to, or had already attempted to, light the paper in the furnace pilot. (The victim has had no further contact since our canvass.)

On its face, this scenario may not seem like much to the casual observer. Because of our past experiences with unusual activity such as this, we tend to take a little closer look. Not too much time had passed when we had a similar set of circumstances present themselves on the east side of our city. We had received calls concerning a prowler lurking in a middle-class residential neighborhood late at night, but no one could actually describe him or her. Then one night this large thirteen-year-old male prowler, a resident of the neighborhood, crawled through a front bathroom window, armed himself with a large butcher knife from the kitchen, entered the bedroom of a sleeping middle-aged female, probably to sexually assault her. As he slipped his hand under her top and began to fondle her breast, the startled victim awoke from a deep sleep in a panic. The powerful 6'2" youth thrust the butcher knife's blade through the terrified woman's chest. She eventually succumbed to her wound.

Our investigation revealed that this same prowler had peeped into another woman's residence and had stolen a long-bladed hunting knife from that victim's master bedroom. Our investigation further showed that this youth had been drawn to the deceased victim's daughter for a period of time. He would, in fact, watch her from behind a block wall that surrounded their house. You can now see why in our job we cannot take anything for granted. Experience and intuition based on perception go hand in hand to save lives.

When we interviewed our youthful killer, it was as though we were talking to a robot. As he related the steps he took to commit the crime, he showed absolutely no sign of remorse or other emotion, for that matter. Unfortunately, Terry and I had seen this type of detached response in other killers that we had interviewed, but not in one this young. This prompted us to fill out an awareness form directed to California's Violent Criminal Analysis Program (VICAP) housed at the Department of Justice in Sacramento so that this individual could be tracked when he got out of prison—in his case the California Youth Authority (CYA). We also asked to be made aware when he was due for release. (Because of his age, he would only be housed until he was twenty-five-years old and then would be released back into society.)

When he came up for release, we were notified and heard something else we found prophetic. We were told that, while in custody, our young stalker/predator had continued to exhibit the same emotionless characteristics that he had shown before going into prison, and he hadn't changed his stalking/peeping behavior. Apparently, he had been found a couple of times under the floorboards of the women's prison guard shower stalls while they were in use.

We feel that another type of predator that falls into our stranger stalker category is the pedophile (child molester). Many people do not associate the word *stalking* with pedophilia because a large number of molestation victims are relatives or family associates. But there is another group of sexual predators out there that do in fact stalk their young victims for a period of time before striking. They follow, catalog, and often compile diaries and writings concerning their prey, who in most cases knows nothing of the stalker until it is too late. Some of these predators actually make contact with the victims prior to attempting or completing molestation, but it is usually a very indi-rect or very casual contact such as sitting or standing next to the child or walking past him or her on various occasions.

I recently got a referral from one of the professors of the colleges where I conduct seminars. The woman the professor had referred to me had a young child that had been stalked without the knowledge of the family. This sexual predator had written a letter outlining his desire for the child and what he was going to do to him when he kidnapped the child. In the diary notes the predator indicated that he had some concerns about his ability to kill this child once he had completed his molestation. A law enforcement interview with this same subject revealed that he claimed to have molested well over two hundred children and could not stop himself from continuing to accost children. This stalker was placed in a mental evaluation facility. While there, he wrote a letter to the poten-tial victim's mother stating that he would continue to fantasize about her child and that there was nothing that she could do about it. The mother had the predator served with a restraining order while he was in the facility. She told me that stopped the letters from coming.

This mother was curious to know if I felt this was a stalking, and if there was anything in the California stalking statute that could be used to get this individual arrested. The answer was yes, we felt it was definitely a case of stalking in its purest form, but because there had been no attempt to make contact with the victim—in this case her child—the jurisdiction where the stalking was taking place could not pursue a criminal charge under the current California stalking statute.

I would like to take this opportunity to revisit this mother's con-cern. I personally feel that there should be legislation that would allow for the prosecution of stalking once a stalking plot is discovered, either by accident or direct investigation. If we can demonstrate that a course of conduct and planning existed for a period of time, but had not yet reached the completion of a direct act, why not eliminate the threat? At least have the individual evaluated and/or attend counseling ses-sions designed to try and break down or eliminate this behavior. I refer to counseling with some skepticism because, to my knowledge, persons with this type of obsession are rarely cured, but they can possibly be controlled for a period of time.

We should note that stalking a child twelve or younger is specifically defined as a crime under section 22-19A-7 of the South Dakota Codified Laws. Another law we found concerning the stalking of children comes from the Michigan Statutes Annotated under section 750.411h(2)(b): "If the victim was less than eighteen years of age at any time during the individual's course of conduct and the individual is five or more years older than the victim," the crime of stalking becomes a felony. In New Mexico, if the child is under sixteen, it is a felony stalking. Even though these laws are a step in the right direction, they both appear to also have the caveat that the child must be threatened and aware of that credible threat before a stalking can be charged.

This brings up another example of a stalking that occurred in a neighboring state. According to the investigator that I talked to, this stalker had lived next door to a family with a very young girl. For unknown reasons, this male neighbor, at the time of writing in his late thirties, had become enamored with this little girl, and over the course of several years stalked her. The investigator said that the stalker believed he was married to the young girl and felt they should be together. He would send her gifts, cards, and notes while maintaining continual surveillance of her comings and goings. He was recently prosecuted for felony charges stemming from the stalking of the girl, who is now in her teens.

Unfortunately, there are still too many of these parasitical stalkers slithering around in our midst. Most pedophiles we have encountered have stashes of child pornography, magazine articles with cutouts of children that look like the subject they are pursuing, and diaries that they must chronicle to promote their obsession and excitement fantasies surrounding the child. It has been our experience, as well as that of the experts we have talked to over the years, that incarceration seems to be the only way to stop the pedophile from exercising his trade. Most states don't have laws that allow them to warehouse pedophiles and other sexual predators for the rest of their lives in order to protect society. However, such states as Kansas, California, Minnesota, New Jersey, Florida, and Wisconsin have "Sexual Predator Commitment Laws." These laws allow the state to civilly commit a person who has been classified as a sexual predator in a custodial treatment center for periods of time past their initial criminal commitment.*

Pedophiles are not the only type of predator-class criminals that stalk before committing their crimes. Even though this class of criminal does not follow the precise definition of stalking that we presented in chapter 1, these criminal stalkers still exhibit stalking behavior by going after their targets in a violent manner. They follow, they surveil, they document, they plan, and they pose a very credible threat to their victims. Some serial killers as well as some types of rapists stalk their victims before raping and/or killing them. We have investigated cases where individuals were killed by murder-for-hire suspects who "stalked" the victim and, in one case, family members of the victim before committing the murder.

Let me try to illustrate my point with yet another instance of predator stalking that I investigated. This was a stalking that the stalker did not plan to make known to the potential victim before killing him. Because I was also trained as a bomb investigator, I was assigned to investigate the detonation of an explosive device at a local high school, where a homemade device with a time-delay fuse was used. The device was simple but quite effective. During the course of the investigation, I was able to narrow the scope of its potential designer to a very intelligent young student who attended that particular school. Once in contact with this particular individual, I was able to find a cache of pipe bombs, explosive ordnance materials, and logs concerning his intended use for these weapons.

After going through the logs and paperwork, I was able to ascertain that this subject had been monitoring—stalking, if you will—the comings and goings of one of the teachers at the school he attended. The youth did not like the teacher. He had drawn a schematic for an explosive device that would be attached to the teacher's vehicle under

---

* For more information on these and other states' "Sexual Predator Commitment Laws," search the Internet under that topic. One site is www.wa.gov/wsipp/reports/predlaws.html.

the hood wiring system. The device had both a pipe bomb and a set of propane tanks set in series. The propane tanks would have greatly enhanced the explosion with a powerful thermal reaction. According to the bomb disposal and ordnance experts we queried concerning his plans, the device was sound and probably would have been killed the teacher and destroyed a great deal of his car. Our young bomber, who had done a tremendous amount of planning and research, was very proud of all his projects. He had compiled his entire bomb-making data without the use of the Internet. Our investigation revealed other instances of explosive device detonations he had set off, not only at the school but elsewhere as well. He appeared to be experimenting with various types of explosives as well as developing various trigger mechanisms. We surmised that these test detonations were precursors to the planned killing of the teacher. The youth was arrested and prosecuted on felony charges for possession and manufacturing of explosive devices. He was housed in juvenile hall for a period of time, where he received counseling, after which he was placed on probation.

FEMALE STALKERS

We have dealt with female stalkers since 1991. Even though stalking is predominately perpetrated by men, women are also well represented. Until recently, though, few if any studies had been done that specifically targeted the role of the female stalker. Therefore we feel it is necessary for us to give equal time to women who perpetrate this crime.

We recently supplied information on many of the female stalkers we have investigated over the years to Dr. J. Reid Meloy and another of his associates, Cynthia Boyd, who holds a Ph.D. in clinical psychology. Dr. Boyd is currently working in a clinical position at the University of California at San Diego's Department of Neuropsychiatry and Behavioral Medicine. Dr. Meloy and Dr. Boyd have just completed their study, which was also Dr. Boyd's doctoral thesis, titled "Characteristics of Female Stalking Perpetrators: Behavior, Psychology, and

Violence Risk." In May of 2002, I interviewed Dr. Boyd concerning Dr. Meloy's and her findings, which I found to be quite interesting. Dr. Boyd affirmed that their research covered samplings in the United States, Canada, and Australia. The following are some of their findings:

- The average age of female stalkers was in the late thirties.
- Most were single white heterosexual females.
- One-third of these women had children of their own at the time of the stalking.
- The majority of their male victims were white heterosexual males, usually in their forties.
- Close to half of the male victims were married at the time of the stalking. None of the female stalkers were married to the men that they stalked.
- Dr. Boyd advised, "Even though we had limited psychiatric data, we found one out of five had a delusional disorder." Dr. Boyd said that the way in which their survey was structured allowed the "respondent" (a police detective or other professional involved with stalkers) to use a check box concerning "psychotic symptoms" with a space for describing the mental condition of the stalker at the time of the stalking. She said some of the responses they obtained in the study were Erotomanic-Type disorders and Grandiose-Type delusional conditions.*
- The majority of the females were not "psychotic" at the time of the stalking. (For a definition of this term, refer to the section in this chapter titled "Psychological Terms That Apply to the Pathology of Stalking.")
- 48 percent of the female stalkers surveyed had a "Borderline Personality Disorder." (Again, refer to "Psychological Terms That Apply to the Pathology of Stalking," this chapter, for a definition of this term.)

---

* According to psychologists we talked to, the Erotomanic-Type disorder revolves around an individual's delusional belief that another person is in love with them. Most of the time the person the subject, in this case a stalker, has fixated on is of a higher social position or status than that of the stalker. In regard to the Grandiose-Type disorder, we are told that many persons diagnosed with this disorder believe they are persons of power or wealth. In a case of stalking, the stalker suffering from this delusion believes she is having a relationship with a person who is in fact rich, powerful, and/or famous.

- About 27 percent of the females had a substance abuse problem at the time of the stalking.
- About half of the female stalkers had a high school diploma or GED equivalent.
- 38 percent were either college graduates or had attained advanced graduate degrees.
- Dr. Boyd explained that in their study they divided their stalkers into four classifications: Acquaintance, Prior Sexual Intimates, Stranger, and Family. The study showed:
  - 49 percent of the stalkers were found to be of the Acquaintance variety—who had had no previous sexual contact with the victim, but who could be coworkers or associated in other ways.
  - 27 percent were Prior Sexual Intimates—persons that had had an intimate relationship with the victim and/or had lived together.
  - 21 percent of the stalkers were Strangers—i.e., completely unknown to the victim before the stalking took place. Dr. Boyd noted that many of these victims were in the "media world," but not all.
  - 2 percent of their sampling consisted of family members.
- One of four female stalkers in the study was violent. The study showed that the highest rate of violence was found in the Prior Sexual Intimate category, with 55 percent exhibiting some type of violence. (Again, we are seeing the greatest amount of violence in the domestic violence stalking situations.)
- Female stalkers tended to call or send e-mail rather than follow their male victims.
- Dr. Boyd said that one of the disturbing behaviors of the female stalker was that "the majority made daily contact" (via mail, faxes, phone calls, etc.).
- The average time that the female stalker pursued her male victim was from one to five years.
- Of the eighty-two case studies involved in this study, there were three homicides committed by female stalkers.

- Dr. Boyd stressed that one of the more important findings that came out of Dr. Meloy's and her research was that "males tend to pursue to maintain intimacy, and females tend to pursue to establish intimacy."

Some of the study's findings can be found in the May 2002 issue of *Men's Health* in an article titled "Mad About You." The article gives the reader a good overview of some of the problems faced by the male who is not only being stalked by females but by other men as well.

We in the law enforcement community find such studies extremely helpful when developing our profiles on stalkers. The more empirical studies there are on the stalking phenomenon, the better it is for everyone concerned—except for the stalker, of course.

WHY STALKERS STALK

As we stated at the beginning of this chapter, one of the most often asked questions is, why do stalkers stalk? Perhaps we can best shed some light on this question by exposing the reader to some of the statements made by the various types of stalkers either to their victims or during interviews we have conducted with them.

Domestic violence stalker: "I don't know why she is doing this to me." "I really love her." "She has caused me to follow her." "I pulled the phone lines out of the wall because I just wanted to talk to her." "She knows that she belongs to me." "She just needed my help, so I directed her." "I can't live without her." "Can't you see she is the one stalking me?" The domestic violence stalker seems to believe the root of his problem lies with the victim, not the other way around.

Even though we are not psychiatrists, we are trained observers. We see the following characteristics with DVSs: a desire for extreme control; obsessive behavior; vengeful attitudes; an inability to handle rejection; and an assumption of little or no responsibility for his or her actions.

Acquaintance stalker: "She loves me, she just doesn't know it yet."

"We are married and have two children, but my family is keeping them from me." (This female was talking about being married to an individual whom she never married and referred to children she never had. Obviously, this person had more problems than a simple case of obsession.) "I know I am the right person for her." "I know she is completely in love with me; I seem to affect all women that way." "She causes these things to happen because of the way she presents herself."

We have observed the following traits among ASs: an inclination toward fantasy; obsessive behavior; and personality and/or mental disorders ranging from simple to extreme.

Stranger stalker: We would have to group the SS's behavior in the same category as the AS—fantasy-oriented and obsessive, with definite personality disorders or mental disabilities. Here are a couple of gems we've collected over the years: "I am watching you." "I like the red panties the best." "I don't like that dress on you." "I know the elementary school she goes to and what class she is in." "The thought of kidnapping and raping him is very sexually exciting to me." (A pedophile's entry, found in his diary.)

The mental health experts we have queried say that stalkers suffer from a variety of conditions. These include, but are not limited to, paranoid schizophrenia, delusional disorders, and a series of personality disorders, such as narcissistic personality disorder and borderline personality disorders, which seem to be a few of the more prevalent disorders encountered. (These same experts tell us that some stalkers may exhibit more than one personality disorder.)

PSYCHOLOGICAL TERMS THAT APPLY TO THE PATHOLOGY OF STALKING

We feel strongly that it is important for you, as well as any investigator assigned to work these kinds of cases, to familiarize yourselves with some of the psychological disorders that any of us may come in contact with when dealing with stalkers. Therefore we are going to make an attempt to define and hopefully clarify these conditions for you, the reader. The work the forensic psychologist and psychiatrist compile aids us in our job. However, I need to put their findings in a much simpler format so that I, and hopefully others, can digest their words of wisdom. Our plan is not to take you through the entire pages of the *DSM-IV-TR* (*Diagnostic and Statistical Manual of Mental Disorders*, fourth edition); rather, it is to familiarize you with some of the terminology as well as some of the conditions we see manifested in the majority of the stalkers we encounter. Our purpose here is to provide you with a closer glimpse into the often twisted mind-set of the stalker. This is a realm that we who investigate the stalker must enter in order to better understand and then to stop or prevent this type of predator's activities.

Psychotic: "A person who is afflicted with a psychosis." A psychosis is "a severe mental disorder of organic, psychological functional cause, or the combination, that leads to bizarre mental states and behavior. Signs may include confusion, delusions, hallucinations, incoherence, phobias, mood swings, mutism, violence."[11] We investigated a stalker whose psychiatrist informed us he was no longer able to treat him because he was refusing to take his medication and having too many psychotic episodes. When we contacted the parents of this individual, they told us that they had attempted to get their son additional medical attention, but he was often too delusional and uncontrollable to receive such help.

While waiting in the courtroom to testify against this stalker in his most recent case, I advised the deputies that were monitoring him to pay close attention to what he was doing. The stalker, who was sitting by himself, began to talk to a nonexistent entity that he perceived to be sitting next to him. After a short period of time, their "conversation" became more and more heated. We could overhear our stalker telling his hallucination, "No, no, I am not going to do that." I explained to the deputies that whatever the stalker was being told to do was agitating him a great deal, so they needed to pay a little closer attention. As we all know, things can get violent in the courtroom. I have already had one defense attorney stabbed in the neck by his client in another non–stalking-related case I worked, so I didn't want anyone hurt on this case.

Schizophrenia: "A complex group of psychotic conditions associated with such symptoms as disorganized speech, inappropriate behavior, delusions, hallucinations, emotional flatness, and lack of motivation."[12] We hear a lot about this condition in the media and elsewhere, but quite frankly, we do not see a great deal of this behavioral type among the stalkers we encounter. Media personalities seem to be more often the unfortunate prey of the schizophrenic and other psychotic stalker types. (That is not to say that celebrities or other public figures cannot be stalked by individuals with other types of mental illness.) Schizophrenics are often depicted by the media and others as having a split personality. However, that is not the case. They do in fact have bouts of "auditory hallucinations," during which they hear voices that are not really there. Sometimes these voices tell them to commit violent acts, as was alleged in the recent case of Andrea Yates, who reported that she heard voices telling her things that she claimed caused her to drown her children. You may sometimes see these people having conversations with an unseen entity, even arguing with a nonexistent person or being. They may slur or jumble their words or get off track when talking to you. They may have very unusual beliefs, such as that someone or something is going to kill them or that they are missing certain body parts when they are not.

In order to give the reader a more in-depth view into the world of the "paranoid schizophrenic," let me discuss another of my cases; although not a stalking case, it should help you better understand the violence that can stem from this disorder. This case involved a 6'6", twenty-five-year-old male diagnosed as a paranoid schizophrenic, who lived at home with his parents, sister, and brother. He was under the care of a psychiatrist who had prescribed medication that he wasn't taking at the time of the incident. His father was dying of cancer, the type of which that caused him to purge blood occasionally. Our subject heard voices that told him that his brother, who was into medieval lore (the study and collecting of medieval armor, items of wizardry, and other such trappings), was casting a spell on his father, causing him to become sicker. One morning, our subject went into his brother's room, took one of his twenty-four-inch replica swords off the wall, and rammed it up through his brother's ribs and out his back. The brother fled his room and proceeded to bleed profusely throughout the house. When I arrived on the scene, there was a thick coating of blood throughout the floors and walls of the house. Unbelievably, the stabbing victim survived. It took five uniformed officers to take the stabber into custody. When I interviewed him, I talked to him as though he were a young child, thus creating a comfortable environment for him to talk to me. He admitted to stabbing his brother, but he claimed that he had to do this to prevent his brother from conjuring up spells to speed up his father's demise. Our schizophrenic stabber was sent for a mental evaluation and was later convicted of attempted murder.

The *DSM-IV-TR* explains in some detail the other forms of schizophrenic behavior patterns. This invaluable reference guide can be located in most libraries and book stores. I found schizophrenia to be a particularly interesting disorder. It is estimated that as many as 2.5 million people in the United States suffer from the disease. If you are interested, you can gather more information by calling the National Schizophrenia Foundation at 1-800-482-9534, or by accessing the Web site sanonymous.org.

OTHER ENCOUNTERED DISORDERS

Sadism: "1. Denoting cruelty in general. 2. Preference during erotic activity to punish, humiliate, or hurt the sexual partner."[13] We find this type of activity taking place with many of our domestic violence stalkers. They need to both verbally and physically degrade their victims. In these environments we find victims complaining that they are tied down, beaten with objects (many times telephone receivers), pinched, gouged, sodomized, etc. An example was a case in a Los

Angeles community where I was called in to act as an expert. The assistant district attorney, who had attended one of my seminars, called and told me she had a stalker who was a "three-strike" candidate. (This stalker had two previous convictions for violent felony crimes, one of which involved following women home, forcing entry into their homes, slashing them, and sexually assaulting them.) If convicted on this charge, he was going away for twenty-five years to life. The assistant district attorney informed me that this stalker had been following a young female over a period of a time. On one occasion he had followed her home and attempted to gain entry into her residence. The assistant district attorney also noted that to complicate matters, this stalker was living with a female detective from another, adjoining agency, who was creating problems by interjecting herself into the case. The case was resolved when the stalker was put away for a very long time.

Sadomasochistic Personality Disorder: We look on this disorder as a kind of Jekyll-and-Hyde relationship. Simply put, these are individuals who get pleasure from both receiving and giving pain. In Dr. Otto F. Kernberg's book on personality disorders, *Aggression in Personality Disorders and Perversions,* the author states, "The sadomasochistic personality has much more capacity for in-depth relationships with others; he is dependent and clinging."[14] Kernberg, a well-known psychiatrist and professor of psychiatry at Cornell University Medical College, also states that the sadomasochistic personality "typically shows alternating masochistic and sadistic behavior towards the same object."[15] Kernberg makes the point that "the difference between normal and masochistic falling in love is precisely that masochistic personalities may be irresistibly attracted to unresponsive objects."[16] In other words, they fall for a woman or a man who will likely never return their advances. We feel this is definitely what we would refer to as a "love hurts" relationship.

We have run across this sadomasochistic type of stalker. One individual in particular comes to mind. He would force his way into his victim's apartment. He would then turn on her air conditioner to muffle her screams, pull the phone jacks out of the wall, monitor her answer machine messages, and later call any males who left messages on the machine to confront them. He would then physically assault the victim and demand sex. He would also complain that everything that happened to him was because of what others, especially the victim, did to him.

We also knew that his mother was still taking care of all of our stalker's problems. In fact, we found him to be quite a "momma's boy." When we conducted a search warrant on his condo that his mother had purchased for him, we were confronted by his seventy-plus-year-old mother, who had come over to clean her boy's house: something she did for him on a regular basis. She claimed her son was the "salt of the earth" and a good church-going boy. The truth of the matter was that her son did in fact go to churches, but he did so to meet his potential victims. He also was very much into pornography, especially women with very large breasts. When we pulled up the carpet in his condo and showed his mother all the pornographic magazines, she was shocked. I felt very sorry for her because she had to clean her thirty something son's condo, including the discarded facial tissues on the floor, under the bed, and in the trash cans. It indicated to us that our stalker was continually masturbating throughout the house. Mom was undaunted, and her hovering didn't stop there. After his arrest, she went out and got him an attorney, paid for a whole new wardrobe of clothes for the victim, helped the victim with her bills, and housed her in the hope that she wouldn't testify against her boy. You'll be glad to hear that didn't work; the stalker pled guilty to four felony counts.

Obsessive-compulsive disorder (OCD): To best define OCD, we are going to break the definition down into two parts. Obsession consists of "persistent ideas, thoughts, impulses, or images that are experienced as intrusive and inappropriate and cause marked anxiety or distress." Compulsions "are repetitive behaviors—hand washing, ordering, checking—or mental acts—praying, counting, repeating words silently—the goal of which is to prevent or reduce anxiety or distress, not to provide pleasure or gratification."[17]

The reason we have referred to this definition is because we will see this type of behavior exhibited to some degree in many of the stalkers we encounter. For example, we arrested an ex–federal parole officer who was a bodybuilder. It took two sets of handcuffs hooked together to span this guy's back and hook him up. We knew that he was another stalker who had some obsessive-compulsive traits. He could not stand to have his clothes, especially his motorcycle boots and jacket, touched by anyone other than him. We also knew he couldn't stand having anyone touch his food, including his stalking victim, with whom he had regularly been intimate for a few years. He also would vacuum the living room floor over and over again without cleaning any other room in the house. These were all things that assisted us during our contact and interview with him. When we arrested this individual in a motel room he was staying in, we made sure we systematically touched each and every personal item while he sat in the room watching. We paid special attention to his motorcycle boots and jacket.

Another example of this same type of personality disorder occurred one day in our jail. I had brought in a 6'4", three-hundred-pound biker type, whom I had just arrested for stalking yet another demure female victim. I told my partner Terry to just stand back and watch, because we knew from our profile what unusual proclivities this stalker had. After the jailer fingerprinted the stalker, he walked over to the sink to wash his hands. Once he cleaned his hands, he put hand cleaner on a wet paper towel and smeared the cleaner all over the entire sink counter and proceeded to scrub and wash the counter. He then took paper towels and wiped everything dry, after which he washed his hands again. A couple hours after putting him into a holding cell, we came and checked on him. We found that he had taken all the toilet paper off the roll and placed it on his cot so that he didn't have to lie on the mat without some kind of cover.

Antisocial personality disorder: A personality disorder "characterized by chronic and continuous antisocial or delinquent behavior not due to severe mental retardation, schizophrenia, or manic episodes. This behavior pattern, more common in males than in females, starts before age fifteen with conduct disorders including lying, stealing, fighting, cruelty, truancy, vandalism, theft, forceful sex, drunkenness, or substance abuse."[18]

One of the things that bothers us the most about the individuals that exhibit the symptoms of this particular disorder is the frequent total lack of remorse expressed toward their victims. You have heard the phrase "He used her like a doormat!" That pretty much sums up this kind of disorder. Some people still refer to a person with this disorder as having a "sociopathic personality disorder." The psychologists I consulted with on this book told me that they no longer use this term as a classification. (We should note that we have found some type of antisocial behavior in all of our stalkers. That does not mean they all suffer from this type of disorder.)

Histrionic personality disorder: A person with this disorder often demonstrates the following symptoms:
- Is uncomfortable in situations in which he or she is not the center of attention.
- Interaction with others is often characterized by inappropriate sexually seductive or provocative behavior.
- Displays rapidly shifting and shallow expression of emotions.
- Consistently uses physical appearance to draw attention to self.
- Has a style of speech that is excessively impressionistic and lacking in detail.
- Shows self-dramatization, theatricality, and exaggerated expression of emotion.
- Is suggestible, i.e., easily influenced by others or circumstances.
- Considers relationships to be more intimate than they actually are.[19]

We tend to find this disorder in the female stalkers we've encountered rather than in the males. Recall the twenty-two-year-old female exotic dancer we discussed in our section on the AS. This female would dye her hair in a variety of colors, wear the most provocative clothing, and talk in a sexy, sultry voice. According to those we interviewed, she loved to dance nude and would go to a motel room and give her clients a very intimate lap dance. When we arrested her, she was disheveled from trying to stay one step ahead of us. Because we knew about her condition from our profile, we told the jailer to allow her additional time in the bathroom before he took her mug shot. As we suspected, she went in looking like a worn-out street waif but came out looking like a cover model. Most female suspects could care less how they look for a mug shot. Because of this stalker's disorder, we knew she did care, and wanted to look the best she could.

Another stalker that exhibited some of the characteristics of the histrionic disorder is one who recently pled guilty to felony stalking. He came back to the police department after doing his jail time to tell one of my other partners, Family Protection Unit Detective Cliff Williams, why he really wasn't a stalker. It was all just a misunderstanding. According to those we interviewed concerning this individual, he would spend hours each day pressing his clothes. He reportedly spent more time in the bathroom primping and fixing his hair than his female stalking victim(s). He could not walk past a mirror without stopping and admiring himself. One quirk that even I had a hard time believing was that he had his eighteen-year-old son dye his chest hairs back to their original color because he didn't want to look old.

When we conducted our threat assessment interview with this stalker's primary victim, we felt that our stalker may have been having a sexual identity crisis as well. According to additional interviewees, we were not wrong. They informed us that our stalker was bisexual. Just to show how much these individuals cannot stay away from their victims, I received a call from Detective Williams, who stated that this stalker had his mother, over whom he has a great deal of control, call the victim's place of business. The stalker, whose voice is known to employees at the business, could then be heard in the background giving instructions to his mother on what to say in order to get information on his victim. Keep in mind that this stalker has just pled guilty to felony stalking, done two to three months in jail, was just placed on formal probation, and was looking at a prison sentence, if convicted on this violation, of around fifteen months. This is just another example of what we say about stalkers over and over again: *they just don't get it!*

We should also mention that, to us, the histrionic personality disorder and the one we are going to discuss next—the narcissistic personality disorder—seem to have some similar characteristics.

Narcissistic personality disorder: The following comprise a set of symptoms derived from the *DSM-IV-TR:*
- Has a grandiose (larger-than-life) sense of self-importance (e.g., exaggerates achievements and talents, expects to be recognized as superior without commensurate achievements).
- Is preoccupied with fantasies of unlimited success, power, brilliance, beauty, or ideal love.
- Believes that he or she is "special" and unique and can only be understood by, or should associate with, other special or high-status people (or institutions).
- Requires excessive admiration.
- Has a sense of entitlement, i.e., unreasonable expectation of especially favorable treatment or automatic compliance with his or her expectations.
- Is interpersonally exploitative, i.e., takes advantage of others to achieve his or her own ends.
- Lacks empathy: is unwilling to recognize or identify with the feelings and needs of others.
- Is often envious of others or believes that others are envious of him or her.
- Shows arrogant, haughty behaviors or attitudes.[20]

I know that everyone reading this book knows someone with one, a few, or all of the nine symptoms we have just laid out for you. My wife has accused me of having a few of these nine, and I will admit to at least a couple. That doesn't mean that you or I have the disorder, nor does it mean we are going to be stalkers. I would say that there is definitely a lot of good old human nature rolled up into this disorder. In fact, the only person I can honestly say doesn't exhibit any of these symptoms is my partner, Terry. (I have no idea how that happened— maybe he thought I had enough arrogance for the both of us.)

The main point I would like to make about this section is that we see some of these described behaviors in a few of our stalkers, male and female. Remember, I have already pointed out that stalkers may have one or more of these personality disorders show up in their profile. Therefore we may find histrionic behaviors mixed in with narcissistic and antisocial personality traits. From what we can see from investigating these people and learning more about these disorders, formulating a diagnosis is not an exact science.

Let me give you an example of a stalker who epitomized the narcissistic disorder. This individual was stalking a female broadcaster. He still lived with his mother. He dressed well, was intelligent, claimed to be a writer of books, and believed he was a true expert on women. He also believed that he was the best person suited for this woman. According to him, she had a cold heart, even though she didn't know it at the time. He researched everything about her, including trying to run a genealogical survey on her ancestors, which he somehow believed she had commissioned him to do. This individual continued to stalk this female and was later investigated by the jurisdiction in Florida where the stalking was taking place. We do not know what the outcome of that particular investigation was.

Borderline personality disorder: We have reviewed several definitions of this disorder, but we like the way the *DSM-IV-TR* lays them out best:
- Frantic efforts to avoid real or imagined abandonment.
- A pattern of unstable and intense interpersonal relationships characterized by alternating between extremes of idealization and devaluation.
- Identity disturbance: markedly and persistently unstable self-image or sense of self.

- Impulsivity in at least two areas that are potentially self-damaging (e.g., spending, sex, substance abuse, reckless driving, binge eating).
- Recurrent suicidal behavior, gestures, or threats, or self-mutilating behavior.
- Affective instability due to a marked reactivity of mood (e.g., intense episodic dysphoria [i.e., unhappness], irritability, or anxiety) usually lasting a few hours and only rarely more than a few days.
- Chronic feelings of emptiness.
- Inappropriate, intense anger or difficulty controlling anger (e.g., frequent displays of temper, constant anger, recurrent physical fights).
- Transient, stress-related paranoid ideation or severe dissociate symptoms. [Ideation is simply the process of forming or developing ideas or images; for purposes of this definition, they would be paranoid images or ideas.][21]

We have encountered stalkers that exhibit many of the borderline characteristics. During the course of their interviews they talk about continually feeling lonely and unable to live without their victim. Many of them have tried to commit suicide but in ways in which they'll likely be discovered before they actually succeed (e.g., cutting of wrists; sitting in a car in a garage with the engine running, but with someone in the residence at the time of the attempt; drug overdosing where someone—they hope the victim of the stalking—will find them in time to save them).

We have found that these disorders may be exacerbated by alcohol and other drugs. We have discovered that many of the male stalkers we have investigated have been self-medicators. Alcohol, methamphetamines, cocaine, and marijuana seem to be the most common drugs used by the stalker. We have also encountered steroid abuse among three of our bodybuilder stalkers. One of these walking brain trusts was doing steroids and methamphetamines at the same time. Steroids, used to promote weight gain and muscle mass, and methamphetamines, used to reduce weight and speed up your metabolism, can both (when used separately or in combination) cause violent mood swings. Used in quantity, they can also cause severe physiological damage.

During the tenth annual Association of Threat Assessment Professionals Conference, held in September 2000 in Anaheim, California, I was once again privileged to hear from Dr. Meloy. He explained that over the past ten years, the research on the stalking phenomenon has begun to accumulate, thus producing a growing body of useful data on why stalkers do what they do as well as how to better assess their threat potential. What we found comforting, for lack of a better word, was that many of these studies, performed not only by Dr. Meloy but also by others in the field of forensic psychology and other associated disciplines, tend to reflect the experiences we who work stalkers in the field encounter on a regular basis. We have discovered that many stalkers who are not mentally disordered are of at least average intelligence, and many of them have higher-than-average intelligence. Many who threaten do not follow through with their threats. Many have had multiple "targets" (stalking victims) in their stalking careers. Dr. Meloy pointed out that there is still a great deal to learn about the "obsessional follower, and nothing is an absolute. Again, we find these clinical studies to be very helpful because they tend to validate our impressions of stalkers.

When we conduct a background history on stalkers, we look for and often find issues such as child abuse, a broken family home, early drug or alcohol dependency, and/or other types of traumatic illness or injury that could have played a role as one of the causative factors for his or her strange behavior. We are investigating an acquaintance stalker who has harassed one woman for over ten years. We found that during his teenage years he had a brain tumor removed; according to relatives, his behavior dramatically changed after the operation. We had another case that, when researched, revealed that the stalker fell off a horse at about age ten, causing severe head trauma. His relatives, who were very afraid of him, said that he had not been the same since. *Don't get us wrong, this doesn't excuse what these individuals do*—but we believe this information might help explain some of the factors causing certain individuals to become stalkers. We should also like to make clear that just because a person has a childhood illness or suffers head trauma does not mean that person has a proclivity for becoming a stalker.

We would also like to point out that that some of the research done on serial killers has indicated that certain types of trauma brought on by injury or illness may number among causative factors producing their behavior. We feel the more science delves into these areas, the more useful information will spring forth. Again, we make no prediction that a stalker will evolve into a serial killer, just that there are some interesting parallels in some of their behavior patterns.

We also know that stalkers come from all walks of life, from professionals to the transient to the somewhat dysfunctional. These ranks have included police officers, lawyers, and judges, as well as well-heeled business professionals. We investigated a case in which a wealthy seventy-five-year-old funeral director, a DVS, was stalking a fifty-year-old female businesswoman. During the course of the stalking, the stalker began attempting to contact the ex-husband of the female victim. This terrified the victim because during their relationship, the stalker had told the victim that he could easily abduct her ex-husband, take him to one of his cemeteries, and cremate him, and no one would ever be able to locate his body. He told the woman he would do this for her so that she would be rid of the ex-husband and possibly reap some insurance benefits from the situation. Another veiled threat the stalker made, which caused our victim a great deal of concern, was when the funeral director sent booklets for planning one's funeral to the victim's healthy son. (I know that this sounds like a screenplay for the HBO series *Six Feet Under*, but it is true.) This stalker was the oldest individual we have investigated to date, but we did find at least one additional stalking victim in his past. In that stalking, he reportedly jumped atop her moving vehicle, reached into her partially opened driver's side window and attempted to pull the female victim out of her car by her hair. On another occasion he also was able to kidnap her and hold her hostage for a period of several hours. He was arrested for those crimes and placed on probation. He was arrested on our stalking charges, and due to a plea bargain, pled guilty to lesser charges and was placed on probation.

At this point let us again advise you, the reader, that just because we have listed a certain behavioral trait under a specific class or genus of stalker doesn't mean that any of these stalkers won't, at any one time, exhibit all or some of these behaviors. We are by no means dealing with an exact science. When we conduct a seminar, we tell our audiences to look at the overall behavior of the stalker, not just a single aspect.

MENTAL ILLNESS AS A LEGAL DEFENSE

The key issue for us in law enforcement is, Do these personality disorders or other forms of mental illness present a viable stalking defense in a court of law? We don't claim in our police reports that an alleged stalker has this type of disorder or that type of mental disability, but we can quote from the experts. Therefore we decided to query two such experts, one on the mental health side, Dr. Kris Mohandie, and one on the prosecutorial side, Los Angeles County Deputy District Attorney Rhonda Saunders,

During our interview with Dr. Mohandie in August 2002, we asked him about the insanity issue. He told us that "mental illness and the legal concept of sanity are two different issues" and should be treated that way. Dr. Mohandie went on to say, "Sanity is simply whether a person understands right from wrong." Mohandie said that many times, even persons who have been diagnosed as having mental illness "may have some recognition that what they are doing is wrong." He also said, "Some in fact are rational enough that they [the stalkers] don't want to go for a mental defense because they realize that it might result in an indeterminate sentence." (This means that, instead of being sentenced for a set number of years and then being eligible for release, their release would be predicated upon review of the mental health personnel who were treating and monitoring them.) Mohandie gave examples of Steven Spielberg's and Madonna's stalkers, stating that even though they both exhibited signs of mental illness, they were successfully prosecuted and sentenced for their crimes.* Mohandie pointed out that Madonna's stalker, who believed Madonna was his wife and bore his child, was still cognizant enough to know that if he served his entire jail sentence, which Mohandie says he plans to do, he would get out of prison and would not have to report to a parole officer or have any type of mandated supervision.

In regard to the mental illness issue as a legal defense for stalking, Rhonda Saunders made a very cogent point, stating, "They [defense attorneys] always try a psychiatric defense, but the stalking is so premeditated and takes so much thought that we never have a problem overcoming the defense tactic when we put this in front of a jury." Saunders gave an example of the stalker that was arrested for stalking Steven Spielberg. She said that on one occasion he came to the Spielberg residence claiming to have a delivery from a well-known music producer. On another he conducted an extensive search for an expensive rental car that looked exactly like Spielberg's wife's car, hoping when he drove it up to the gate, the guard would believe it was her and would not pay attention to the occupant, allowing him into the compound. According to Saunders, he did obtain a vehicle just like Spielberg's wife's car, but was turned away when he drove up. Of course, he was also caught later with handcuffs, a knife, duct tape, and razor blades, along with paperwork laying out how he was going to kidnap and assault Spielberg; he was promptly taken into custody. This stalker is currently doing twenty-five years to life due to convictions on other criminal behavior. Saunders also noted that although this individual was cunning, he had mental problems, such as believing he was Spielberg's adopted son.

CHAPTER 2 SUMMARY

- We have grouped stalkers into three specific categories: domestic violence, acquaintance, and stranger stalkers. Dr. Michael Zona and John Lane, principals in the Omega Threat Management Group,

---

* To date, none of the stalkers we have prosecuted who exhibited signs of mental illness have incorporated mental illness as a viable criminal defense.

have generated stalker typologies that are used throughout the industry: Simple Obessional, Love Obsessional, Erotomanic, and False Victimization Syndrome. There are at least twelve different suspects or stalker perpetrator typologies in existence.

- Stalkers can be driven by several different factors. There can be one primary driving force or a combination thereof. Some of these factors include fantasy, rage, obsession, sexual perversion, and sometimes revenge.
- Some stalkers have diagnosable mental illnesses such as schizophrenia. Most seem to have one of many personality disorders such as obsessive-compulsive, borderline, histrionic, narcissistic, or anti-social personality disorders.
- Most stalkers don't take responsibility for their actions and blame others for making them do what they do.
- Most stalkers have stalked more than one person in their lifetime.
- Stalkers that have had an intimate sexual relationship with their victims have been shown to be much more aggressive and violent with their victims. This includes both male and female stalkers.
- Drugs and alcohol often act as a catalyst in increasing the intensity of the stalking.
- Stalkers are obsessed with their victims. This obsession is expressed in many ways.
- The inability of the stalker to formulate coping mechanisms when he or she is rejected plays a major role in many stalking scenarios.
- Sometimes incidents of stalking increase around birthdays or anniversaries, or particular times of the year.
- The majority of stalkers are domestic violence stalkers. Domestic violence stalkers tend to demonstrate more violent behavior than other classifications of stalker, although other types of stalkers can be violent as well.
- A growing number of forensic psychologists and other clinicians are conducting research into the stalking phenomenon, thus greatly assisting those individuals who work to protect the stalking victim as well as those involved in their counseling and care.

- New research into the nature of female stalkers shows that the majority are intelligent, single white heterosexual women in their thirties; at least a third have children. About half of them stalk married white men in their forties. About 50 percent of the men they stalk are from acquaintance-type contacts.
- The juvenile population in the United States is growing, and so is the number of violent crimes committed by these youthful offenders. Therefore we are seeing and expect to see more domestic violence, or intimate partner, stalking perpetrated by this segment of our population.
- Mental illness and legal insanity are separate issues. Many individuals who exhibit mental illness are nevertheless considered culpable for their crimes.

CHAPTER 3

TOOLS OF THE STALKER

Now that we know more about where the stalker is coming from, and why he or she stalks, we need to discuss the tools of the stalking trade. Keep in mind that stalkers are very good at what they do. For those who have never encountered a stalker, this chapter should be viewed as another segment of Stalking 101. For those of you that are currently or have been a victim of stalking, you will probably be nodding your head, saying, "Been there, seen that." As we go through this stalker laundry list, we may associate a certain tool with a certain type of stalker. This is because we've seen a pattern develop with a specific type of stalker, but again, nothing is cast in stone—any stalker could use any of these tools at any time. Stalkers are always full of surprises.

GIFTS AND NOTES

As we have mentioned earlier, many times stalking begins with small gifts or notes either given directly to the victim or left on the front porch, on the victim's car, etc. These notes and gifts can be pleasant, sexually oriented, or simply off-the-wall, depending on the stalker. If the stalker is continually rebuked, the gifts and letters can turn more toward the dark side: a stuffed bear hanging from a door knob, painted black or with dead roses; the victim's photo with an X through it; letters with direct or veiled threats, such as "R.I.P." written next to the victim's, a spouse's, or significant other's date of birth, etc. (See Figures 4 and 5 for examples of threatening letters sent to victims by stalkers.) Stalkers will also use these notes and gifts to inform you that they are back in your life if they were away for a while for whatever reason.

For instance, a victim who has been stalked by the same male for the past several years knows her stalker has returned when she finds matchbooks lying on her lawn from neighboring cafés and restaurants. The victim initially met the stalker while the victim worked as a waitress. The stalker believes by bringing up the past (i.e., by using restaurant matchbook covers as his calling card) that he is able to play on her mind. We have arrested this particular stalker on more than one occasion. Each time he has done sixty to eighty days in jail, which seems to have little or no effect on him.

Until just recently, this terror-monger was again out of custody and began stalking another victim who lived out of our jurisdiction. When that particular victim got in touch with us, we were surprised to find out that she had in fact married him. We felt it must have been a very short courtship, because this particular stalker usually showed his violent, controlling stripes early in his relationships. This victim told us that she had met the stalker through a church contact. He seemed nice at first, but later after they were married, he turned into a monster. This woman told us he would continually threaten her, push her around, break up furniture, surveil her at both work and elsewhere. She said that she was terrified of him and wanted to know who he really was. That was when we invited her down to our police department. When she arrived, we sat her down in front of our big-screen television and played a couple of videos for her. One was when the stalker was profiled on *20/20*. After the viewing, she sat hunched over in disbelief. She had no idea this was the man she had married. This poor woman broke down in tears and began telling us about how she divorced this subject and was now being continually threatened and stalked by him. We then began assisting this victim with her stalking case. We contacted the law enforcement agency that was investigating her case and offered our assistance. Again, the stalker was convicted on lesser charges and received a minimum sentence.

Too often, as we have stated before, we run into a form of stalking prosecution resistance from some outside jurisdictions that don't take the issue seriously enough. I have had numerous conversations with other investigators who are deeply committed to investigating stalkers within their own communities. They are continually frustrated when dealing with stalkers that cross jurisdictional lines because they have to coordinate with some police agencies that, shall we say, have not yet put a priority on working the stalker. Again, having made this observation, we also need to applaud these same agencies when they see the light and become more aware of the problem.

Another example of stalkers: we investigated a stalker who produced several collages, made up of hundreds of photos, drawings, and cartoons cut out of numerous magazines and periodicals (Figure 6). After hours of arduous work, the stalker would then hand-deliver these collages to the victim's residence. The victims in this case were husband and wife. This particular stalker's psychiatrist told us that the stalker was a paranoid schizophrenic who would not take his medication and thus had become psychotic. That same doctor said he would no longer treat our stalker because he was being nonresponsive and was considered to be a danger. Our boy was placed on formal probation. As a side note, last year we got a call from our victims. The stalker wanted to rekindle a relationship with the woman, whom he had known in high school over thirty years before. He wanted the woman's husband out of the way so that he could reignite that relationship. The victims stated that they had once again been contacted by this individual. We are currently continuing to monitor this case. (This is just another example of a stalker returning to his original, or genesis, victim. His probation time is up, so he is back.)

One more example: an AS we investigated was pursuing a female

LiFe is ShorT,
Very ShorT !
Too Short !
11-20-43 (47) P.J.D.R.
12-29-60 (30) R.T.H.
7-5-55 (36) R.H.P.

Chickasaw Dr.
WesTminsTer, CA. 92683

7-5-55 R.I.P.
- -91 R.H.P.

LiFe is Indeed

Very Very ShorT !

Figure 4. Stalker's threat letter to victim's husband, whose birthday is 7-5-55. (Courtesy of the Westminster Police Department)

REVENGE

JUST A BIT PSYCHOTIC
A LITTLE OUT TO LUNCH
BENEATH MY 3LB. SLEDGE HAMMER
YOUR KNEES BEGIN TO CRUNCH...
YOU MADE ME VERY ANGRY
TO MY SHEER DELIGHT
YOU DONT THINK ID HURT YOU,
YOU NEVER WERE THAT BRIGHT...
YOU THINK I CAN NOT FIND YOU,
I DONT KNOW WHERE TO START
YET WHEN YOU LEAST EXPECT IT
I'LL TEAR YOUR SOLE APART!
I CREEP AMONG THE SHADOWS
THROUGH THE DEAD OF NIGHT
HIDING IN THE BUSHES
STAYING OUT OF SIGHT
I DRAW MY SMITH & WESSON
AND AIM IT AT YOUR HEAD
ADD PRESSURE TO THE TRIGGER
I WATCH YOU FALL, YOUR DEAD!!
LYING IN A PUDDLE
YOUR BLOOD IS RUNNING THICK
YOU NEVER GOT TO SEE IT
YOU DIED TOO FUCKING QUICK!!

Figure 5. Poem sent from prison to a victim.
The inmate was charged with making criminal threats.
(Courtesy of the Fullerton Police Department, Fullerton, Calif.)

Figure 6. Stalker's threatening collages left on the victim's doorstep. (Note: It is not important if you can read what the stalker has written, only to see how much effort stalkers put into the stalking process.)
(Courtesy of the Westminster Police Department)

he'd had a crush on in high school some twenty years before. Even back then the crush was one-sided, and the female, a popular cheerleader, had no knowledge of the infatuation. Initially she did not know the man had been watching her at the supermarket, but shortly thereafter, her mother began receiving oranges and avocados, along with other gifts left on her front doorstep late at night and in the early morning hours. Evidently, the stalker was not aware that his victim had married and no longer lived with her mother.

When we finally identified the stalker and questioned him, he told us the victim contacted him in the supermarket and began a conversation and a relationship. However, this contact never took place. He refused to explain why he was leaving the items at the victim's mother's house. We then requestioned the victim and learned that she had in fact bought avocados and oranges one day in a local market but she neither had been approached by nor had she even seen the stalker. Due to this stalker's violent criminal history, we had the victim obtain a restraining order that also covered her mother and her mother's residence. We told her that we strongly believed the stalker's pathology showed he would violate the restraining order sometime around Christmas of 1997, because the stalker had started his initial stalking pattern around Christmas of 1996 and had stopped his stalking behavior shortly after that. Remember we said that dates and times mean something to these individuals for some reason, and they reactivate their old behaviors when these dates or times cycle around again. We also expressed our theory that the stalker would continue to stalk her sixty-eight-year-old mother in order to gather more information on the victim. Unfortunately, we were right on both suppositions.

In late December 1997, the stalker dropped off a Christmas card addressed to the victim's mother. In the card he discussed the fact of being served with a restraining order and then brazenly invited the victim's mother out for coffee. The stalker also dropped off an old box of high school memorabilia. One of the items in the box was a couple of ticket stubs for a high school football game.

We believe the stalker would pull out his box of old high school junk and begin to reminisce about his high school days. This would also allow the stalker to keep fantasizing about the cheerleader that he longed for but couldn't have. The box being dropped off was his strange way of communicating his feelings toward the victim. We also felt that for this particular stalker, high school and the years surrounding his attendance there obviously meant a great deal to him. They may have been a good time in his life. We believe he mentally traveled back to that period in his life to regain some stability.

Due to the increased stalking activity, we initiated a combination search and arrest warrant. When we served the warrant, we found in the stalker's possession well over 450 rounds of ammunition, a stun gun, a homemade zip-type gun, numerous large hunting and assault-type knives, as well as equipment normally used by telephone repairmen, which could be used to tap into phone lines. The stalker had as pets a large pit bull and a huge Oscar-type fish. (This is a fish that looks similar to and has some of the same vicious characteristics of a piranha.) We also located a cassette tape with the stalker screaming at another female to open her door or he would kick it in. He told her that once he got in he was going to "fuck her in the ass." Our search also revealed another photo of a female who appeared to be of college age. When we showed it to the mother of our initial stalking victim, she identified it as a photo of her *other* daughter, who had been attending college when that photo was taken. This Charles Manson look-alike pled guilty, was sentenced to jail, served about four months, and was then placed on formal probation.

Another unusual personality quirk of this stalker was that he would take on his brother's identity. He might have done this possibly to throw off anyone he really didn't want to talk to. I record most of my calls with potential suspects, murderers or stalkers. When I first called this stalker he claimed to be his brother, Ben (not the stalker's brother's real name), telling me that he had no idea where his brother John, the stalker (not his real name), was. I had such an in-depth telephone interview with our stalker while he was in his "Ben, the brother" mode, I wonder if this stalker is one of those individuals that actually uses another personality from time to time, in this case that of his own brother. When we confronted him about acting or claiming to be his brother, he said he had no idea what we were talking about and his brother didn't live with him. There is always the possibility this stalker was intelligent enough to feign being his brother to avoid confrontation or prosecution, but in this case, I feel the stalker is more mentally disordered than blessed with a high IQ.

VANDALISM

Vandalism is another common tool of the stalker. The damage the stalker causes can create a tremendous amount of emotional and financial wear and tear on the victim as well as those who must assist in repairing the damage. Think about it: even if you have never been a stalking victim, imagine yourself one day going outside and finding that somebody has "keyed" your car (i.e., has dragged a key along your car such that a line of bare metal shows through the paint). First comes the blind anger that causes you to think about inflicting the most excruciating torture imaginable on the person responsible for the damage; then comes that feeling of absolute frustration and helplessness, because you have no recourse against the idiot who did the keying, either because you have no clue who did it, or, more likely, due to an absence of witnesses. Now try to put yourself into the shoes of the stalking victim who is faced with these feelings on a regular basis. We had one stalker who had fashioned a specific tool shaped very much like a small, chrome, flat-headed screwdriver used to pry open the tops of paint cans. When he dragged it along the body of the car, it would leave about a quarter-inch-wide gouge the entire length of the car. Another stalker we investigated would put plastic quarts of motor oil behind the tires of the victim's parked car. When she backed out of her driveway the oil containers would explode, splashing oil all over her tires, car, and driveway. The oil would also soak into the driveway, leaving a stain that is difficult to get out.

Stalkers are experts at destroying property. They put superglue in your car door locks as well as garage padlocks. They don't puncture the tread of your tires; they puncture or slash the side walls of your tires so that you have to replace, not repair them. We've seen them cut brake lines, and slash water hoses, urinate on computers, and put sugar into gas tanks. (Putting sugar into a gas tank causes the sugar to dissolve in the gas. When the mixture is ignited during combustion, it forms a heavy carbon residue that clogs the piston walls, ceasing the engine.)

During one investigation, we found that a stalker had broken into his victim's house; found her computer, which she normally hid; superglued the keyboard, and poured cola into the workings of the computer. The stalker in this case knew that the victim had worked hard for months to save enough to purchase this computer. This was just another way of causing mental anguish and emotional distress during the course of the stalking.

In another stalking, a female stalker threw a softball through the victim's front apartment window while he was having sexual relations with his fiancée. The stalker used a softball because she knew the victim was an avid softball player (again, a little added symbolism by the stalker). The male victim said when the ball struck the window it literally exploded the glass. "Needless to say, it got my immediate attention," the victim said, "and I checked both me and my fiancée for bullet wounds, because we thought we had been shot." On another occasion, this same victim tried to remove this same persistent stalker from his apartment after she had entered, taken off all of her clothes, and demanded sex. When the victim attempted to remove his nude stalker, the resulting struggle caused them both to fall into the blades of a large commercial fan that had been placed inside a doorway to cool off the apartment, fortunately only slightly injuring both of them.

Let us return for a moment to one of the problems sometimes faced by stalking victims—ineffective police intervention. We have touched on this earlier, but we still have a need to discuss it further. In the above scenario, our male victim became frustrated with the attitude of the police, who responded to his complaint of an attractive female stalker coming to his apartment, stripping, and then demanding sex. The responding male officer's reaction of "Yeah, so what's your problem?" didn't help his plight. Remember, I said we all need to be educated.

Once these officers realized the potential problems involved with this type of stalking, their response was a great deal more helpful to our victim. One of the ways we educate officers about the stalking phenomenon is by training. To train the officers, we often use a portion of the videotape I helped develop through POST (Police Officers Standards and Training). A portion of that training video shows a segment based on a true stalking of a uniformed officer. The officer was stalked by a very provocative sixteen-year-old female, who for unknown reasons had fixated on this poor guy. During the course of the stalking she wrote numerous amorous letters, attempted to contact his wife, called his station over and over again, and would follow him while he was on patrol. She would even pull up in her car behind him at night without her lights on while he was trying to make car stops. This is extremely dangerous behavior, putting both the stalker and the officer's life in jeopardy. This officer had a great deal of difficulty getting his superiors to believe he was the victim in this case, not to mention the stress this stalker put on his home life. (My wife thought that I was married to my partner, because we spent so much time together. I would not be here to write this book if she thought I was doing something I was not supposed to. I can only imagine what this officer's life was like after his wife was contacted by some young female, attractive or not.) He was finally able to get the stalker arrested and placed into custody, where she began stalking other personnel involved in the daily administration of the law enforcement system. The look on our officers' faces after they have seen this video tells it all. It gives them a whole new respect for the stalking victim.

To finish our story concerning our softball-throwing stalker, we eventually arrested her. During her psychiatric fitness hearing, we were told when the judge asked her a question, she turned to the wall and began a conversation with her shadow. Feeling that this was not quite the response he was looking for, the judge remanded her to a California psychiatric prison hospital for prolonged treatment and evaluation. Not too long after her evaluation commitment, she was returned for trial. She pled guilty to all charges, was placed on formal probation, and was not allowed to enter our city. She continued to call the police department, complaining that we put her in jail for over eleven months. She also claimed to be stalked by a male in the San Diego area, and—would you believe it?—wants us to work her case! She was given the San Diego Police Department's phone number. (As a final note, I was advised in September of 2000 that this same subject has been recommitted because she had begun to stalk her therapist.)

SURVEILLANCE

Most stalkers could make fairly good trackers. Certainly all of the stalkers we've investigated and profiled have done some type of surveillance. They follow, they peep, and they record. These individuals keep logs or diaries, or they memorize as much about the victim they are surveilling as is humanly possible. We learned about this behavior from all the items we have recovered when serving search warrants on these stalkers. Some will take photos of their victims with or without their knowledge. The following are a couple of examples of stalker surveillance patterns and the techniques they use:

We had a well-educated thirty-five-year-old business manager who had an extreme fetish for long-legged, large-breasted women. Now just because a man admires an attractive female doesn't make him a stalker or even someone with a fetish. This guy would date women primarily with these requirements, but if the women didn't have exactly what he wanted, he would try to coerce them into getting their attributes augmented. We had suspected that he had been photographing women who fit his particular set of requirements without their knowledge.

When we conducted a search of his car, we found a quality 35mm camera with a very good telephoto lens, a set of high-powered binoculars, and a yellow legal pad next to the driver's side of the vehicle. On the pad, our stalker had written some names of women with their physical descriptions, including the size of their breasts, etc. He had also listed other physical attributes of women whose names he didn't have or know, noting the date and time he had apparently viewed and/or photographed them. When we conducted another search, this time of his house, we found several photos of women that had obviously been taken at the beach while they were sunbathing or roller-skating. When we interviewed him, our stalker developed a case of what we call "convenient amnesia." He said he had no idea who these women were, nor could he remember why he had these photos in his possession.

The second example we would like to present is the stalker who liked to confront his victims about having sexual encounters with more than one man at a time. This stalker would hide a microcassette recorder in the bookshelf or under the bed of the female that he was starting to stalk. He would recover the tape and then play it back for her, accusing her of having these sexual encounters. The victim said all she could hear on the tape were television programs that she had been watching, and had not had any type of sexual encounter at those times. During our investigation we were able to obtain one of these tapes on which our stalker swore he heard his stalking victim having sex with multiple male partners. I listened to the tape in its entirety, but to the best of my knowledge, episodes of *This Old House* have never included orgies. (Obviously, our stalker has a better imagination than most of us do-it-yourselfers.)

We would also like to point out that it is not unusual during these surveillances and information-gathering sorties for the stalker to go through the victim's trash or the mail she receives. (Your trash can reveal a great deal about you. We will discuss what to do with trash in the chapter concerning safety strategies.)

CONSTANT COMMUNICATION

The stalker works at harassing the victim with a continual stream of information so that she knows her assailant is always lurking out there in the urban mist. This communication can be accomplished through letters or notes, as previously discussed, but it occurs most often by telephone, cellular phone, or pager. Nothing is more disconcerting to a victim than for a stalker to call and comment on what she is wearing, where she went, or the people she was with.

One stalker who watched a specific woman in a shopping center come and go from her workplace used to leave a photocopy of his erect penis on the windshield of her vehicle, sometimes with notes discussing how he felt about her. We finally caught this individual while he was sitting in his car with a fresh run of copies.

On occasion stalkers have friends or associates call and relay messages from the stalker. Sometimes the friend thinks he is doing the stalker a favor and is merely acting as a go-between in a relationship. In other situations, such as the stalker who had his elderly mother call the victim at work, the mother knowingly did this to harass the victim. We recently had a case in which the stalker paid a younger male to repeatedly slash the victim's tires as well as make over five hundred phone calls to her place of work.

The DVS also uses this line of communication to bully and threaten. It is extremely tiring to the victim and those around her to continually receive hang-up calls at all hours of the day or night. The stalker may use these calls as a means of tracking where the victim is at a specific time of the day. The stalker will also make calls to friends or relatives of the victim to continue the harassment. Frequently these phone calls will follow the victim to the workplace. These contacts can come in the form of faxes as well as numerous unsolicited calls. This harassment definitely causes friction at the workplace and has resulted in some victims being dismissed from their jobs because of workplace disruption.

Another example of an SS we would like to discuss had a very unusual way of making his presence known to the victim. Since people know what I do for a living, I am contacted on a regular basis for information as well as advice. In this scenario, I was contacted by an employee of a business whose services I use. The female employee mentioned that over a period of four weeks she had been stalked at her place of work. She said that when she would come in around 7:30 each morning to open up her store, she would find one or two used condoms attached to the office's front doorknob. This obviously both disgusted and alarmed the lone female, but she had no idea who was doing this. The victim said that after about a week of getting these "messages," a male who worked as a maintenance person in the same business center started coming into her store by himself right after she opened. He would stand in the corner of the store and just "stare" at her. The victim said that a short time after this took place, as she walked from her car in the morning to open her store, the stalker would pop out of the bushes, walk right toward her, and then veer off without saying a word. The victim said she felt he was trying to convey a message of control and power by scaring her all the time. The stalker was confronted by the victim's boss, who had found out that this individual had several children and was at that time married to a young female, even though he was much older than his wife. The victim also noted that once the stalker stopped pursuing her, she heard that he had begun doing the same thing to another woman who owned a shop in the same center. We get complaints of this type from many females who work in shopping centers as well as malls. Unfortunately, these predators are shopping as well, and these women represent a smorgasbord of easy targets for these types of stalkers to select from, since the nature of their work causes them to be so available.

TROPHY COLLECTION

Some stalkers will commit burglary both to further their information gathering as well as to spur on their fantasies. For example, during the course of one stalking investigation, we located several pairs of the victim's panties and pantyhose in the stalker's residence during a search. The stalker had cut or eaten through the crotches of the panties and was masturbating through the holes. One of the questions we routinely ask our stalking victims is "Do you have any panties or other undergarments missing?" Once we have them check their clean garment drawer, we ask them to check their dirty laundry. One of the items we have found to be most often taken by the stalkers we investigate are undergarments, clean or otherwise. These items are removed by both DVSs and SSs. We have also found that most of the women we have contacted in a stalking or panty-burglar type of investigation know how many and the brand names of the undergarments they have, and they can most often identify them when seen again, especially if they were gifts (unlike most men, who give us a bewildered look when that question is raised; men seem to have no clue about such issues, except maybe to tell you they wear boxers or briefs and some had holes in them).

Another example: We have investigated a stalker who appears to be some type of a cross-dresser. He reportedly goes into clubs his victim frequents dressed as a woman so that he can observe her. This represents one of the more extreme measures these individuals will take to surveil their victims. This victim has had several pairs of Victoria's Secret-brand panties taken from her home over several months. We are not sure what he is doing with these garments, but we have a pretty good idea.

One of the things that had frightened our victim the most was when a state investigator called this woman's home; he talked to a "woman" claiming to be the victim's mother. The "woman" was reported to have spoken very good English without any accent and gave out information only personal family members would know. However, on the day the state official had called, no one was supposed to be home. Furthermore, the victim's real mother speaks with a very heavy foreign accent that cannot be mistaken. Although we could not prove it conclusively, the victim and I believe our stalker had been inside her residence conducting one of his trophy collection forays and for some reason decided to answer the phone and act as the victim's mother.

Another of our most frequently asked questions, especially for DVS victims is "Did you or do you have any nude photos or videos of yourself with or without your stalker? Why?" Remember, fantasy is one of the things that seems to drive these individuals. When we write our search warrant affidavits, one of the things we generally ask to search for are photos, nude or otherwise, of the victim.

One DVS we had profiled had entered his ex-wife's house after he was served with a restraining order. Once in the house, he took a video containing footage of him and his ex-wife having sex several years before. She did not want him to have the video, so he took it without her permission. (Because California is a community-property state, and there was no civil distribution order concerning the video, we could not charge him with theft and/or burglary. We could and did, however, charge him with violation of a restraining order once we found the video in his possession.) Because of the nature of this stalker's behavior, he still wanted to have sex with his ex, continually commented on her breasts, and was inordinately jealous of any male contacts, no matter what their purpose. We felt he had taken this video to perpetuate his fantasy about her. I also suspected that he would have this video set up in his residence so that he could watch it regularly, probably while in bed. When we served the warrant, we found the tape still in the VCR of the television facing the bed in the stalker's bedroom.

When stalkers enter a victim's residence to collect trophies, they may also engage in actions designed to subtly terrorize that victim. This is accomplished by moving items that the stalkers know hold some type of value for the victim. They do something to the item, as simple as turning it a certain way, or noticeably damaging it. They also leave items in the house to create fear. For example, we once investigated a DVS who would enter the victim's apartment with a key he had stolen. He would leave photos he had taken of the victim months before taped to the front of her refrigerator. He would also leave notes reminding the victim of the time they had been traveling down the freeway and he stuck a gun in her face, stating that if he couldn't have her, no one else would. Unfortunately, this victim stopped cooperating with us, because she had a new boyfriend and felt this would end her problem with this stalker. On the contrary, we felt there was a tremendous likelihood that she would end up badly injured or even worse. What we know about this stalker's profile, including his past use of a gun, caused my partner and me a great deal of concern. In fact, at the time of writing, we were again contacted by this victim, who stated that the stalker was again bothering her. However, we are still waiting for her cooperation, which we may never get. This is one of the frustrations that we are sometimes forced to live with. It is not uncommon for those of us who deal with the domestic violence victim, such as this particular female, to continually have to urge her cooperation, especially when it comes time for prosecution. There are a number of victim dynamics at work in these types of cases. Some victims have serious problems confronting their stalkers at any time, let alone through the rigors of the judicial system.

HARASSMENT TACTICS

We have found that many stalkers like to use the following tactics to both harass and control:

Small claims or other legal actions against the victim. We had a DVS give several gifts to a victim over the course of their relationship. Finally, when the victim initiated a stalking investigation with us, the stalker filed a small claims action to try to recover the gifts. Obviously, there would be no chance of recovery on such an action once the items were shown to be gifts. We had another stalker who would sue all of his victims for defamation of character. Shortly before the case would come to trial, the stalker would drop the suit knowing he had no case whatsoever. Although the suit was dropped, he had still obtained his goal of harassing the victim. These actions caused the victim both stress and, in some cases, financial burden. For stalkers, the courtroom can again provide an arena to harass and control their victims. The suit forces victims to show up and again face the stalkers, empowering the latter. In the case where the stalker sued in small claims for his gifts to be returned, we had the assistant district attorney handling the victim's stalking case show up at the court on her behalf. He explained to the judge there was a restraining order against our stalker as well as an ongoing criminal case. The judge then postponed the hearing of the facts on the civil case until the criminal case was adjudicated.

Fraud. We have seen several types of fraud perpetrated against the victim as both a revenge and a harassment tactic. We investigated a protracted domestic violence stalking in which the suspect had recorded a great deal of financial information concerning his victim. With this information he was able to get money transferred out of one of her checking accounts into her ATM account, where he then removed the cash. He would also have other females use a fake credit card he had made up with the victim's name on it so that she would be hounded by bill collectors. Another common fraud tactic stalkers employ is to run up large bills on the victim's calling and credit cards. Some stalkers go through their victim's mail, find credit card applications, fill them out, and return them using either the victim's address or another. If they can get the card when it comes in the mail, they will make a series of charges. Stalkers also subscribe to magazines using the victim's name and address. The magazines mean nothing in and of themselves, but are simply another harassment tactic when the victim begins receiving unsolicited periodicals and bills for them.

We had a case in which the male stalker, who was stalking another male, would fill out magazine subscriptions in the victim's name. The stalker subscribed to magazines that contained hardcore pornography, child pornography, and gay and lesbian material, as well as white supremacist material. The stalker sent these subscriptions to the victim's place of business, causing the victim a great deal of difficulty; especially because he worked for a large corporation heavily involved in developing weapons systems for the federal government.

Pager harassment. We have seen stalkers use the pager as an electronic tool of harassment. The stalker does this in one of two ways. One way is for the stalker to call other individuals or businesses with phone messaging capabilities. The stalker leaves the victim's pager number or cellular phone number. The victim is then deluged with returning calls to her number. The stalker also might call the victim's pager and leave valid random numbers. When the victim calls them back, the people she is calling are clueless as to why they are being called. Either way, it causes a great deal of frustration for the victim and those with whom she comes in contact as a result of the stalker's phone plants.

Disruption of services. We have had stalkers contact various utility companies and have the victim's service disconnected or in some cases have repairmen sent out to the victim's house, causing both the utility company and the victim grief.

Harassment of family members and significant others. Usually a stalker will begin harassing the victim's family members for one of two specific reasons: if he is not able to contact the victim directly, he may decide to send a message in an indirect fashion by harassing a family member. Secondly, the stalker may go after a family member merely for effect. That means even if the stalker has access to his primary victim, he still may go after a family member to cause the victim additional stress. This is especially true in cases where the victim has young children, whether these children are also the stalker's or not. Stalkers, especially those whose primary goal is revenge as well as control, can easily instill instantaneous terror in the victim by targeting the victim's children. As a result, the protection of these children is a very high priority on our list when we deal with a stalking situation.

Unfortunately, we have found among some cultures that stalker contact with the victim's family members may cause some of these family members to try and coerce the victim to cooperate with the stalker. For example, we have investigated cases in Asian-American communities where family members—when harassed by a male stalker—have told the female victim to go out with the male and try to work out their differences. These same family members have told the victim never to contact the police concerning these incidents. Fortunately, through acculturation and community-sponsored education, we are experiencing more reporting from those cultures that previously felt the act of stalking was some type of romantic interlude. As we indicated before, we have been interviewed by Japanese media, who are very interested in the stalking phenomenon, because, they informed us, thus far the act of stalking has been looked upon as an element expressed in some courtships in their country. We are not saying that these behaviors pervade or are completely accepted in these cultures, but we have experienced these attitudes on more than one occasion.

A stalker will also frequently go after the victim's significant other. She usually does this because she sees that person as a barrier between herself and her victim. One of our male victims had several of his lady friends' vehicles damaged by the female stalker who had been plaguing him for five years. The stalker actually believed she was married to our victim, even though that could not have been farther from the truth. This stalker would also contact the various females and threaten them in an attempt to keep them away from the victim. We had arrested this female stalker on several occasions for violation of a restraining order, simple assault, and trespassing. We had to intensify our response when the male victim she was stalking got married and then had a child, because our profile predicted that if the stalking victim were to get married, the stalking would escalate. The stalker would see his new wife as a definite threat to the stability of her relationship with the victim. We felt she would try to eliminate the new wife and kidnap their child, believing that it was hers.

It is not uncommon for the significant others to receive death threats, and in some cases, the stalkers act those threats. During the course of pursuing a stalker, we uncovered an additional victim who told us the stalker we were investigating had run one of her boyfriends off the road and then threatened him with a handgun. Unfortunately, some stalkers are successful in their quest to eliminate a significant other. Too often we hear of the death of a boyfriend, girlfriend, or spouse in connection with an enraged stalker.

Harassment of family pets. Stalkers have been known to take their victims' pets. We have heard of the stalker holding a pet for ransom, the payment of which is the victim's meeting or being with them. Stalkers have even tortured and in some cases killed these animals. The only purpose for this type of cruelty is to terrorize and cause a tremendous amount of mental anguish to the victim. Keep in mind that many people—especially those without children—treat their pets as family members. To them the death of a pet is just as devastating as losing a family member. If the victim has children, often the stalker achieves a double whammy by injuring or killing a pet: the victim must then deal not only with her own grief but that of her children's as well. Again, we must remind you of the insidious behavior stalkers are capable of.

The use of extortion generated by libel and/or slander. The stalker may make slanderous remarks to the victim's friends or associates, thereby causing the victim damage both in interpersonal relationships as well as associations in the workplace. The stalker may also do the same thing in print or via photographs, thus libeling the victim. The following are a few examples: we had an individual call two of our victim's boyfriends and tell them that she had AIDS. On another occasion, we had a DVS post nude photos of his victim on telephone poles in the area of a main highway with the victim's home phone number. He then informed the victim he would tell her where the photos were if she got back together with him. We have also had a male stalker hang photos of a coworker with a statement that he was a homosexual looking for company. We are currently consulting on a case where a county employee has been stalked by an ex-girlfriend. His nude photos have not only been distributed all over the neighborhood where he works but also sent to administrators at the local schools in the area. The female stalker had written the employee's name and the office where he works on the flyer. We had another female stalker begin showing up at her victim's workplace telling fellow employees that she felt abused by this individual. She also began sending nude photos of herself to his place of business, as well as to him over the Internet. This caused a great deal of embarrassment to the victim. The female then sent letters and photos to the victim's new fiancée, which again caused him a great deal of difficulty. This spurned female stalker advised that she would stop doing these things if he would just come back to her and marry her.

Just a word to the wise: think before you make any promises you are not about to keep. In this particular stalking case, the victim told the stalker he was going to marry her, even though the victim apparently had no intention of doing so. The victim knew that the stalker was very possessive and was having mental problems before making that statement. Obviously, the victim's statements alone cannot be enough to condone the female's stalking behavior, but one can see that affairs of the heart are always a delicate matter that can produce tremendous emotional imbalances. So, gentlemen, be careful about what you say and do. The same rules apply to men as to women: don't exacerbate the situation by opening the door wide open to the stalker and inviting her wrath. In other words, don't be the match that lights the fuse to the powder keg.

One of the most unusual forms of libel-type harassment we have seen to date occurred when an Asian-American media personality was being stalked by an estranged boyfriend. The stalker and his assistant made up and distributed a flyer that was disseminated throughout this particular Asian-American community. The flyer falsely linked the victim to the Communist Party. This type of linkage, if believed, can be extremely detrimental to the victim's success within this tight-knit community. We also treated this use of the flyer as a criminal threat because it could easily lead to physical harm coming to the victim.

The DVS will often indicate to the victim that the libel or slander will stop if the victim capitulates and comes back to the stalker. However, it can also occur in both the AS and SS scenarios as well. If employed by the AS, it seems to be used as a tool to persuade the victim to be more open to the proposed relationship with that stalker. On the other hand, we have seen the SS use all forms of photo or other written documents (for example, a casual snapshot of the victim with her head cut off) against the victim, more for a tool of terror than for the purpose of bonding with that victim.

Violence or threats of violence. Many stalkers will threaten violence against the victim or persons close to the victim. These threats may be born out of frustration, or may in fact be a calculated way of trying to get the victim to do the stalker's bidding. Domestic violence stalkers especially use this tactic. Some stalkers do intend to carry out their threats. We have found weapon stockpiles in the possession of many of these stalkers (see Figure 7 for an example of the weapons kept by a stalker).

One example of this behavior was a case handled by one of our homicide detectives because of the high potential for violence. The following are some of the recorded messages left on the victim's tape recorder by a female stalker: "I have called you 100 times; you have not called me back." "You want to cause me a problem, I will cause a bigger one for you." "I will use a knife to cut your face open." "If you don't drop the charge, you will have a problem; you will have to deal with me." "You give all your money to that rotten, infectious pussy bitch." "If you don't give me money, then I'll just throw your boy in a trash can or bury him." "Wait until I find you all." "I will beat her up, cut her face open." "I will hire someone to kill you all." "The executioner will never get caught because the killing will be well planned." "Watch out, I will make your life miserable." This stalker's last statement was rather prophetic.

Another example is of a young male stalker who made a series of phone calls to his young female victim. He started out by saying that he still loved the victim and wanted her to call him so that he could "feel better." He then began sobbing on the phone. The stalker continued to make several calls expressing his love and the injustice of her dumping him. He then started saying that his life was over and that he had nothing else to live for. He went on to say, "I could have any girl I wanted, but I only want you." Over the period of a couple of weeks, the stalker's mood drastically changed. He said that he was going to use a "forty-four magnum" on both the victim and her parents. He began to demean her, calling her a "bitch" and a "whore." He blamed her for everything that had happened to him. This is classic DVS behavior.

Now that we have discussed a few examples of direct threats being made by stalkers, let us take this opportunity to remind you that not all

Figure 7. Cache of weapons found during a search.
The stalker had made a sword out of a metal fence post.
(Courtesy of the Westminster Police Department)

stalkers use violence, and some never make a direct threat to their victims. Nevertheless, even though those who make no direct threat or commit violence still harass and often follow, surveil, and continually try to communicate with their victims, thus becoming a very real emotional and psychological threat to the persons they stalk. Also keep in mind there are stalkers who make no direct threat but do in fact commit acts of violence against their stalking victims, for instance the stranger stalker who makes his presence known but never makes a direct threat, then suddenly physically attacks his victim.

As we have said before, stalkers may convey threats via third parties. They do this by telling another person something threatening directed toward the victim, knowing full well that by communicating this threat to this specific person or family member, the threat will find its way back to the intended target or victim.

Cameras. We also want to take a special moment and talk about the camera as being a particular tool of choice for a certain type of stalker. The circumstances surrounding the death of Princess Diana in 1997 make relevant a brief discussion about a portion of the press known as the paparazzi. We want you to use what you've learned thus far in this book to contemplate whether or not an individual who follows, harasses, or, at times, even threatens the safety and well-being of the public person he is photographing in fact qualifies as stalking that public figure. It makes no difference whether or not that figure is royalty, a media personality, or another public figure. We feel that in searching out and harassing their subjects, some of these photo hounds do in fact use their camera as a license to stalk. Some of the news interviews conducted by the media with some of these press photographers bore out our feelings. These individuals firmly believed that a photo opportunity created by any means was perfectly within their rights. However, even some of their colleagues totally disagreed with their argument. Even though this type of activity takes place every day, I believe that it took Princess Diana's tragedy to put the spotlight on this issue. We feel that this is something for legislators and law enforcement personnel to think about.

CHAPTER 3 SUMMARY

- Stalkers use a variety of tools to perpetuate their stock and trade:
  - Gifts
  - Vandalism
  - Surveillance
  - Constant communication
  - Trophy collection
  - Nuisance tactics, which can involve harassment of family members, significant others, and pets, including legal action, fraud, pager harassment, discontinuation of utility services, and extortion and defamation of character via libel and/or slander
- Violence or threats of violence are also tools used by many stalkers. These threats can also be directed to family members, significant others, or children belonging to the victim.
- Not all stalkers actually perpetrate a form of violence toward their victims. They may not verbalize or issue a direct threat against their victim, but their course of conduct does establish the needed credible threat in order for a stalking to have legally taken place.
- There are stalkers who never make direct threats but still carry out acts of violence against their victims.

CHAPTER 4

LIMITING YOUR STALKING EXPOSURE

Now that we've established what stalking is, as well as why stalkers do what they do, we need to discuss some ways to reduce the chances of being stalked. Let us start out by saying that these precautions may or may not stop a stalker from taking a fancy to you, but they should help lower your odds of that taking place. As you read on, you will discover much of what we are going to suggest is based on common sense—but you'd be surprised at how many people play down its importance in life.

No! The first and most important tool in your antistalking arsenal is the word "no." One of the first things we discuss when we lecture a group about stalking exposure is the word "no." If you have kids, I'll bet you've used, or at least thought about using, this phrase over a thousand times: "What part of the word 'no' don't you understand?" Well, that is what you must be able to convey to a potential stalker, in no uncertain terms: "No!" Maybe even "Hell no!" Either way, you must send a clear and concise message to that individual that you are definitely not interested in his advances.

Too often, when we ask our victims if they actually told the suspect in no uncertain terms that they were not interested, their replies are invariably something like "Well, I told him I was currently seeing someone." The stalker then thinks, "Well, she is seeing someone now, but there will be an opening for me later." Another common response is "I'm busy now," or "Now is not a good time for me." Obviously, this type of response indicates to the stalker literally what you said: now is not good, but tomorrow may be. Come on, folks, you have to be firm and tell the flake to take a hike! In our society, we try to let the potential suitor off as gently as possible so as to not hurt his feelings. I'm afraid, though, that that tactic doesn't always work anymore, and you must get past the notion that saying no to a come-on is impolite. Trust us, there is absolutely nothing wrong with telling someone no if you are not at all interested in that particular individual.

Pump up your sixth sense. Cops will often tell you that after only a few years on the job, they develop a strong sense about the people they deal with as well as the environment in which they function. Some develop their perception better than others, even to the point of having this sensory ability being described as uncanny. The streets are a mean teacher, so this sense must be developed quickly. Over the thirty years we have been involved in law enforcement, we have learned that the sixth sense is merely utilizing a combination of some or all of the senses the human animal possesses. That's right, the human animal. Think about it: how many times have you watched a dog or a cat, or any other animal, come upon a scene that stops them dead in their tracks? They sniff the air, take a good look around, and then quickly make a decision to avoid the potential danger they have just perceived. They work off instinct in averting danger, and so should we. This may sound strange to most readers, but when my partner and I came upon a fresh homicide scene, we would ask everyone, if possible, to leave the crime scene so we could soak up as much of what was offered to our senses. In a way we were trying to let that scene, as well as the deceased himself, impart as much information to us as we could assimilate through our sensory radar. (Just so there is no confusion, when we say that the deceased gave us information, we don't mean that he sat up and answered our questions. What we are talking about is body position, the condition of clothing, wound positioning [or lack thereof], as well as what was left on or in the body.)

We all have this ability, but for the most part, due to societal mores as well as other factors that have been ingrained in most of us, our sensitivity quotient has been dulled over time. How many times have you met someone who caused the hair on the back of your neck to tingle? How many times have you entered into a situation where every sensory fiber in your body says, "This isn't right—there is possible danger here!" But our usual tendency is to fight back those incredibly strong and often very accurate urgings and stumble right into a position we wouldn't be in if we had simply forgotten our "manners" and acted on our gut feelings. Trust your instincts!

In this day and age, if you ain't safe you're tempting fate. If it doesn't feel right, don't do it, and for your sake as well as those near and dear to you, don't close down your sensory radar. Listen to your inner self. Remember, first impressions are usually good personality indicators. There is nothing wrong with sizing up those you encounter while wading through life in order to avert danger for you and your loved ones.

Don't advertise. How many times have you seen a personalized plate with the driver's name on it? Many of these same people go an additional step by adding even more information about themselves on the license plate holder. For example, the plate reads "Randi," and the license plate frame states, "Bakers make more dough." This now lets anyone who takes an undesired interest in the owner of that vehicle to have enough information to start building a stalking plan of attack. A stalker now follows the victim into her apartment complex, contacts the manager, and says he is looking for Randi, a fellow baker, but has lost the apartment number. (Remember, many of these slime merchants are smooth talkers and charming!) The "helpful" apartment manager gives the stalker all the information he needs to develop a stalking file on Randi.

We in law enforcement continually encourage parents not to put their children's names on their clothing. This helps avoid the possibility of strangers calling your child by name. The same holds true for adults. This is one of the reasons the rich and famous are susceptible to being stalked. Their notoriety is like a beacon drawing the wayward, unwanted stalker into their port. As we discussed in the second chapter, because those in the media are in the public eye on a regular basis, those stalkers that feel a need to feed on the rich and famous are continually stimulated by the media personality's exposure in talk shows, interviews, etc.

Occasionally I work with media personalities. One of the points I stress to them is to try to keep a low profile whenever they have a chance. We realize that a big part of their job is exposure, but they and their publicist need to try to control what information is actually presented to the public, at least by them. All the personalities that we have talked to know that fame can be a double-edged sword, but it is a price that must be paid for success.

One of my kids recently came up to me and said, "Hey Dad, when you are on TV, why don't you say anything about us? I thought you were proud of your kids." I explained that especially in my line of work, I need to limit my family's exposure. This also holds true for celebrities, be they in the entertainment industry or elsewhere in the public spotlight. I cringe every time I see a media personality doing a walk-through of her home, especially when it is presented on a program where one can obtain a videotape of that segment just by calling in. That program gives the potential stalker access to places he or she normally wouldn't know about. I also am very disappointed when I see a commercial or a monologue where the celebrity shows or uses his children in the piece. Again, this allows the stalker to develop multiple targets. I am sure that these celebrities are proud of their children, but fame and other media exposure causes a whole new set of security rules to come into play.

As human beings we all have our uniqueness, but sometimes what we are, what we do, and where we do it should be kept to ourselves until we are sure we can trust those we come in contact with. That doesn't mean we need to become paranoid, just more cautious. In other words, before telling someone your whole life story and jumping into the jaws of a relationship, test the waters for sharks. We often give people we meet more information than is needed, or in some cases even wanted.

When making purchases, even in the local grocery store, try to use cash, a debit card, or credit card rather than a check. When you use a check (which usually requires that you show a picture identification or driver's license), you are giving away vital information about yourself—telephone number, address, etc. Although this is beneficial to the store, it can also be extremely helpful to a potential stalker. Your check also contains your bank account number and the branch of the bank where your account is held. Stalkers (as well as those interested in consumer fraud) can use all the information you have given on a check to their advantage; all they need is the account number, your name and address, and the bank routing number off your check. Armed with this information, they can fraudulently obtain merchandise or services such as a prepaid phone card. How is this possible? Most banks in the United States have contracts with corporate clearinghouses. When you call a company you want a product from and give them the information we just described, the company runs that information through their designated clearinghouse. If the information given to the clearinghouse matches, and there is money in the account, the clearinghouse will authorize the debit to that account without requiring any further security information. Usually the thief does not ask for a large amount on any one single purchase so as not to alarm the clearinghouse. Unfortunately, my wife and I had to find out about this process by becoming victims ourselves of identity thieves running this con.

Credit cards, especially those with your photo on them, are usually accepted for purchases without additional identification. (Obviously, if you have a problem paying off your credit card, you will need to rethink this tactic.) Some credit card companies do not put your photo on the card. For those cards, I write "Check Person's Identification" in the space reserved for my signature. This way, the person taking your card has to verify via photo identification that you are the one that is actually using the card. We should note, however, that credit card numbers can be stolen; still, bank information, home addresses, phone numbers, and even driver's license numbers, which can be found on personal checks, are not shown on a credit card, nor are they required when making most purchases with one.

Be wary of cyberstalkers. We have placed the topic of cyber-stalking following the section called "Don't Advertise" because this is where it seems to fit the best. Those of you that surf the Internet have a tendency to feel safe telling someone your innermost feelings because you're insulated by the phone or cable line. But are you really? We have already dealt with cases of cyberstalking. In fact, we recently investigated a case in which a lesbian couple broke off a stormy five-year involvement. This relationship involved vandalism to vehicles and one of the partners stabbing the other with a screwdriver, who then retaliated by striking the first one in the head with a two-by-four. A portion of the victim's business was conducted through the Internet. She had a Web address where her stalker would send electronic messages to her, threatening both her and her new female lover. The suspect would send these e-mails on a daily basis and would not make any attempt to disguise who she was while continuing her stalking behavior over the Internet. In this scenario, the stalker could be charged with terrorist threats and stalking directed at both the victim and the victim's new significant other.

It has been our experience that people get on the Internet for a variety of reasons, one being loneliness. People want to reach out and figuratively touch somebody, and the Internet provides them with an opportunity to do so, usually without worrying about the consequences of a real, three-dimensional relationship. The same was and is still true for many CB (citizen's band radio) operators. They can jump on the airways and talk to someone for fun without having to worry about what that other person looks like, what their foibles might be, or even if they are telling the truth. The CB operator can live in a fantasy world without, for the most part, the fear of being found out. However, the Internet can do so much more than what the CB used to do, and it can do it all over the world with just a few strokes on the keyboard.

If all that occurs during Internet chats is a harmless, fun conversation, no one is hurt. Where the fun stops and the danger begins, though, is when one person on-line is a predator, not a fun-loving "webster"— a term we like to use for a person that surfs the Web with legal and innocent intent. Does this mean that everyone you meet on the Internet is a potential stalker? Hardly, but unless you personally know each individual, each must be treated as a potential threat. Why? Because most likely, while staring into the magic computer screen in the safety of your room or home office, you poured out your thoughts, sometimes very intimate ones, to someone you thought you'd never meet or have any more than a cyber-relationship with. Even if you don't believe you are giving out too much information, you probably are. Let's say, for example, that while in a chat room "Gena" tells a potential stalker she loves going to the beach. Some time later, the stalker, who has already figured out where Gena may be living based on detailed notes from previous e-mail or chat conversations, then tells Gena he likes going to a beach in an area where he believes she might reside. Gena then, without thinking, says something like, "Oh, that's not too far from where I go. Are you familiar with lifeguard stand 47?" Remember, patience and stealth are a couple of the stalker's primary skills. Now he has enough information either to set up a meeting with Gena or just show up and begin surveilling her. It does not take much for these cunning predators to spin the webs they need to ensnare their victims.

According to both of my brothers-in-law, who have degrees in computer science, math, and microbiology—and who don't seem to breathe the same air I do—the Internet will develop more sophisticated personal protection buffers in the not too distant future. They believe that the Internet is still in a major growth phase, and as a result, no one has directed a lot of energy toward these problems. They predict that like anything, a greater demand will generate a better product or system.

An *Oprah Winfrey Show* titled "Child Stalkers Online," which aired April 17, 2002, was dedicated to exposing the ever-increasing use of the Internet by child predators. We strongly recommend the purchase of the videotape of this program on-line at oprah.com or through their fulfillment house so that you can play it for your child and then have a discussion about what is presented on the tape. Detective Mike Sullivan was profiled on this particular show, and he had some of the computer safeguards he recommended placed on Oprah's Web page. Some of those safeguards are listed below. (Detective Sullivan also wrote a book titled *The Safety Monitor: How to Protect Your Kids Online*.)

- **McAfee NeoTrace Pro:** "This tracking program allows parents to identify who's communicating with their children and where they are coming from." It is designed to backtrack the sender's e-mail. Visit www.neoworx.com for further details.

- **PowerTools for AOL:** "Every time your child has an instant message with someone, this program saves it as a simple document on the hard drive that you can open later and read like an e-mail or text file." Visit www.bpssoft.com/PowerTools/pt_comp.htm for further details.

- **Cyber Sentinel:** "This internet software filters out sexually explicit material and protects against exposure to on-line predators and pedophiles in chat rooms, instant messaging, and e-mail." Visit www.securitysoft.com for further details.

- **Child Safe:** "This computer monitoring utility can block websites, capture screenshots, and log keystrokes." Visit www.webroot.com/childsafe1.htm for further details.

- **McAfee Privacy Service:** "Privacy computer application that features different access levels, website blocking, content filtering and information protection." Visit kids.mcafee.com for further details.[1]

We should state that to the best of our knowledge, none of these devices claims to protect your child 100 percent of the time, but they should certainly help.

Now if you or your child runs across someone on the Web who begins to exhibit some weird behavior through threatening or harassing e-mail, these are just a few tools you can use. Your local computer store should have the programs we listed. If not, you might go directly to the company's Web site to obtain their product. On another note, one of the Web experts we contacted wanted us to make sure we mentioned to those purchasing items over the Web that the sites mentioned above use a "secure server" for accepting purchase orders and when taking any kind of personal information. The expert advised that the company you are purchasing from should have these servers available. By the way, it is always a good idea to check with your Internet provider to see if it has a policy of sharing or selling your profile information and/or e-mail address with anyone else. It is better if they don't, but if they do, see if you can block that kind of activity, or change your provider.

At this point, we thought it would be appropriate to discuss three cyberstalking cases. All three involve Internet stalking, but show two different techniques used by stalkers to perpetrate their crimes.

The first case, which took place in Irvine, California, in December 2001, was profiled on *The Oprah Winfrey Show* and *Dateline NBC*. The primary detective on the case was Irvine Police Detective Larry Montgomery. During the early stages of this investigation, Detective Montgomery said he received assistance from the Newport Beach Police Department as well as the University of California at Irvine Police Department. Since Larry and I have been colleagues for years, I invited him over to my home so that I could interview him on this case. This case is an excellent example of how a casual Internet chat room experience can go horribly wrong.

For a period of about $1\frac{1}{2}$ weeks, a fifteen-year-old female struck up a conversation with a male who described himself as being about eighteen to nineteen years of age. The female, who was interested in having a relationship with a young man, began telling the predator a great deal about herself. According to the victim, the predator sounded like a nice person, so she decided to meet him at a location in the city of Orange. She went to the location but was not able to locate him. She returned home, got on the Internet, and asked him what had gone wrong. The stalker said that he had been there and had in fact seen her, but for whatever reason he didn't contact her. (I believe this may have been a trial run for the stalker, so that he could observe his potential victim. It could also mean that the stalker felt that the proper conditions were not optimal for him to make his move on the victim.)

The stalker then set up another date with the victim at the same location, and this time he showed himself. The stalker convinced the girl to enter his car and go to a college campus where he both studied and worked as a part-time parking attendant. Once in the parking lot, the stalker convinced the victim to get into the back seat of his vehicle so that she could give him a backrub. The stalker then got into the back with her. Once in the back seat, he produced a knife, held it to her throat, demanding that she do everything that he told her to do. The stalker had brought duct tape with him, which he used to wrap her hands and cover her eyes.

Once the victim was secured, he pulled off her skirt and panties. He removed his belt and began striking the victim with the buckle end of the belt over and over again. The stalker concentrated his blows on her thighs, vaginal area, and pelvis. As he struck her without mercy, he would call her "slut," "whore," "bitch," etc. When he struck her he would yell "Yee-ha" or something similar, as if he was striking a horse or another animal. Detective Montgomery said when the stalker began striking the victim in the pelvis, she put her bound hands down to try and protect herself. This enraged the stalker, who then told her to remove her hands, striking her in the mouth with the belt buckle and breaking off her front tooth, which he made her swallow.

Over the course of the beating, which took about two to three hours, the stalker would force his hand and fingers into the victim's vagina on multiple occasions, injuring her in the process. At one point he forced her to orally copulate him. The victim also said that when the stalker would get tired of beating her and seemed to need rest, he would lie on top of her and kiss her. Once rested, he would continue to beat her.

During the course of the assault, the stalker became increasingly angry, took his knife, and cut a swastika into the victim's cheek and forehead, telling her that this would make her even uglier than he thought she already was. The victim also told Detective Montgomery that during the course of the assault, the stalker would put his face down to her buttocks, and demand that she "fart on him." She said that he would then do the same to her. The victim said that when she complied, he would snort around like an animal while smelling her.

Detective Montgomery told me that the victim thought she was going to die, so even though she was reeling in horrible pain and was completely terrified, she had enough presence of mind to try a technique that probably saved her life. When the suspect again lay on top of her, exhausted from his repeated, brutal onslaught, she kissed him back when he mouthed her and said something kind to him. This caused the stalker to change the entire way he acted toward the victim. She said that he stopped calling her names and began to actually treat her with some compassion. He then redressed the victim and let her get out of the car.

I feel that up to this point, the stalker had only looked at her as being an object for his control, rage, and disgust. Once she did something that caused him to realize that she was a real person, it brought him back to reality, thus changing how he related to the victim. The victim was very wise to respond to the stalker in this fashion. Let me try to explain this phenomenon a little further. Over the years of interviewing hundreds of violent criminals, I have noticed that some have been able to better articulate their feelings than others. They describe either being totally out of control—in a rage—while committing acts of violence. Others describe being totally in control of themselves, but totally dissociating—i.e., separating—themselves from the individual they are doing these often brutal things to. Some liken the feeling they have to being in a void, with no outside stimulus bothering them at the time they are perpetrating these acts. This female victim was, however, able to bring this stalker, whom we believe to be a sexual sadist, back to some sense of reality.

Montgomery, a soft-spoken and very thorough homicide detective, said that during the course of the investigation, he was able to get the victim—whom he praised for her courage—to try to communicate with the suspect again on the Internet in the hopes of drawing him out. Montgomery said that a few days before Christmas he was still in his office (an occupational hazard) when he got a call from the victim. She had made contact with the stalker in the same chat room as before. Unbeknownst to the detective, the victim had a friend who was also connected to the chat room talking to the same suspect in the hopes of helping draw the stalker to her, and thus helping her friend. Montgomery said he was now on a three-way hook-up, with the victim's aunt and the victim's friend, as they drew the stalker into their trap. During the course of the Internet conversation, the stalker decided he no longer wanted to talk to the victim but instead began arranging a meeting with the victim's girlfriend. Once that was set, Montgomery contacted an arrest team, and they proceeded to a mall in Orange, where they took the stalker into custody as he was waiting for the initial victim's friend to arrive. The victim of the brutal attack was in the car with Detective Montgomery and was able to positively identify him for officers at the scene. Montgomery noted if she had not been with him assisting in locating the suspect, they may not have located him, because he was driving a different vehicle than the one he had used during the kidnapping and assault. Montgomery said that when they arrested the stalker, he had duct tape in his pocket and had the knife "ready to go" laid out next to the driver's seat.

Because I am very interested in what makes stalkers tick, I asked Detective Montgomery about the stalker's background. I knew that there had to be some type of fantasy planning on the part of this stalker before he committed his crimes. Montgomery related the following: the stalker was a twenty-year-old male, and the fifteen-year-old-female victim was of a race different from that of the stalker. The stalker lived with his parents in an upscale area of Orange County. He was a college student with a good grade-point average. He had never been in trouble, nor had he had any law enforcement contact. He had few friends, kept to himself, and seemed quiet. I then asked Montgomery about any diaries or pornography: I knew that there had to be something unusual about the stalker. The detective then noted that they had in fact obtained a search warrant and seized his computer. In the computer they found all kinds of Web sites devoted to rape and bondage that he had accessed. (For me, this helped to explain the stalker's behavior. This is a twenty-year-old male with no apparent sexual relationship who sits at his computer, surfs rape and bondage sites over and over again, and downloads information from these sites, which feeds his fantasy life.) I told Montgomery that I felt that was why he wanted to have the victim pass gas for him, because he had seen it on some site and wanted to know how it smelled and if it would arouse him sexually. That was also the reason I believe he didn't have sexual intercourse with the victim but only digitally penetrated her. I felt he was a novice, based on the way he explored the victim sexually. In short, he was on a highly perverted quest of sexual experimentation. (Those are obviously my professional observations. As we have said before, this type of dissection or postmortem of the crime helps us to interview the suspect and understand why he does what he does. It is never intended to excuse or downplay the horrible trauma this victim or anyone like her goes through at the hands of this or any other perpetrator.)

Montgomery said that during his interview with the stalker, he admitted to cutting her face, using a swastika because that was a sign of "hate." He admitted to breaking her tooth but said that "that was just an accident." Montgomery said the stalker's parents had no idea that their son was involved in anything unusual. Montgomery said his investigation also revealed another victim, whom the stalker had picked up the same way he did the fifteen-year-old. He also transported that victim to the same college campus parking lot, but according to that victim, he was "acting so crazy" (for example, talking to himself) that the female—very smartly—fled before any assault took place.

There are millions who surf the Internet. Many who enter and view porn sites never cause another human being any harm. However, for a certain percentage of the population, the Internet is a virtual cornucopia of deviant pleasures; this is what makes it so scary. You have a twenty-year-old male subject who now doesn't have to travel to some low-life part of town to buy this type of pornography. The Internet made the material available to him in great abundance, and probably for not a great deal of money. All he has to do is go on-line. In fact, in a chat room, he could talk to people who are into the same type of perversion he is, and get ideas from those supposedly more experienced than he. Once his fantasy is properly fueled, the Internet gives him access to a significant number of potential victims. So, as in this case, when the predator-class stalker decides to make his fantasy a reality, he can ply his trade fairly easily.

The second example of cyberstalking I wanted to relate was a case investigated by the Los Angeles Sheriff's Department along with the FBI. It was reported by the *Los Angeles Times* staff writers Greg Miller and Davan Maharaj on January 22, 1999, as the first California cyberstalking case. The facts are simple but appalling. A twenty-eight-year-old female had turned away the advances of a fifty-year-old security guard. He placed her name, address, and phone number on the Internet, saying that she had rape fantasies. According to the *Times* article, several men showed up at the victim's apartment trying to assist her in her supposed fantasies. The victim received several rude and annoying phone calls concerning this issue. According to Dr. Kris Mohandie, who discussed this case during a presentation at the 2002 Threat Management Conference, this woman finally put a sign on her front door stating not to bother her and that all the postings on the Internet were a "hoax." Mohandie said that when the suspect found out about this, he wrote another posting in these sadomasochistic chat rooms. He stated that the sign was to "separate the men from the boys" and that the victim still would welcome being forcibly raped.

What makes this case so unique is that the stalker got his revenge on this poor woman by entering into Internet chat rooms that discussed or catered to those interested in rape and acted as though he was she. Obviously, this type of stalking is somewhat Machiavellian, because the primary stalker would resort to any means to achieve his end, including having complete strangers conduct his campaign of terror and extreme emotional distress without physically stalking the victim himself.

Our third example concerns a cyberstalker going after a celebrity. For this, we contacted Los Angeles County Deputy District Attorney Rhonda Saunders, whom I have known for years and who is renowned for handling many of these types of cases. Rhonda told me that not too long ago, she and her team of district attorney investigators, along with the Los Angeles Threat Management Unit, got a call from Jeri Ryan, one of the attractive stars of a *Star Trek* television series produced by Paramount Studios. Apparently Jeri and her boyfriend, Brannon Braga, the show's producer, were being stalked by an individual later found to be from the San Francisco Bay area. Rhonda said this stalker, who knew his way around a computer, was sending thousands of e-mails to both Jeri and Brannon. The stalker was e-mailing Brannon with threats such as "I am going to cave in your cranium!" or "I am going to tie you up and put you next to a hot fire." The stalker was sending very sexually explicit e-mails to Jeri, who played "Seven of Nine" on the show. The stalker also sent Jeri nude photos of himself. When the stalker was initially contacted and advised to stop sending e-mails and gifts to Jeri, he started a campaign of extortion via the Internet. He said something to the effect of, If you want me to stop, make me a charity and give me $100,000 so I can get a car and find a girlfriend. The stalker, who was a physical health nut and heavily into the martial arts, said he had never had a girlfriend.

This stalker was eventually arrested for stalking and extortion. He was placed on formal probation and was told that he could no longer have any access to any electronic device that transmitted any wireless information. You guessed it, not two weeks later, he was back on the Internet sending e-mail. When he was arrested the second time, he told the arrest team, "I didn't think you were going to catch me again." He is currently serving two years in prison on his probation violation.

Since most cyberstalking is directed toward the young, let us give you some interesting statistics. These findings can be found in the June 2000 report titled "Online Victimization: A Report on the Nation's Youth,"[2] compiled by the Crimes Against Children Research Center.

- Nearly twenty-four million youth ages ten through seventeen were on-line regularly in 1999, and millions more are expected to join them shortly.
- Approximately one in five received a sexual solicitation or approach over the Internet in the last year.
- One in thirty-three received an aggressive sexual solicitation—

a solicitor who asked to meet them somewhere; called them on the telephone; sent them regular mail, money, or gifts. (Parents, if your children start getting phone calls from people you don't know, or you find gifts and/or other items in the mail by persons your child said they met on the Internet, be very, very concerned. First speak to your child and then contact local law enforcement concerning these solicitations. Remember, these are all preludes to further contacts, stalking and possibly worse.)

- One in seventeen was threatened or harassed.
- Approximately one-quarter of young people who reported these incidents were distressed by them.
- Less than 10 percent of sexual solicitations and only 3 percent of unwanted exposure episodes were reported to authorities such as a law enforcement agency, an Internet service provider, or a hotline. (You can report these incidents to the National Center for Missing and Exploited Children's (NCMEC's) CyberTipline by going on-line at www.cybertipline.com or simply by calling (703) 274-3900, or you can contact your Internet provider, who should also be able to get you in touch with other cybertip-type organizations.)
- About one-quarter of the youth who encountered a sexual solicitation or approach told a parent. Almost 40 percent of those reporting an unwanted exposure to sexual material told a parent.
- In households with home Internet access, one-third of the parents said they had filtering or blocking software on their computer at the time they were interviewed.
- 97 percent of the solicitors were strangers.
- The methods of delivery or contact on these unsolicited exposures to youth were as follows: 71 percent occurred while the youth were surfing or searching the Web, with the rest occurring through e-mail or instant messages. In 67 percent of the incidents, youths were at home when the unwanted exposure occurred; 15 percent while at school; 13 percent in someone else's home; and 3 percent at the library.

Internet Safety for Children. Earlier, we recommended viewing with your children the *Oprah Winfrey Show* program entitled "Child Stalkers Online." One segment of that program was an interview with Mike and Cassandra Harris, a law enforcement husband-and-wife team from Colorado. These two investigators for the Jefferson County district attorney's office have been very active in the investigation of the cyberstalking of children. In May 2002 I called and talked to Mike Harris concerning some of the issues he had faced. I also asked him to give me some suggestions on what advice I should provide to parents reading this book whose children were on the Internet. Investigator Harris directed me to a Web site where he had posted a letter. This letter, titled "Internet Safety," can be found by going on-line and simply keying in "Jefferson County Colorado district attorney," then clicking on "Internet Investigations." Investigator Harris also advised that he gave the producers of the *Oprah Winfrey Show* a great deal of this type of information, which they then put on their Web site, which was mentioned earlier. The following are some of the points Investigator Harris laid out in both his Web site, "Tips for Parents with Children on the Internet," and the one listed at oprah.com, "What to Teach Your Children."

- Place the computer in the family room or other visible area, not in a child's bedroom.
- Use gender-neutral screen names. (Don't allow your child to use screen names that denote their sex or express sexual connotations, for example, "love-dog," "slut-monster," etc. Some of the other computer experts we talked to also advised using screen names that were hard to remember or that didn't really make sense, such as "2*C+," etc.)
- Talk to children about Internet safety and participate with them online. If they know more than you, let them teach you. (Now I don't know about you, but I am fifty-five years old, and most of the time, I can barely figure out how to turn the computer on and off. One of my boys, whom I unfortunately have recently found chatting in a few of the wrong chat rooms, is way ahead of me

on this technology. He also programs my VCR, so don't feel embarrassed about sitting down with your kids and asking them how to use the Internet. It will tend to bring you closer together, because you know they always like to be in a position to teach you something, especially when they know it is something you are clueless about.)

- Children shouldn't believe anything said to them over the Internet from an unknown source.
- Tell children they do not have to respond to messages sent to them, whether by e-mail or instant message.
- Children should never give out personal information, screen names, passwords, or credit card information online. (This is especially true for phone numbers, addresses, or other personal information that can be tracked.)
- Use a good virus detection program.
- Supervise children's computer usage. Don't rely on filtering software to do the work. (We also suggest not allowing your children to compose their own computer profiles, if you decide to let them have a profile.)
- Know who your children are communicating with on-line. Get to know their on-line friends just as you would their other friends.
- Promote an environment where your children can talk openly with you. (As a parent, you should know this is the key to everything. My teenager told me in a recent conversation that people use abbreviations in chat rooms to speed up the conversation or to stop other people from checking on what they are doing, such as *LOL* for "laugh out loud," *G2G* for "got to go," or *PIR* for "parent in room.")

Investigator Harris also said to be aware of children turning off their computer when you come into the room or being on the Internet when they are not supposed to be. He advised parents to be mindful of any unusual phone calls showing up on their bill, or any mail or unusual items sent to their children. We suggest that one adult in the home be made responsible for getting and checking the mail. Make it clear that that individual is the only one who picks up and sorts the mail, every day. This hopefully will dissuade children from intercepting the mail. The events following September 11 also make it a good idea to have this policy in place.

Harris said that their experience in dealing with cyberpredators has shown that children in the following categories seem to be more at risk for being stalked than others on the Internet: those who are shy, withdrawn, and/or who have low self-esteem; those with a weight problem; and those who have divorced parents. We in law enforcement continually encounter such youths, who become victims not only of stalking but also of other crimes associated with being bullied and harassed, usually by their peers. They are continually searching for acceptance.

One last thing we would like you to keep in mind concerning use of the Internet, whether you are a child or an adult, is the use of the Web camera. This is a digital video camera that can be attached to your computer that allows you to see the person you are chatting with on-line. These cameras have been around a while and are great for seeing your loved ones, but they are an open window for not only stalkers but also other predators laying traps in the Web. The Web camera allows the predator greater intimacy with the potential victim. It allows him to see and read facial expressions or how the victim just reacted to a question. Obviously, it also allows the predator to con individuals on the other end of the camera to expose more than just their face.

When I asked Investigator Harris what new trends he was seeing lately in youth cyberstalking, he informed me there was a marked increase in pedophiles using Web cameras. He advised, as we have previously discussed, that they want to see more and more flesh on the camera. Again, victims think that because they are in the privacy of their own home, exposing themselves does not create a problem; obviously, however, it could.

Even though it will take law enforcement time to react to cybercrimes, due to manpower and funding shortages, you still should contact them when a problem arises. Remember, when you're out there surfing the Web, all that flops onto your proverbial beach is not going to be friendly.

Monitor your trash, both at work and at home. Here's one that gets a lot of raised eyebrows in our seminars. Take a moment and think what you put in the trash: banking information, utility bills, credit card information, medication bottles, notes and personal letters, motor vehicle information, etc.—all of which are a veritable jackpot to a stalker. Get the picture? "Dumpster diving" is one of the stalker's best tools for finding information on you. For instance, we investigated a stalker who obtained phone numbers as well as social security information on a female victim, along with information on the person she was currently living with—all this was garnered from their trash. This information was used by the stalker against the victim, causing both her and her new live-in boyfriend a great deal of consternation. The stalker would make comments to the victim about things that she and her new boyfriend were doing and what they were paying for certain items. Because she and her boyfriend had no idea how the stalker was obtaining this information, they became very upset, to the point of always looking over their shoulder and questioning some of the people who had legal access to this information, when all the stalker was doing was going through their trash late at night. Our investigation showed he was also prowling and watching them at night. (It should be noted that when we conducted a search of this stalker's residence, we located some of the items he had removed from the trash. If we feel that our stalker is trash-oriented, we can include this information on our search warrants.) Another stalker was able to get hold of a credit card application, similar to what most of us receive in the mail on a regular basis, and ordered a credit card for the victim without her knowledge. This stalker used his victim's credit card number to purchase tires and get work done on his vehicle valued at several hundred dollars.

Trash shredders are becoming cheaper and cheaper; if you can't afford one of these machines, make sure you cut or tear up anything personal before tossing it into the trash. (Note: Cross-cut trash shredders are the best type of shredder because the items shredded in almost all cases cannot be put back together, as can material cut merely into strips.)

Be careful with your house keys. Get a key chain that allows you to easily detach your car keys from your house and other personal keys. In fact, it takes no time at all to make a duplicate set, so do it. (Of course, if you have one of the newer vehicles, where a computer chip is embedded in the ignition key, a duplicate can be a little pricey.) This way, when you give your car dealer, mechanic, or valet a set of keys, you aren't giving them access to another slice of your life.

Take a self-defense class. There are hundreds out there, many of which are taught by law enforcement personnel. You don't have to become a black belt to learn some basic defensive moves. These classes may even reinforce some of the common-sense material we have been discussing. If nothing else, they should assist you in developing some type of plan for escape if the need arises. Along these same lines, it doesn't hurt to keep yourself as fit as possible. This not only promotes health but allows you more options if you have to run or defend yourself.

Meet on a first date in a public place. If at all possible, do not invite your new-found friend over to your house to pick you up, and provide your own transportation to and from the date. This may sound somewhat inconvenient, but you cannot really say if this will turn out to be Mr. Wonderful or Mr. Hyde until you've been on a couple of dates, right? If he isn't the right guy, and he turns out to be your worst nightmare, why let him know where you live? Obviously, a couple of dates may not be enough time to really expose the beast, but it still gives you a chance to run him through your sensory radar.

CHAPTER 4 SUMMARY

- Say "no," and sound like you mean it!
- Use all your powers of perception. If it doesn't feel right, it probably isn't.

- Don't advertise who you are to just anyone. Be careful about how much information you give out about yourself.
- Be aware that cyberstalking is on the increase. Follow some common sense steps when using the Internet:
    - Don't believe anything that someone you don't know tells you on-line.
    - Be careful about what information you give out on the Internet. Always think twice about giving out any personal information.
    - If you get unsolicited, explicit, threatening, or distasteful material on-line, report it to your Internet service provider or some other organization, such as the National Center for Missing and Exploited Children (NCMEC; accessible on-line at www.missingkids.com).
    - If you have children who use the Internet, monitor them for the telltale signs that they are in inappropriate chat rooms or on-line with the wrong people.
- Be careful with your house keys.
- Consider taking a self-defense class and trying to keep yourself fit.
- Find a neutral public meeting place for your first date. Provide your own transportation both ways.

CHAPTER 5

WHAT TO DO IF YOU BELIEVE YOU ARE BEING STALKED

If after you've read everything up to this point you feel you're being stalked, don't panic. Keep reading so you can begin to get a handle on your stalker. The goal of this chapter is to help you get some intervention on your side, as well as help you take back some of the control the stalker has taken from your life.

STEPS TO TAKE WHEN DEALING WITH A STALKER

Document everything. Trust us, the key to prosecuting a stalker is to document, document, document, and then document some more. To date, every stalker except one that we have prosecuted has pled guilty prior to trial; most have pled guilty to multiple felony counts. The reason is simple: we bury them so deep in investigative documentation that they could bleed to death from the paper cuts they would receive when trying to burrow out.

Seriously, in short we find out everything we can about our stalkers. *We stalk the stalker.* What we've concluded from all these thousands of hours of laborious work is that you can't give these terrorists (an appropriate name, since they achieve their end by causing fear) a second chance. So, the minute you believe a stalker has come into your life, start to document every event as it unfolds. Think of yourself as a court reporter—everything this individual does must be chronicled. (We suggest you keep your records in a log or diary format, similar to the one illustrated in Figure 8. This is an example of the Westminster Police Department's victim stalking log.) Recently we had a two-day preliminary hearing on an AS who stalked a woman over the past eleven years. Due to the circumstances of the case, if this victim hadn't kept good records, both her testimony and our investigation would have been greatly hindered. As it was, the stalker was bound over (remanded) for trial in superior court on all felony charges. He later pled guilty to felony stalking, served about four months in jail, and was placed on probation, which he continued to violate, each time going back to jail for longer and longer periods of time.

Keep the information you gather on your stalker in a safe place. If possible, make copies and leave a copy in another location. Remember, some stalkers will enter their victim's house and/or car, and they have been known to steal the documentation you have accumulated.

As much as possible, corroborate this documentation with eyewitness accounts or photographs. Go out and buy a disposable camera and keep it with you at all times. Then, when you are confronted by your stalker, take a snapshot, trying to get some type of landmark in the photo as well. Taking a picture is advisable for two reasons. First, there will often be no witnesses when the stalking event occurs—thus a photo is utilized for corroboration. Second, depending on the type of stalker, taking his photo may tend to slow his activities.

Always remember, however, that what works with one stalker may not work with another, and taking your particular stalker's photo may cause a violent response. To date, each time a stalker we have investigated has been photographed by a victim, he has left the area without trying to take the camera away. That is not to say there won't be a time when a stalker takes a camera away from the victim in the hopes of destroying evidence. That is why it is best to be working with a law enforcement professional as early into the stalking scenario as pos-

WESTMINSTER POLICE DEPARTMENT
VICTIM STALKING LOG

Detective assigned to case: _Det. M. G. Proctor_   DR # 03-000

Victim's Name: _Jane Victim (example no such person)_

Suspect:s Name: _Jake Simpleton (example no such person)_

This stalking log is designed to allow you to record and track your stalker. This log is to be filled out as accurately as possible. Please use a No. 2 pencil or black ink when filling out and listing times of occurrence. If you need additional logs, contact Westminster Police Department.

Please use A.M. or P.M. when listing times.

Date of Incident	Time	Type of Contact; I.e. phone, personal, etc.	What was said; occurred	Evidence Collected
09-03-03	1:30 P.M.	Jake called	"You won't see tomorrow"	Taped call
09-04-03	3:05 A.m.	Left card on my car	"I love you, Jake"	Put into a paper bag
09-04-03	5:00 pm	Dropped dead roses off	Knocked on door & said "These are for you bitch!"	Bagged roses & took photo of him running to his car

WPD 30 (2/98)

Figure 8. Example of a victim's stalking log.
This one is utilized by the Westminster Police Department.
(Courtesy of the Westminster Police Department)

sible, so that officers are kept up to speed on events as they happen and so that they can better assist you.

This same set of rules can also apply to the use of a videocamera, which we really prefer. Many times the camera can be set up in such a fashion as to not alarm the stalker. Obviously, this type of visual evidence is very damaging to stalkers' testimony when they are trying to explain that they were not at a certain location stalking you. In one stalking case that took place in another jurisdiction, the victim videotaped her stalker leaving a package that contained a realistic-looking, but fake, bomb. This kind of evidence had a profound impact on the jury at the time of trial.

In 2003 we had a case in which a stalker was continually slashing the female victim's tires while she was at work. We convinced the business supervisor to place her car in such a position as to give us the best of view of the car. We were able to get very clear video of the suspect taking a razor-type knife and slitting the sidewalls of the victim's tires. The video was so good, it showed a close-up of the stalker slashing the tire and then putting the knife in his mouth as he crawled around the car to do the next tire.

Documentation also includes saving anything that the stalker sends, gives, or leaves you. We realize that you are probably not a crime scene analyst, but to better assist law enforcement, we are going to put you through a crash course in evidence collection. (Of course, if you can get law enforcement personnel to respond and collect your evidence in a reasonable time frame, don't move the evidence—leave it in place.) One must collect these items in the following manner:

- All correspondence, cards, glass or plastic items, etc., should be carefully handled so as not to destroy any fingerprints left by the stalker. This can be accomplished by barely touching only one corner or edge of what you are collecting, or by putting regular cellophane tape around your thumb and forefinger before grasping the object. They should be bagged in a loose-fitting paper bag; avoid using plastic sandwich baggies or other plastic products whenever possible, as they tend to adhere to the surface of the item being collected. Avoid showing these items to all your friends and relatives—the less an item is touched before it gets into the hands of law enforcement personnel, the better. At the time you receive these cards, letters, and other gifts, they may not mean much, but over time they do begin to paint a picture of your stalker and will probably help weave the rope needed to secure him to the crime of stalking.

- On the outside of the paper bag, mark with something—preferably a magic marker or other quality marking pen)—the date and time you found or recovered this evidence. When you process this evidence in a professional manner, it will assist your law enforcement first responder greatly. It may also stop her from improperly handling the evidence you have presented, because from time to time, even the law enforcement personnel will forget (not frequently, but it does happen).

- If you locate the above-described evidence in a place other than your mailbox, such as hanging from your door or attached to your car, try to photograph it in place before removing it. If you cannot do this, it is our hope that your first responder will have a camera with him. Many agencies do, but some don't. If you have a small portable camera with you as suggested above, you can turn over the camera as part of your evidence collection. Again, these suggestions may seem a bit much, but just remember, when you follow these suggestions, you are becoming a partner in the investigation.

- If you run across items that are of a fragile nature, such as blood, semen, or feces left behind by your stalker (and you might) *it is much better to leave that for a professional to collect.* However, if it is not possible to get a first responder out to collect this evidence right away, try to secure the sample by putting a box over it or by cordoning the area off from others. Obviously, if for some reason you felt you had to collect this type of evidence— which by the way can contain DNA that can help identify the stalker—then we would suggest using any gloves you have, along with a resealable plastic bag. (This would be the only time we would suggest this type of bag, due to the liquidity of the substance. If the material has dried prior to collection, a paper bag may be used. You can also write with a felt-tip pen on the outside of the bag.) Again, record the date and time of collection, and photograph the evidence in place if possible. We have had examples of stalkers and residential burglars who leave feces both in and out of the toilet when they have entered a residence to collect trophies or to steal certain items. This behavior resembles a wild animal marking its territory. A Los Angeles police agency worked a case in which the stalker was mailing jars of feces to a victim. The jars resembled the type that fruit or soft cheeses are packed into.

- If possible, tape-record the phone calls your stalker makes to you. All of them, including the ones you'd rather not ever hear again—for example, when he is describing how he is going to execute you and your loved ones or relating his latest sexual fantasy. It's amazing what that tape does to a jury when played aloud in the courtroom. We have all of our victims tape-record their conversations with their stalkers; they are allowed to do this without telling the suspect they are being recorded because it is for the purpose of a criminal investigation, not a civil proceeding. However, we must caution you to coordinate with the law enforcement entity in your area to ascertain if this kind of audio taping is legal in your state. (Note: If you start receiving phone communications from your stalker, put an answer machine on that line if at all possible and let the stalker threaten you on tape as much as he wants. Keep those tapes for future prosecution. If possible, record the date and time of the calls when they come in. This is another reason why we have developed a stalking log that our officers issue to potential stalking victims. The victims can then log the calls as well as other stalking events (again, refer to Figure 8 for an example of that log).

We have stalking victims who get voice mail from their stalkers on their cellular phones, save the message, and then tape-record the message onto a cassette before deleting that message. We just worked a case where the stalker was calling a victim from jail with the assistance of a third party. He would call his female associate, who would in turn call the victim's cellular phone, and then the stalker would leave a message on the victim's voice mail. He did this because the victim would not accept any of his collect calls from jail. The victim tape-recorded the calls off her phone, and we convicted the stalker on two counts of violating a domestic violence restraining order, which gave him another three hundred days in jail.

In most states, an extra phone line is inexpensive. You might want to invest in one and give that number out only to trusted friends and family with an expressed request not to give that number out to anyone else. This way you can still communicate with friends and family while your stalker continues to build up evidence for your case on your answering machine. For some reason, most stalkers, especially of the domestic violence variety, like to leave threatening messages on a machine. They tell us that they figure even if the victim is monitoring her calls, she will still hear what the stalker has to say. Each time the stalker calls and leaves a message can mean another count of harassment, making annoying phone calls, and/or violation of a restraining order, if one is in place. All of those charges, however, are what we call "lesser and included" charges in the stalking case.

Another fairly secure medium of communication is e-mail. Most stalkers aren't going to have all your friends' or relatives' e-mail addresses or have a way of monitoring them, unless they are computer experts or adept hackers. Remember, even though we think it is a good idea for stalking victims to avail themselves of a cellular phone, some of these conversations can be monitored via scanners that anyone can purchase, because cellular calls are transmitted on a group of specific frequencies that can to date be legally monitored by anyone. This is why many law enforcement agencies have gone to scrambled radio frequencies. This stops unwanted eavesdroppers, including the media, from listening in on their radio transmissions.

Notify law enforcement. Throughout this book, we have tried to emphasize the importance of connecting with your local law enforcement agency. We realize there are other kinds of stalker interventions; one we refer to as the "axe-handle" type. During the course of our travels, we have heard about incidents of axe-handle stalking intervention, as in, "Yeah, my relatives took care of the problem" (i.e., with an axe-handle). Although smacking a stalker around with an axe handle may be slightly more gratifying than the longer route of legitimate prosecution, we would definitely recommend that you seek out law enforcement intervention instead. Obviously we cannot recommend taking the law into your own hands, because if you do, you will probably end up in a bigger mess than you started with. Thus, as soon as you believe you are becoming the victim of a stalking, notify your local law enforcement agency. Advise them that you feel you are being stalked and ask them to investigate, keeping in mind that all fifty states now have some type of antistalking legislation on their books. As we have discussed in previous chapters, the legal definitions of and the penalties for stalking vary from state to state, but they do exist. And even though most law enforcement agencies throughout the country don't have designated stalking experts or someone that specifically "works" stalking/harassment cases, they should have personnel who are capable of investigating your case.

Admittedly, we continue to hear horror stories about a lack of understanding and empathy on the part of law enforcement personnel for the stalking victim's plight. We have heard from victims all over the state and many parts of the United States decrying the type of treatment they have suffered from what they believe to be callous, uncaring law enforcement personnel. When we first began investigating stalkers and were interviewed on *20/20*, I obtained a letter from a woman in the New England area. This woman poured out her heart explaining that she had been in a dating relationship with a male for a short period of time. Over the next several months, this individual forcibly entered her residence, hid in her closet until she got home, assaulted her, followed her, continually threatened her, and vandalized her vehicle on a regular basis. This woman wanted me to get in touch with the law enforcement agency in her town, because when she went to them with her problem, they said it was only a domestic dispute and would not get involved. This same poor woman even wanted to talk to one of our suspects so that she could find out why he stalked, in the hopes of helping to solve her own problem. Not too long after being interviewed by a *Los Angeles Times* freelance feature writer on stalking, we received a letter from a woman who wished to remain anonymous, thanking us for investigating stalkers and wishing she lived in our jurisdiction so that we could do something about the individual plaguing her. Along those lines, we have had victims advise us that they are going to move into our city from adjoining jurisdictions because they heard we would work their case. A few actually did move into our city. But as we have said before, there are more and more police personnel trained in handling stalking situations, and it is definitely getting better.

Not all agencies are as unaware as the ones these victims faced. Many counties in California, such as Orange, Los Angeles, and San Diego, along with several of our northern brethren, are introducing law enforcement personnel to stalking education in the form of seminars and state-mandated training. While recently conducting our fifty-state survey, we were pleased to find that many states had recognized the importance of the stalking issue. Many had combined their law enforcement efforts with their agencies involved in social and psychological services to pursue these cases. As mentioned earlier, the California POST (Police Officers' Standards and Training Commission), which also coordinates with neighboring states, has trained personnel about stalkers through a workbook and a two-hour videotape. Many other states have followed with this type of training for their officers. We are also aware of other successful programs in such cities as Colorado Springs, Colorado, and Nashville, Tennessee, as well as others that are actively dealing with stalkers, many under the umbrella of their domestic violence units. The word is being preached, and the law enforcement community is listening, although some listen better than others.

So don't despair if you are not satisfied with your initial law enforcement response. Keep trying to be heard; hopefully you will find a law enforcement professional versed in stalking, or at least open to learning about this particular sort of crime. If they are amenable to it, have your investigators call us or any of the other agencies listed in this book's appendix for further information on the subject, including various training materials. We can assure you that most police officers want to help, but they sometimes lack the tools and training needed to get this particular job done. (Incidentally, this lack of training can apply to both judges and prosecutors as well.)

From our law enforcement agency's perspective, whether or not we will take on a stalking case is simple. If just one incident occurred in our jurisdiction, we will contact the agency in whose jurisdiction the majority of the stalking has occurred and request that they investigate the stalking. If they refuse, we will work the entire case, regardless of the fact that the majority of the events in the case took place outside our city. We believe it is our job to help and protect, despite lack of knowledge or politics. However, as with any publicly supported entity, funding, politics, and manpower constraints can affect what types of crimes are to be pursued, and how and when they are going to be investigated.

If it appears you aren't getting anywhere with your first law enforcement contact, which is usually a desk officer, a patrol officer, or a deputy, you might want to try the following:

- Contact the commander of your agency's detective division and explain your problem. Most of the time, this gets results.
- If that doesn't work, contact your local district attorney and attempt to get some assistance.
- You may also want to contact any victim's rights advocate groups who specialize in domestic violence problems and see if they might offer assistance in contacting law enforcement in your area.
- Try contacting your local mayor or congressional representative.

It may not seem right, but sometimes you have to push to get heard. It took us over three months of wrangling with our district attorney's office to get the first stalking case filed in Orange County. The main reason was that our initial contacts didn't understand the stalking issue. Prosecutors had heard of the new stalking law, but no one had actually prosecuted one; therefore they didn't know how to proceed with the case. We finally ended up in "special prosecutions," a division of the Orange County district attorney's office, which at that time handled unusual or high-profile cases. Realizing the stalker had made the victim's life a living hell, the supervising deputy district attorney decided on a plan of action, ordering one of his people to file and vertically prosecute the case. The deputy district attorney assigned to the case did a fine job prosecuting the stalker, who pled guilty before trial.

- Most important of all, keep the faith—as more and more information gets out about stalking, victims will have to do less and less to obtain the assistance they need, not only from law enforcement but also from the prosecutors and probation personnel. We should point out that initially, prosecutors were having some trouble with developing the right format for constructing a stalking prosecution. Once a formula was developed, case presentations became much easier, which allowed for more and more convictions.

For those individuals reading this book who work in the women's advocate field, or who are prosecutors interested in contacting individuals that might assist you in developing some type of antistalking and prosecutorial strategies, we have included a resource section, appendix A. Therein you will find names of female prosecutors who, in our opinion, are leaders in setting a standard for how a stalking case should be formulated and prosecuted. These illustrious prosecutors all teach the process and strive to make it better. Certainly there are other exceptional prosecutors out there, but we have worked with these individuals and can vouch for their courage and overall commitment to prosecuting the stalker.

Don't cry wolf. In other words, make sure you have experienced a true and complete stalking incident before you get the judicial wheels rolling. Don't let your imagination get the best of you. Say, for example, your stalker drives a white subcompact car. Not every white subcompact that comes up fast behind you is going to be driven by your stalker. So make sure you identify your target before reporting a sighting. Positive and accurate reporting helps everyone, especially when your stalker's trial rolls around. Keep in mind that most police investigators have extensive caseloads and need your help throughout the investigation. You will know when they are working hard on your case. Most will keep in touch with you on a regular basis. Help them do their job.

Prosecution. If a stalker commits a crime directed toward you or your loved ones, push vigorously for prosecution of that crime, no matter how small it is. Early intervention is always best when trying to nip stalking in the bud. Perhaps there is not enough evidence to convict the perpetrator for stalking, but there could be evidence to prosecute for vandalism, misdemeanor assault, or making rude or annoying phone calls. Therefore help both the officer and yourself out: cooperate by prosecuting to the full extent of the law. It is our hope this prosecution will end up with some type of probation that requires the stalker to be monitored in some fashion. If nothing else, it introduces the stalker into the judicial system. We have found that for the most part, when the stalker is looking over his shoulder for us or a probation officer, it tends to put less pressure on the victim and more on him.

I recently contacted the supervisor of the domestic violence unit of the Providence (Rhode Island) Police Department, who discussed their encounters with stalkers in their jurisdiction. He said that they don't usually have to conduct an extensive stalking investigation, because they can usually short circuit the case before it goes too far. He noted that when they arrest a potential stalker for a lesser charge such as violation of a restraining order, they are usually able to get a sentence of six months in county jail after conviction. He informed me the courts are very strict with these types of prosecution, and the suspects don't appreciate their time in incarceration. We are glad to see that there are jurisdictions out there that are able to get the assistance they need from the courts. I explained to the sergeant that because our county alone has over 2.5 million people, the sheer number of prosecutions don't lend themselves to the maximizing of first-time sentencing. Instead, the revolving door policy is alive and well in our region of California, as I am sure it is in others. We have arrested one individual for violation of a protective order six times in the last two years. Each time he is convicted, he is given 180 days in jail, of which he serves about half. We are told jail housing is at a premium, so the jail system can only keep him for the minimum duration of his sentence. Once out, he violates within weeks or even days, but the fact is that he is in the system, and we continue to intervene on the behalf of the victim. In fact, we just got him another 240 days in custody because he continued to send letters to her from jail about having sexual relations with her.

We again need to take this opportunity to explain that our criminal justice system is not perfect, but we as investigators and you as victims have to work with the system that's in place. We are continually asked by victims as well as others: "How come he got out of prison?" "He was arrested for felony crimes, why is he out?" It has been our experience throughout the thirty years we have been involved in law enforcement that the judicial system is designed to allow the perpetrator of most types of crimes to indulge and be arrested and prosecuted on multiple occasions before he does any real prison time. Obviously, this does not hold true for murderers, kidnappers, train wreckers, and other crimes associated with much heavier penalties, but it does seem to be the case for those committing most misdemeanors and a great deal of the felony crimes on the books. So don't fall apart if your stalker gets minimal time. The penalties generally do increase with each transgression. If you don't follow through with prosecution, there are no other legal ways of trying to eliminate your problem. Working a stalker is not a one-shot deal. Unfortunately, it is almost always an ongoing process.

You should also be aware that the path the police take may not be one of criminal prosecution. They may well have other alternatives to deal with the stalker, at least in the initial stages, such as a mental health solution. This may work to eliminate your problem. Some agencies, like the Los Angeles Police Department's Threat Management Team, which actively pursues stalkers, utilize a mental health professional in some of their stalker evaluations, thus enhancing the depth of their investigations.

At this point we would like to take a moment to talk directly to those who are being stalked by a DVS. If you were married or had a protracted relationship with this individual, we realize how difficult it is to sever those ties completely, especially if children are involved. But you need to be strong. We don't want to see you injured or killed. Remember, life is much too short to live in fear. So please make a commitment, and don't falter. Work with your law enforcement professional, and *follow through*.

Moving. Most stalking victims either don't want to or can't move; they have jobs, relationships, and homes that tie them to one location. Still, as a last resort, some victims opt to move; but unfortunately, it is not always a guarantee that the stalker won't follow and continue on with his reign of terror. We have found that it is not uncommon for a stalker to pursue a victim out of state. We had one go so far as to become a long-haul trucker, so that he could travel to a series of midwestern states in pursuit of his victim. We initially got involved with a stalker that even traveled all over Europe in pursuit of his victim, who was a world-renowned female figure skater. This is not to say that relocating never works, however, because we have seen some cases where the stalker didn't follow and simply moved on to another victim. It depends on how resourceful and committed the stalker is. Remember, it has been our experience that if the stalker is dissuaded from stalking one person in one state or jurisdiction, he will often revert back to his genesis stalking victim, who could be in another state.

If we have identified a GV in a case we are working, we will get in touch with that individual and keep her updated on our current actions regarding the stalker. This way she will have some forewarning that the stalker may be coming back after her once thwarted by us. It recently took us two months to track down a GV in Texas, so that we could alert her about the stalker that would be looking for her once again.

As law enforcement professionals, our outlook is that moving is not something the victim should have to do, and the very prospect of suggesting that someone move to get away from a stalker doesn't sit too well with us. It is not as if the victim is in the witness protection program. We don't like the fact that someone has to be victimized both financially and psychologically yet again by being forced to relocate. But although we wish we could say that law enforcement will always eliminate the stalking threat, we must be realistic. Still, we would hope that you would give law enforcement intervention a chance to eliminate your stalker before deciding to move.

Seek counseling. Sometimes, during the course of a stalking, victims need to take action to retain their sanity. Many of our victims have opted for psychological counseling through either the county or their private medical plans. While there are many domestic violence counseling centers springing up across the United States, few specialize in stalking victims.

A recent study concerning stalking among a group of women, conducted by Michele Pathe and Paul Mullen, revealed:

- 94 percent significantly altered their social and work lives due to the stalking
- 83 percent felt increased levels of anxiety
- 24 percent thought about suicide
- 37 percent suffered from posttraumatic stress disorder
- 53 percent changed or ceased employment[1]

We have found that these conditions and behaviors are prevalent in our stalking victims as well. We would say that all of our victims suffer from anxiety. Some are so despondent that they feel there is no way they will survive, so they prepare wills and make arrangements with relatives to take care of their children.

We have found that, as in many other traumatic situations, stalking victims like to network. That's right—they exchange information with each other. In the case of one victim, who has been stalked by the same person for about twenty years, she has assisted several other victims to better understand the crime of stalking as well as their own stalkers. We encourage this type of networking and help to facilitate it as much as possible by bringing victims who, in our opinion, have held up well during their stalking ordeal and who are willing to offer their assistance in contact with other victims. In these network scenarios, we feel that both parties benefit. It was the stalking victim we had interviewed in Alabama years earlier who notified all the victims of this particular stalker in the state of California that the stalker was wanted for the beating murder we discussed in the introduction of this book. If the victims had not networked, "Jake" might not have been caught for weeks or months. As it was, he and his accomplice were captured within a few short days of the murder. We feel that we should bring up one point concerning networking in cyberspace: recalling our cyber-stalking section in chapter 4, unless you know exactly who you are communicating with, don't bother. Why take the chance of talking to another stalker—a wolf in sheep's clothing?

HOW WE INVESTIGATE STALKERS

We felt that this portion of the book would be the best place to show you how we have decided to investigate the stalker. My agency, the Westminster Police Department, has seen the growing need for a specific division to work domestic violence and stalking. Therefore the Family Protection Unit was created under the leadership of then Captain (now Chief) Andrew Hall and with the blessing of then Chief James Cook. This unit has its own in-house prosecutor, a detective that works only domestic violence cases, one that investigates only stalkers (that would be me), and one that works sexual assault. The unit also includes a county social worker and a victim's advocate. We find that this gives our victims the benefits of vertical prosecution, as well as assistance in obtaining restraining orders and crisis counseling. Our initial prosecution statistics have been very promising. This style of aggressive prosecution also tends to assist our victims. They only have to deal with one detective and one prosecutor throughout the entire trial process.

In 1995, after working stalkers for about four years, we decided that we needed a set protocol in order to better serve our victims and unify our overall investigative process. I first discussed this protocol in an article I wrote for the *Journal of California Law Enforcement.*[2] The protocol has since been modified, as both the laws pertaining to stalking as well as the crime's investigative dynamics have evolved. It is our hope that you'll understand better why a stalking investigation has to become a vertical prosecution scenario. As noted earlier, by "vertical" we mean that one detective or a specific group of detectives are assigned to the case. They are charged with the sole responsibility of the case and don't pass it off to another unit. When the case is pre-pared for court, it is given to one district attorney, who handles the case throughout its prosecution until the case is finally completed. In this fashion, the baking of the criminal pie is handled by the few and not the many; thus the details are less likely to get lost along the way. This type of case management allows for a much greater proficiency in both investigation and prosecution. This is the way major cases such as homicides, kidnappings, and serial sexual assaults are handled. The following list is an outline of the Westminster Police Depart-ment's stalking protocol. Other agencies have adopted and/or modified this protocol to fit their own stalking investigations. The unique part about investigating stalking is that if an investigator works enough of these cases, she ends up developing something similar to this protocol even if she has never heard of me, the Westminster Police Department, or any other agencies like the Los Angeles Threat Management Team. Why? Because it may be the only reasonable way to control and develop the investigation of a stalking case.

- In the City of Westminster, a uniformed patrol officer is not to take a stalking crime report. The officer, who will be trained in what stalking is, will submit a crime report for whatever specific crime he is dispatched to, such as annoying phone calls, threats, vandalism, etc. In the body of the report, the officer will state whether he believes the crime of stalking is taking place. The reason the officer doesn't try to investigate a stalking case is because he has limited time in the field. The average stalking case that we develop for prosecution is well over one hundred pages in length, and it represents many hours of investigative work. If the officer has an arrestable offense, such as violation of a restraining order, assault, or a domestic violence offense, he should arrest under those sections, but he is not to place the additional charge of stalking on the charging sheet. The detective in charge of the case may do that later, after she has had time to review the case.

- The officer can initiate any emergency protective order (EPO) if he deems it necessary at the time of field contact.
- Once a report is filed by the uniformed officer, the next step is for the detective supervisor to triage and then assign the case she feels has the elements of stalking to a specific predator-crimes detective.
- Once I get a case and I feel a stalking might be taking place, I will call in the victim to conduct what we call a threat assessment evaluation. These evaluations are tape-recorded or videotaped. The purpose of this evaluation is twofold: 1) to find out if a stalking is actually taking place, and to what extent; and 2) if there is in fact a stalking scenario unfolding, to determine the current level of threat to the victim and/or significant others. From this evaluation we should be able to ascertain a course of action, be it immediate or one that allows us to do a more in-depth investigation before submitting the case for prosecution. For example, we are working a case in which the stalker was initially arrested for making terrorist threats against the victim. When he was taken into custody, we took twelve handguns, rifles, and several rounds of ammunition out of his house. The

stalker also had a loaded crossbow sitting next to his front door. The suspect also has a heavy drinking problem, exhibits very low self-esteem, and appears to be very depressed. Therefore we have rated his threat potential as very high. One of the things we have requested that officers do prior to entering this stalker's residence on the search warrant we've prepared is to arrest him outside of his residence, preferably in his vehicle. This type of arrest technique will prevent a potential barricade situation as well as allow us to conduct a search on him and his vehicle for weapons. Once inside the stalker's residence, our technical support staff will be called to photograph and diagram the interior. We do this so that if he does barricade himself in the future, SWAT (Special Weapons and Tactics) officers will be familiar with the interior layout of the house.

- While we have the victim at the police department, we fill out a victim stalking worksheet. This worksheet contains basic information on the victim and family members. It also includes things such as where we can find their dental records (remember, I am a homicide detective first—I need to plan for worst-case scenarios). We log marks, scars, tattoos, and any medical problems. We then ask the victim to have her credit card numbers held with a family member or close friend so that we can run a track on the numbers, in the event the victim comes up missing. Since anything we put into our crime report can be discovered by the stalker's defense attorney, we do not want to record any personal information in the report that we feel the stalker doesn't already have, because it could harm the victim further. Therefore we want access to credit card information in an emergency, but we don't need to put it in our reports unless it becomes a necessity. We then photograph the victim. The set of photos that we ask our identification people to run include a full frontal, full side, and full back of the victim, as well as a mug. (How many people do you know, except for a model, would have these types of photos?) We also fingerprint the victim so that we can easily compare any physical evidence we recover against the victim's fingerprints to eliminate her prints from those of the stalker. (See the section in chapter 6 titled "General Security Measures" for how we handle the victim's children.) We have our identification staff photograph all the cars the victim normally drives. How many times have you watched the evening news with a bulletin stating that the police are looking for a kidnapping victim and her vehicle, which "looks similar to this one." The news then shows a generic Ford, Chevy, etc. When we put a bulletin out, it is a full-color flyer with a front, side, and back photo of the victim, with all of her scars and/or tattoos shown and described. The flyer also has a photo of the victim's car with all its unique features, rims, tires, dents, primer patches, etc. The more exact information we are able to get out to the media in a short period of time, the greater our chances of getting the victim back unharmed.

- Once the threat assessment is completed and a course of action is determined, we may want the victim to obtain a restraining order, which our social workers, housed in our family protection unit, will assist her in obtaining. We may decide not to seek an order. We may want to place the victim and/or her children into a temporary shelter, or make sure they stay at a relative's or close friend's house until we have had time to locate and arrest the stalker. Once the stalker is in custody, we will request the prosecutor have the presiding judge issue a criminal stay-away order. (Refer to chapter 7, "Legal Remedies," for a definition of this type of order.)

- If we have the time, which is usually the case, we complete a detailed background on all the cases we can use against the stalker. We place all these cases into chronological order. We then name this section of our crime book—a large three- to five-inch hardbound binder that keeps our case in order—the "stalking chronology." From this chronology, which serves as a bibliography of the stalking, we write our stalking crime report.

- While we are conducting our criminal investigation, we also profile our stalker. We trace his history as far back as we can in order to better understand him, as well as to find as many other victims in his past as we can. This background information is all articulated into the body of the crime report. It also helps us when we interview the stalker.
- Once the case is ready, we submit it to our vertical prosecution district attorney for filing. This district attorney only prosecutes our stalkers. We also request an arrest and a search warrant for the stalker at the same time.
- Throughout the entire investigation, we remain in continuous contact with our stalking victim.

When we arrest the stalker, we transport him to the police department to be interviewed. The stalker is put through a prebooking process that includes being photographed and fingerprinted. The stalker is then transported to Orange County Jail, where an additional booking process takes place. If the stalker can post the bail assigned to his arrest warrant, he is released and given a date to appear in court. We purposely ask for a high bail, usually $100,000 or higher, so that it is difficult for the stalker to obtain a bail bondsman and get out. The majority of the stalkers we arrest do not have a great deal of money or assets, so they usually stay in custody until they go before a judge one to two days later for a bail hearing. At this hearing, the judge can decide to reduce the bond or leave it at its original amount. The judge can also decide to let the stalker out of custody on what we call an "OR," i.e., on his own recognizance, and give him a date on which to appear with an attorney in court. Fortunately, this does not happen too often. Most of the time, the stalker cannot make bail and remains in custody until his preliminary hearing. In March of 2003, we arrested a stalker on three felony counts, one of stalking and two of making criminal threats. His initial arrest warrant bail was set at $50,000. Once we conducted a search warrant of the stalker's residence, the district attorney charged him with an additional seven felony counts, which included the possession of two banned and unregistered assault weapons. Armed with this new information we submitted an affidavit for bail enhancement. Once the affidavit was presented before the judge, the subject was held without bail, but, at a later hearing, bail was reinstated at $250,000. Due to the violent behavior of this stalker, the judge also ordered the stalker be fitted with an electronic monitoring device and not allowed to leave his residence except in certain authorized situations. (For more information on how a stalking trial is conducted, refer to chapter 8.)

Once the stalker has been arrested, prosecuted, and convicted, there are two sentencing possibilities. The stalker can be put on probation whether he does jail time or not, in which case the detective in charge of the case will contact the probation officer, who will then keep track of the suspect, or else he serves prison time and is ultimately placed on parole, in which case we will contact the stalker's parole officer in order to track the stalker's activities.* All this information is then placed into our existing file on the stalker. We do this to protect both our victim and any future victim(s) that may emerge. A stalker may also be on summary or informal probation, which means he has no assigned probation officer and does not have to report periodically as he would if on formal probation or parole. He is still required not to violate any laws, and many individuals on informal probation have to submit to a search of their property and person by a designated police or probation officer without a warrant being issued. This is commonly known as being under search and seizure, or having no search and seizure rights.

This seems like an appropriate time to mention another measure we take when dealing with stalkers. Because most of them are repeat offenders, we keep "red books," or case books, on stalkers that we feel have the greatest propensity to reoffend. Whenever we get more infor-

---

* For the most part probation occurs when an individual is out of custody on felony or misdemeanor charges and has not served any prison time. He is assigned a probation officer who monitors his activity for the prescribed period of his probation. Parole officers do the same thing with parolees, or persons who have been released from prison and still have a set amount of time left on their sentence. In police jargon, a parolee is referred to as having a "tail" during this time.

mation about that stalker, we then update the stalker's book. These files are not destroyed unless the stalker dies or is in some other way incapacitated to the point of not being able to continue his stalking behavior. This information retention allows us to assist other jurisdictions and victims concerning this predator, giving them insights into the stalker's habits and patterns. An example of why we keep these books up-to-date took place in September of 2000, when we received information on a stalker we worked in 1991. Our informant told us that the stalker wanted to get a gun and obtain a large amount of "prussic acid." The stalker planned to use the prussic acid to put on a steering wheel of a car, hoping that enough would be absorbed to cause the victim heart failure. He also wanted to shoot other individuals. We were able to notify the known victims of this stalker so they could be on the lookout. This is just another reason why we continue to monitor stalkers.

All of the stalking victims we have encountered have at least one thing in common: they are not comfortable unless they know where their stalker is, and are happiest when they know their stalker is securely locked away. We recently arrested and confined a stalker that had been plying his trade on one woman for almost eleven years. When the victim first contacted us, she told us that she was going to kill her stalker—she felt that was the only way she was going to regain peace in her life. We convinced her that was not an option. At that time she was breaking out in skin blotches, was listless, and couldn't sleep. She also reported she was having continual feminine health problems associated with stress. (These types of physical maladies and others are often commonplace among stalking victims.) Once we took the stalker into custody, we saw a dramatic change. She later told us that was the most relaxed and safe she had felt in eleven years. We share this story to offer you a sense of hope; though it may take some time, your situation can change.

CHAPTER 5 SUMMARY

- Documentation is the key to successful prosecution, including the collection of items your stalker sends or leaves you.
- Law enforcement intervention is a necessary tool against the stalker. They need to be notified immediately. Keeping a close working relationship with them is crucial.
- Don't cry wolf. Be certain of your observations; try to keep your paranoia to a minimum. Work with law enforcement, but give them some breathing room.
- Don't give your stalker a second chance. Prosecute to the fullest extent of the law.
- Moving is not always recommended, but it is an option that some victims may opt for to try to alleviate their stalking situation.
- Seeking out professional counseling or working with other stalking victims may greatly assist you in dealing with the psychological trauma associated with the stalking phenomenon.
- Some agencies, like the Westminster Police Department Family Protection Unit and the Los Angeles Threat Management Team have set protocols for investigating and assisting in the prosecution of the stalker. This better enables the agencies charged with helping the stalking victim in controlling and prosecuting their stalkers.

CHAPTER 6

REDUCING SECURITY RISKS

Anyone can take significant measures to reduce the risk of break-ins or other security problems, whether at home, at work, or on the road. Many of these are common-sense measures, but in a stalking situation they become even more critical, since the risk of exposure is already substantially higher. We realize you may not be able to follow every single one of these suggested procedures, but complying with as many as you can will only help you. We are very aware of all the high-tech security equipment that is now available. When I consult, I have access to a group of skilled technicians that can wire just about anything in your home or office as well as your car and person. Obviously, these experts don't come cheap. We will endeavor to discuss a few of these higher-tech security measures; however, as we said before, we are trying to keep it simple and as low-cost as possible.

One of my special assignments early in my police career was serving as crime prevention officer. I was in charge of educating and coordinating all the neighborhood block captains. Block captains are those citizens who volunteer within their neighborhood to disseminate crime prevention information and bulletins supplied by the police department to the residents in the area. They also provide a "safe house" for those children going to and coming from school to report to if they are being followed or harassed. Part of the job involved attending meetings held within these various neighborhoods and lectures on how to prevent either recurrent problems that the residents were facing at the time or ones they could and would face in the future. During my tenure in this position, I was able to glean a good deal of information on security planning as well as many of the devices that could implement these plans. I hope to share this knowledge with you so that you can better protect yourself and your loved ones not only in a stalking situation but also in your daily lives. In other words, even though this chapter is geared toward the stalking victim, it should help anyone who reads it to better prepare and safeguard his or her family and home.

GENERAL SECURITY MEASURES

Family notification. Make sure your significant other, close family members, and those you most often come in contact with are aware that a stalking is occurring. Give a brief rundown on what has transpired between you and your stalker. Show them a photo of the stalker if possible. If not, you can identify your stalker by describing him, or possibly pointing him out to these individuals. By taking these steps, you accomplish two goals: first, you derive the support you need from these people; second, you are putting them on notice to be on the lookout for any contact with the subject they might experience. Recall from chapter 1 that family members and significant others many times become targets themselves of the stalker.

Children. Children require some extra attention in a stalking situation. Once we have determined that a stalking has been taking place, we find out if the primary stalking victim has children. If she does, the following steps are taken:

- We photograph the child. These photos are similar to the photos we take of the primary stalking victim when we catalog her. Full frontal, side, and mug shots are taken. The primary reason for these photos is so that if a child is abducted, we can get the photo and information out in an "Amber Alert" broadcast.*

- We then fingerprint the child. If the child's fingers are too small to have a significant ridge count, our identification technicians opt to take a whole handprint on a palm card. There have been times when the child was so young that we had to take their inked footprints on a palm card instead. A palm card is a stiff, white piece of card paper on which we normally place the inked palm of the right and left hand of a suspect during the jail booking process. This card is then placed on file with the suspect's fingerprint or ten card. However, we also take prints of others we want to keep track of. Have both your and your children's fingerprints taken; most police or sheriff's departments will do this either for free or for a nominal cost.

- With the advent of DNA testing as an ever-increasingly important part of the legal process, we are currently mulling over whether or not we should obtain a DNA sample that can be stored by the parent. How many times have you read about child abductions taking place where none of these means of identification were available to the law enforcement entity assigned to work the case?

Even though the majority of the children we catalog are toddlers and young children that we feel might be most at risk, we have also cataloged entire families, including spouses and teenagers. This is rare, but it was the directed procedure when we were consulting on a couple of SS cases in which the stalkers were stalking public officials. Because we had no idea at the time who the stalkers were, we felt the family members, which included older siblings, could be at risk, too. We would also advise this type of cataloging process be conducted

---

*Amber Alert is a system devised by NCMEC (the National Center for Missing and Exploited Children) in the fall of 2001 and named after a young Texas girl, Amber Hagerman, who was kidnapped and murdered in 1996. Whenever a child is taken, the system uses the emergency broadcasting system in the state to send out a description, including a photo of the missing child, within a very short period of time. In the states that have adopted a form of the system, such as California, Utah, Georgia, and others, it has proven to be effective. The national Amber Alert law was signed into law by President Bush on April 30, 2003, so now all states will participate.

with those in the media who are being stalked. I always approach a stalking scenario through the eyes of a homicide detective. Thinking worst-case scenario causes me to dot more i's and cross more t's.

If your law enforcement professional has not cataloged you as well as your children, we would suggest that you invest in a good-quality full-length photo as soon as possible. Many chain department stores offer photo packages at a reasonable price. Make that photo available to the law enforcement personnel you are working with. If the stalking is protracted (occurring over a period of months and/or years) update your child's photo periodically. As you know, kids' appearances seem to change almost daily.

If you have a photo of your stalker, take it to the school your child attends and make the school staff aware of the problem. Tell them that under no circumstances are they to release your child to that person. Make a concerted effort to take your child to and from school personally. If another person must pick up your child, let the school know exactly who will be assigned that task.

Explain to the child why you are taking these extra precautions. Remember, some stalkers will go after your child, either to get at you or because, due to mental illness or some other proprietary feelings, they believe that the child is somehow theirs. For example, we had a female stalker who felt that she had children with the male victim, whom she had dated for a very short time and never married. When we conducted an in-custody interview of this stalker, she "explained" to us that she had two children from this relationship with this male, but she believed her mother and her sister were somehow able to hide these offspring from her. Our investigation was able to show that the two children she spoke of were nonexistent figments of her fantasy world. This stalker also believed she was married to the victim, who was in fact married to another woman. The stalker also thought the couple's newborn was hers and threatened to take the child. We have experienced this same phenomenon with male stalkers who believe that their victim's children are somehow their own offspring. The victims are understandably terrified when they learn of the stalker's feelings for the children.

We also have problems DVS cases where the male has had a period of contact with the victim's younger child or children. The problem arises when the stalker believes, not necessarily because of any mental illness, that he has a right to see these children, even though they are in no way his. The stalker will try to see these children even when told no, persisting even when civilly restrained from doing so. Some have even tried to go to court in an attempt to obtain some type of visitation rights to the child they have fixated on. When we interview these individuals, they inform us that because they spent time, money, and effort on this child, they have developed an emotional "parenting" connection to the child. In short, they tell us that this investment of time affords them a "right" to access. To date, however, we have not seen any attorney take this type of case, nor has any court allowed a stalker this access.

This brings up a few points we need to discuss concerning child abductions. According to the U.S. Bureau of Justice Statistics, most child abductions are perpetrated by people who the children know or who are related to them. They estimate that approximately 354,600 children are abducted by a family member each year. About five thousand are taken by people who have at least some association with the child, and only about two hundred are taken by a stranger. One of the most terrifying statistics I have come across is that 74 percent of the children murdered by non-family members are killed within the first three hours of their abduction.[1]

Trip itineraries and personal information. Whenever you are going on a trip, give a trusted friend your itinerary so that the friend can notify authorities if something goes wrong. You may also want to entrust this person with a photocopy of your driver's license and credit cards. As we have discussed before, these can be given to law enforcement personnel if the need ever arises, as they can quickly trace the use of your credit card.

Variation of routine. If you are a creature of habit, as most of us are, try to change some of those patterns and routines to throw off your stalker, for example, take different routes to work each day, come home a different way, etc. Another thing we recommend is to take a defensive surveillance posture when you are returning to your neighborhood, especially when you have been away for a longer period of time. This means simply that you should not go directly back to your house when you return to your neighborhood; instead, drive around the area a little first. Sometimes stalkers set up a position in their vehicle on the street a few blocks away from your residence so that they can better watch you.

Cellular phones. Obviously, we like and recommend the use of cellular phones. Portability is the key with these communication devices. You can carry one with you virtually everywhere, some now even while swimming. Remember, this phone can be used inside your residence even if your phone lines are cut by the stalker. As more and more calling plans come on the market, they are becoming an easily affordable commodity. Our agency, along with many others involved in domestic violence cases, is supplying used cell phones to our social service coordinators. These phones are then modified by local carriers, at no cost to the phone holder, to be able to specifically dial 911 and summon police assistance for those stalking victims that cannot afford a phone. If you have an old cellular phone, think about donating it before you just add to the landfill problem. My wife and I have supplied at least five phones since our program was initiated.

Remember when we talked about carrying around a small single-use camera to take photos of your stalker if he approaches you? Now they have new cellular phones that can also take digital photos. You may want to invest in one of these devices if you can afford one.

One other thing we would like to discuss in regard to cellular phones is a new technology that allows a global positioning device to be attached to your cellular phone. This device is then supposed to pinpoint the location of the phone when you activate a special 911 button attached to the phone. We have never seen this technology at work, but we are assured that it does work. The more advanced cellular technology becomes, the better the tracking technology will become, we feel. (For information on this device, we suggest going on-line and visiting www.fonefinder.com.)

HOME SECURITY MEASURES

We are now going to focus on home security measures and describe several different security devices available to you, depending on your pocketbook. Our discussion of security plans and devices will range from the simple to the more complex and high-tech. It is up to you, the reader, to decide what you can best afford, and what you think will work the best for you. Think of this section of the book as the "security supermarket." It is up to you to walk down the aisles and fill your cart with the items you like. However, we suggest that you always become familiar with a device's application and mode of operation before implementing it or any other security plan we are going to present.

Post office boxes. We used to advise victims to get a post office box for mail delivery, preferably *not* one connected with the U.S. Postal Service, because when you get a U.S. postal box, it has to say "P.O. Box" on the address. With private mail drops, you used to be able to list the address of the business as the physical address where the mail is delivered, with your box number listed as a suite number (for example: 12741 Barney St., Suite 101, Fantasy Land, Rhode Island.) It also used to be the case that you could walk into a commercial mail receiving agency (CMRA) and obtain a mailbox without filling out much paperwork or showing photo identification. However on April 26, 1999, House Joint Resolution 55 changed all that. Now you must fill out Form 1583 and present two forms of identification, one of which has to be photo identification, along with proof of residency.* If the box is to used for business purposes, you must state that on Form 1583. For now, you have to list your personal mailbox with the letters "PMB" on a separate line of the address, or the postal workers don't have to deliver the mail to your box. This requirement was added because boxes were being used by the criminal element of our society for a variety of purposes, primarily fraud, and therefore the system had to be changed. So check with your private mailbox provider as to what they will allow

---

* Please go on-line or contact your local post office for a copy of the regulations on private mail boxes. Be sure to read all the requirements to make sure this is a viable option for you and that you can comply with all the requirements of Form 1583.

you to do. Even with this new postal change, we still feel a private mailbox is the way to go. One of the primary reasons for this is that it allows mail to come to another location other than your home, thus maintaining more anonymity and security from theft for you. Another reason is that you can have mail and other couriers' products delivered to the box located in an area near you, not a centralized, frequently out-of-the-way post office. (Federal Express and UPS will not deliver to a P.O. box, but they will deliver to CMRAs). Because this law creates problems for persons legally seeking anonymity from predators, domestic violence groups are looking into trying to change or amend it.

Be aware that we have had stalkers enter a victim's residence and steal P.O. box keys. We even had one take an extra set of keys that the victim had apparently forgotten about. Thus the stalker had control of his victim's P.O. box for several weeks until she finally figured out what had occurred. The moral here is to keep track of your P.O. box keys, and don't label them as such. Also be aware that depending on the nature of your stalker, he may surveil your private mailbox center to see if you show up—so stay alert. Some stalking victims have had all their mail sent to a close friend or parent, but that still doesn't stop certain stalkers from surveilling those locations.

You should also be aware that California and other states have developed a program that allows victims of either domestic violence or stalking to have their mail sent to a neutral place. This is the "Safe at Home" program, which in California is handled by the secretary of state's office. The program was first developed by legislation in 1998 to assist victims of domestic violence and later included stalking victims in 2000. Here is how it works:

- Once a stalking victim applies at a designated victim assistance facility and is accepted to the program, she is issued an official authorization identification card containing a substitute address. This address can be used by the victim for business or public transactions requiring a residential or mailing address. State and local agencies are required to accept the Safe at Home address when the victim presents her card.

- When first-class, government, served, or certified mail is delivered to the victim's Safe at Home address, it is then forwarded to her confidential address within forty-eight hours. Junk mail, periodicals, and packages are not forwarded. I spoke with a Safe at Home representative who advised they will not accept packages for the victim. They may call the victim if they get a mail pouch in order to verify authenticity, but for the most part they advise the victim to have any packages delivered elsewhere.
- The Safe at Home program also allows victims to request their voter registration information be kept confidential at the same time they sign up for this program. Once the request is processed, they will be sent an absentee voter form each year that they are in the program.

For more information on this program, please contact the California Secretary of State at (877) 322-5227 or go on-line to www.ss.ca.gov/safeathome/. (Other states that have similar programs include Nevada, Washington, Florida, Rhode Island, New Jersey, New Hampshire, Vermont, Maine, Massachusetts, and Indiana.)

Confidentiality. Apply to have your voter registration information made confidential (explained above). Unfortunately, many states still allow some types of Department of Motor Vehicles information to be obtained by persons other than law enforcement or other government agencies. Check on the requirements for DMV information retrieval in your state, and see if you can have these records blocked.* If you move, don't leave a forwarding address. Contact your credit bureau and ask to have a hold put on your application information. Rent an apartment using someone else's name. See if a parent or other close relative, preferably with a different last name from yours, agrees to rent the apartment in his name and then let you live there. This would include having them named on the utilities. Keep in mind, though, that whoever signs the lease or rental agreement is responsible for that agreement. Have all

---

* Go to the Web page www.ftic.gov/privacy/protect.htm#Motor to obtain information on your state's DMV privacy rules.

names taken off rental or condominium-type message boards. Transfer all your property into a trust, so that if a legal search is done, only the trust name will appear. Of course, we suggest you consult with an attorney before enacting this legal strategy; you don't want to make an error that would jeopardize your standing in regard to any property you might own. We know that some of these changes are a real hassle, but then so is being stalked. It is up to you how far you want to go.

Doors. Before we get into the proper door fortification hardware, we need to describe the different types of doors. When you take a stroll through your neighborhood home improvement store, you will see a variety of doors. Each type of door has a specific use within your home:

- *Hollow-core doors.* These doors are used primarily as pass-through doors for bathrooms or in tract-housing bedrooms. Many have a pattern embossed on them by the manufacturer. These doors look nice but have little resistance to force. They are easily penetrated, even by putting a fist through the core of the door. They do not hold security hardware in place when forced.

- *Solid-core doors.* These doors are manufactured in such a way that there is a solid wood or composite core sandwiched in between two pieces of laminated material. These doors are heavy and tend to hold security hardware in place much better than hollow-core doors. Often they are only a few dollars more than the cheaper hollow-core door.

- *Steel-cased doors.* We recommend these doors as entry doors. Most are solid-core doors cased in metal, but some are cased over fiberglass. They cost $300 or more, but they wear well and don't usually flex when struck.

- *Fiberglass doors.* These doors are actually quite strong and need little maintenance.

- *Heavy-clad steel doors.* Most do-it-yourself stores don't carry this type of item; instead, you will probably find these doors at a commercial door outlet. Your local locksmith should know where they can be purchased. Expect to pay $500 or more for the door plus installation. We have seen them used in high-end homes, especially for what we call "safe rooms" (which we will discuss later in this chapter). Again, this is a pocketbook issue. If you want something like this, it can obviously afford you the best security of all the types of doors mentioned here.

- *Security screen doors.* While on the topic of doors, we would also like to suggest that you obtain a metal security screen door that is attached by bolting its frame over your existing front or back door frame. These heavy-duty screen doors have a deadbolt lock assembly. The screen is constructed from heavy-gauge metal fabric, not your average flimsy, light-weight window screen material. These doors are usually designed to let you see out as well as to allow ventilation anytime the need arises. The beauty of the door is that they can be securely locked with your front door open and still allow air to circulate through your residence.

Now we need to talk about what you put in your entry doors as far as decoration. We fully understand that you may want to beautify your home. We are also aware that you may not want to make your home look like a fortress. However, you need to be aware of the problems associated with door inserts, which for the most part are made of glass. These inserts, although very nice-looking, are easy to break out. Therefore if you are going to get inserts, think about getting them small enough so that your assailant cannot squeeze his hand or other body parts through the opening in the door. You should also have a double-locking deadbolt on these types of doors. (This type of deadbolt is described below.)

Another type of insert is a door viewing device. You have all seen these peephole-type devices for sale and installed in doors. They are cheap and easily installed, and they do not weaken the structural integrity of the door when properly installed. Again, think about what you are doing when you use this device. First look through the peephole and verify who is there before allowing whoever is there to know where you are. Obviously, if your residence is set up in such a way to allow viewing the entrance area from another, unobtrusive window, by all means use this option to check on the person outside.

We are now going to discuss the different types of locks and hinges you can either have installed or install yourself in or on your door:

- *Dead bolt locks*. Dead bolt locks are manufactured by several different companies and vary in quality. Stick with a brand name such as Baldwin, Quickset, or Schlage. The bolt should be made of case-hardened steel. It should have a cut-resistant roller pin inserted in the middle of the bolt. This feature is a deterrent to anyone trying to cut the bolt. The pin spins when the cutting tool touches it. The cylinder guard should have the outer edge tapered or angled. This outer ring should also revolve when any type of clamping tool is placed on the ring in an attempt to twist it off. The case or trim should be constructed of solid brass, bronze, or steel. The exterior part of the lock should be connected to the inside portion of the lock with connecting rods or bolts at least one-fourth inch in diameter. We feel assured when you walk into your local hardware store armed with this information, you should walk out with a quality dead bolt, not one that the kid from the local high school picks off the wall and tries to sell you.*

- *Double-locking dead bolts*. This is the type of dead bolt that requires a key to open either side. We recommend the use of these locks for doors with glass panels. If the intruder breaks the glass, he cannot reach inside and pop open the lock. It is recommended that you keep a key for this type of lock hanging somewhere in reasonable proximity to the door. This will allow you to open the door in case of emergency. All the other specifications we laid out with the other dead bolt still apply.

- *Double security lock*. This is a common lock set on many homes, especially those that have double entry doors. This is a lock with

---

* All the locks we do not show you in photos can easily be found in your local home supply, hardware, and lock and key shops. Try to purchase a quality lockset; you get what you pay for. If you can't install it yourself, get a reputable firm to do the work.

a dead bolt on the bottom and a lever lock on top. Most of these lock sets have a simple, short throw bolt on their lever lock similar to a standard door lock. The more costly sets have an instant lock-release feature. This feature permits you to unlock both locks at the same time. Some also have rectangular dead bolts with single or double case-hardened roller pins inside the bolt.

- *Rim locks.* Rim locks, both standard and "jimmy-proof," are designed as secondary door locks that supplement the use of dead bolts. The rim lock has two separate parts: one attaches to the door, and the other to the door frame. Once the door is shut, a vertical dead bolt slides through a minimum of two securing rings, thus forming a tight fit for the door. The jimmy-proof rim lock attaches to the door frame almost like an additional hinge and has a key locking mechanism. One of the locksmiths we talked to said that if you live in an area where your home shifts a lot, rim locks would not be the best choice. When the house shifts, the locks may have to be realigned.

- *Padlocks.* We thought we should also advise you of padlocks as another door-locking mechanism. When buying a padlock, most people don't pay much attention to how it is made, even though they should. The padlock should be constructed of case-hardened steel, with at least a $\frac{9}{32}$-inch shackle. Stainless-steel shackles usually afford the best form of security. The shackle— the curved piece that slides through whatever you are securing your item with—should lock at both the heel and toe of the lock. The lock should have a pick-resistant tumbler with at least five pins. If the lock is activated by a key, it should have a key-retaining feature. This system prevents the key from being removed until the padlock is completely locked. If you are getting a combination padlock, which we prefer because we don't have to carry around a bunch of extra keys, make sure it meets all the requirements we pointed out for the key lock.

- *Double-door locks.* When you have a set of external double doors, you need a way of securing both doors. The door that is opened only to allow for additional access, the stationary door, is usually secured with interior flush bolts. These bolts are mounted at the top and bottom of the door. Obviously, the longer the throw—i.e., length of the bolt—up into the door frame and jamb, the better. If your door does not come with that type of hardware, and you don't want to pay to have it installed, you can go to cane bolts. These bolts attach to the outside of the door. They should be mounted to both the top and the bottom of the door. The sliding portion of the lock goes through a loop that is screwed into the door jamb at the top. The bottom slide should go into a loop on the door and be inserted into a hole in the flooring or threshold. Unfortunately, the cane bolt is usually only as strong as the screws that are set into the door.

- *Portable security door lock.* We also want to mention those door security devices that you can take with you when you travel or are at a friend's house. A few lock companies such as Master have developed a portable door lock. The lock design is that of an adjustable steel rod. One end of the rod attaches to the doorknob. The rod is then adjusted at an angle from the doorknob to the floor. The floor end of the device has a foot that, when laid in place, stops the intruder from being able to force open the door. It is like wedging a strong stick against the door, but much more effective. There are also other mechanisms, such as portable door alarms, that attach to the doorknob. When the knob is twisted or moved, a loud alarm activates.

- *Sliding glass doors.* Security manufacturers have developed all kinds of locking devices for sliders. We are going to discuss some of the simple to the more expensive ones. In this case, we think simple works fairly well. The first thing you want to prevent with a sliding glass door, as well as any type of sliding window, is to stop the suspect from lifting it up out of its travel carriage. You can achieve this by screwing two or three number 8 or number 10 sheet metal screws into the upper track above the door itself. These screws should protrude just far enough so that the top of the slider just clears them when pushed along the carriage (Figure 9). The next thing is to install a patio door lock (Figure 10). This lock has a post that screws into the bottom of the slider. It is easy to install. You can also drill a hole large enough for a metal dowel—they can be purchased at any hardware store and come in a variety of sizes—at the top of the sliding glass door's track and place the dowel through the holes across the track, so that the door cannot be pushed open. One of the newest slider locks on the market is one that is snapped into the frame of the slider so that it cannot be forced along the carriage. Some of these devices have a key lock on them. Some can be totally removed from the door and taken with you on a trip. Others are screwed into one half of the door and then are just pulled down and popped into place. We are seeing more and more of these being installed in hotel and motel rooms. One other lock that we like is the lock that lies in the bottom of the slider carriage track (Figure 11). The slider can move back and forth over the mechanism, but when activated by simply pressing on one end, it will act as a stop. This way the slider cannot be forced back into an open position. Obviously, a sliding glass door can be broken to gain entry. However, we do not find this to be the most common method used by the criminal when gaining entry into a residence. Breaking a slider makes a great deal of noise, and those individuals who use this method often cut themselves while entering the residence.

- *Garage doors.* Garage doors can be secured in a couple of simple ways. The first is by putting a padlock on the door. The second is by drilling a hole in the interior garage door spring bracket and the garage door frame. Make sure the hole is big enough for a $\frac{5}{8}$-inch bolt to slide through both the spring bracket and the door frame (Figure 12). Once the bolt is in place, the door cannot be pulled up. Another possibility is to attach a hasp to the middle of the wood header that runs the length of your garage door. Attach the male portion of the hasp to the garage

Figure 9. Photo showing how to insert a number 8 sheet metal screw into the upper track frame of a sliding glass window or door.
(Courtesy of Duck Works Criminal Consulting)

Figure 10. Photo of locking-barrel sliding glass door lock.
(Courtesy of Duck Works Criminal Consulting)

Figure 11. Pop-up sliding glass window door lock.
(Courtesy of Duck Works Criminal Consulting)

Figure 12. A $\frac{5}{8}$-inch bolt placed through both the garage door frame and the
spring mount, thus securing the door from the inside.
(Courtesy of Duck Works Criminal Consulting)

door, and then padlock the door.* Since most people do not want to padlock their garage door every day, we suggest you purchase a garage door opener that is designed to change its activation frequency every time it is activated. This way an intruder cannot just drive up to your house with a generic garage door opener and attempt to gain entry by running codes through the opener. Make sure that when that garage door goes up, the lights in the garage go on. We have had several occasions where stalkers and other predators have gained entry to the victims' garage and lay in wait for them to come home at night. Make it a point of activating your garage door opener far enough from your house so that you get a good look before you pull in. You might even want to avail yourself of one of the new garage door opening systems that also turns lights on in and around your home once it is activated.

If you sense someone is periodically entering your residence, but you are not seeing any signs of forced entry, try putting a small piece of clear tape across the door and door frame—toward the bottom so it won't be conspicuous. Your suspicions will be verified if, when making your daily inspection, you find the tape has been torn away from either the door or the frame. This will assist you in determining the point of entry when you call your local police department to make a burglary report.

Security lights. Add motion detector lights in areas where your stalker might attempt to gain entry to the property. These lights can now be purchased in a solar-powered package, thus eliminating costly wiring and allowing for installation almost anywhere. The lights have solar batteries, which charge during the day and allow activation at night.

We also want to discuss installing low-voltage exterior lighting. This type of lighting is also available with solar-powered batteries.

---

* A hasp is a locking bracket that comes in two parts. One part attaches to a portion of what you want to secure, and the other attaches to the other part; a common example is found on a gate post and a gate. The two parts are secured when a padlock is placed through the hasp ring, thus holding the parts together.

Use timer lights inside your residence. These are good to use not only when you are out but also when you are there. This comes in handy when you have gone to bed at, say, 10:00 P.M., and a couple of low-impact lights stay on in your house for a few more hours as you are getting to sleep in another room. With the advent of compact fluorescent bulbs, the energy used will cost you only pennies, but the additional light may give you peace of mind. Remember, for the buck, lighting is one of the best available deterrents against intruders.

Windows. All of your windows can be secured, even if they did not come from the factory with locks. For those of you that don't have factory locks, please take note of the following locking techniques for windows:

- *Sliding windows.* Insert a number 8 sheet metal screw in the upper track of sliding windows, allowing just enough room for the window to slide, but not enough for anyone to pry the window up and out. This is the same process we described in securing sliding glass doors. Obtain window clamps that attach to the window slide at the bottom and then are twisted tight with your thumb and forefinger. This stops the window from being slid open. The slides are also handy because you can adjust them all along the track, thus allowing for ventilation when you are in your residence. You can also drill holes through the top of your sliding window or door and apply a nail or aluminum door pin to stop the window or door from being opened farther than desired. If the only thing you have available is a stick to put in the window or door track, use it. If you decide to install burglar bars on your windows, please make sure you follow the strict fire safety code that governs these devices.

- *Double-hung windows.* If you have older, double-hung windows, you can secure them by first drilling a hole, about the size of a sixteen-penny or slightly larger nail, that angles downward through the bottom of the window. Then place a nail or a metal dowel into the hole. This will prevent the lifting of the window from an outside intruder. You can also drill other holes on either side of the casement about an inch or so up. This will allow you to pin these holes in such a fashion as to allow ventilation.

- *Casement/crank windows.* For the most part, casement windows are easy to secure. First, make sure all your cranking hardware is in good working order. This will eliminate any play in the windows. Keyed locking handles are available if you wish to increase your security. Some casement windows have standard lock loops that you can put a padlock through.
- *Louvered windows.* Louvered windows are by far the worst windows to secure; their single panes can easily be removed by an intruder. When my family and I lived in Florida, just about every house in the neighborhood had this type of window. They were always cracking and being broken. If possible, these windows should be replaced. However, if you cannot bear to replace them, there are some things you can do to secure them. Place metal bars or grates over the windows. There used to be a locking bar available that could be placed alongside the lever that opens the louvers. However, we could not determine if the lock is still available.

Home alarm systems. If possible, have a home alarm system installed. These days you can pick up a basic intruder system from an electronic parts store or a mail-order supply house. If you feel comfortable with that type of system, and it is the only thing you can afford, by all means do it. However, in this day and age you can hire the services of an alarm company that has a central monitoring system—one that monitors your residence and notifies law enforcement if the alarm is activated—for a fairly nominal installation fee. Alarm companies today are interested in developing their customer base through monitoring fees, not necessarily through the equipment you purchase. A relative of mine just had an alarm system installed in his daughter's condo for around $100. In fact, many of the alarm companies now lease the alarm sensor equipment they install and then charge for any maintenance they have to do through a contract.

Features you want to look for in a simple alarm system include the following:

- Exterior sensors located at each entry door, including the door leading from an attached garage into the residence, and on all windows that are accessible to at least street-level entry.

- Motion detectors placed in such a fashion as to cover the main traffic areas of the residence. Exterior sensors and motion detectors, in conjunction with a loud siren, can usually be enough for your basic coverage and peace of mind. If you have pets that walk around at night, make sure that you have zoned the house so they don't set off motion detectors. Or, you can shut down motion detectors and just have windows and doors activated when you are sleeping, so you don't activate the alarm during a late-night food or bathroom run.

- At least two alarm control pads. We suggest one be placed in the master bedroom, and the other in the area where you most often enter your residence. Most monitored systems will have a panic sequence on their keypads; make sure yours has one of these. When it is pushed, the monitoring agency should immediately contact law enforcement to respond.

- Some other features that are nice to have, but not a must, include smoke detectors that can transmit sensor information back to the monitoring station in case of fire; and a radio transmitter backup system to the alarm, which we really like. This system is designed to send an alarm activation via a wireless transmitter, even if your phone and power lines are disabled. If for some reason your phone lines are cut or don't work, your alarm activation will not be monitored by the central system. Of course, the radio transmission system costs more.

For those of you who want more, the sky is the limit. We are not going to describe everything that is available, but we are going to give you just a taste of what is out there.

- *Pad sensors.* There are alarm systems that not only have window, door, and motion sensors, but also pressure pad sensors, which are installed in the floor or under the carpet and activate when someone or something applies pressure to them.

- *Laser sensors.* If you have watched any television at all, you have seen these alarm sensors: invisible laser beams that, when broken, activate alarms. By the way, any of these sensors can further trigger a myriad of other alarm devices in the home, such as strobe lights, cameras—both still and video—along with voice activators. In other words, once an alarm is tripped, a set of microphones in the residence or business turn on. They can hear whatever you and/or the intruder is doing, and the alarm company can talk to you or the intruder.

- *Internet alarms.* The latest type of alarm monitoring system is set up on the Internet. At the time of writing, it is mostly being used in the business community to reduce theft both from within and without. The company that provides the monitoring can be housed anywhere in the world. They install active video—a connection through which they can both see as well as talk to whomever they are watching—in the business via the Internet. Once they perceive a problem, they can notify the law enforcement agency in that jurisdiction or talk to the suspect committing the crime, or both. Obviously, deciding on when to contact the suspect while he is still in the store would depend on the gravity of the crime. We wouldn't suggest talking to the suspect when he is in the middle of committing an armed robbery, but making contact during a simple shoplift is probably fine. These monitoring systems may be available for use in homes. The only problem I could see with this type of system in residential usage is deciding when the monitoring should take place. To eliminate the "Big Brother" aspect, the users' residence would probably be monitored only when they were away or when they requested surveillance done to a potential threat, such as a known stalker possibly lurking in the area. Some of the people that do avail themselves of these residential Internet security systems use them for just that purpose. They have cameras set up both inside and outside their primary and secondary residences so that they can monitor these locations from remote sites, e.g., while traveling or at their office.

Once you have installed an alarm system, you may want to notify your trusted neighbors that your system is in place. You might want to tell them that you are currently having problems with a stalker, so they might be a tad more sympathetic when the alarm goes off. Make sure you have a battery backup, and keep the entire system in good working order to prevent false alarms. Many law enforcement agencies have initiated alarm ordinances, which allow police departments to bill you for a false alarm response they had to make to your residence. However, this usually occurs only after a "grace period" of two or so responses. Check with your alarm company on their false alarm policy. Post a couple of alarm signs in visible areas.

One of the best house alarms known to man runs on four legs: that's right, Bowser. Man's best friend can be a definite asset to your home security force: when the dog barks, it not only alerts you to possible danger but likely also causes some uncomfortable feelings for a potential intruder.

Telephone security. Have the telephone company put your phone box in an area that doesn't allow easy access to the stalker, such as in the arch of your house's eaves. We have had stalkers cut the phone lines before attempting entry into a victim's residence, but it is doubtful they would carry a ladder around with them. If you are able, padlock your phone box. Many newer homes now have underground cable and phone lines to add to the aesthetics of the neighborhood. These new homes usually have access panels built into the frame of the structure, with panels on the outside. Most of these panels can be secured with padlocks. Along these same lines, we suggest you also padlock your fuse box.

If your state allows having caller identification (a system that permits you to see the number of the person who is calling before answering the phone), see about getting it installed on your phone. Some caller ID machines have memory capabilities. It is important to your law enforcement professional that they get those numbers. We ask victims of stalkers to bring their caller ID boxes into the station with them so that we can activate the numbers and then copy them for evidence. However, this works only if you have a battery-operated caller ID machine or one that has a battery backup system available.

Look into getting a star (*) feature such as "star 82" placed on your phone. In other words, the caller must hit *82 before dialing your number, or else you will not accept the call. This feature allows you to screen your calls before actually picking up. This feature is supposed to work even if the incoming number is unlisted. (Always remember to log your calls when you believe it is the stalker who is calling.)

Pick-up. When you are going to be away from home for any length of time, have someone pick up your mail and newspapers as well as any flyers left at the door or in the driveway. If you can't get someone to pick up the mail, put in a request with your local post office to hold your mail for the length of time you will be gone. Remember, it is not unusual for stalkers to steal or at least go through your mail. If you donate magazines or take them to work for others to read, make sure to take off your name and mailing address.

Along the lines of "picking up," we want to remind you also to take a look at your backyard. If it looks like a jungle, with vines and bushes covering windows and doorways, take the time to either remove them or cut them back. I don't know how many cases we have worked where the victim or her neighbors complained about the stalker hiding in or around bushes next to windows. Why help them conceal themselves?

Weapons. Always check with your local law enforcement agency to ascertain the legality of each of these weapons before you obtain them in your jurisdiction or state. If you have decided to have firearms in the house for protection, consider purchasing a semiautomatic handgun. That way the unloaded weapon can be kept separate from the loaded magazine until such time it is needed. These handguns can be loaded in a very rapid fashion, making them safer than a wheel gun (revolver). Look into the use of low-impact rounds—ammunition that when fired will stop an assailant but does not have a great deal of extra penetrating power. Therefore the slug has less of a chance of going through walls and doors, which will limit the chances of injuring innocents. This type of ammunition is marketed by manufacturers such as Glaser Safety Ammunition and Strike Three Ammunition. (If you don't think you can take a human life, and you are not completely comfortable with the use of handguns or other firearms, we strongly suggest you rethink having one for home protection. As I always tell my sons when we shoot, *never pull the trigger unless you are sure of where that round is going!* Because once it's gone downrange, you can never bring it back, and there is definitely no "oops" in the language of shooting.) Of course, there is also a broad range of "nonlethal" weapons on the market, such as stun guns and taser weapons, which have electronically charged darts that are shot into the assailant, usually rendering him helpless. Other so-called nonlethal weapons include a gun that propels beanbags with compressed nitrogen gas, pepper sprays, tear gas, and foam foggers.

Many police departments have opted to shoot suspects with wooden and/or beanbag projectiles whenever their policy calls for this type of projectile to be used. For example, they might use this type of weapon instead of having to subdue a combative, threatening suspect with a club. These weapons, although not usually deadly, can cause death, depending on factors such as distance from target and location of impact. I mention this as food for thought. When you strike or shoot someone with any type of defensive weapon, there is always a risk of severely disabling and/or killing your assailant. Because of this, it might not be a bad idea to become familiar with the self-defense statutes in your state. Each state is different, but most are very specific when it comes to what force you may use when a predator enters into your residence.

No matter what your weapon of choice, make sure you and anyone else who has access to the weapons attend a certified training class in the use and care of that weapon system. *And of course, make sure all weapons are kept secure away from children!* Some states, such as California, have strict laws governing accessibility of loaded handguns to children, particularly in your home. There are gun safes available that allow you to store a gun securely but have easy access to it.

The safes have push buttons, either mechanical or electronic, that allow you to quickly activate the combination, thus allowing easy access to the weapon. These safes fit easily into a bedside or office drawer. Some are designed to be placed into a wall and look like a wall hanging or a picture in a frame.

One item that we especially like is the new personal sound activator that can be attached to your key chain or hung around your neck. Once the pin on the module is pulled, a loud, penetrating, and at times unbearable squeal is emitted. It should startle your attacker and hopefully allow you time to get away, or at least cause someone else to come to your aid. This device would also work well outside as a non-lethal protection tool.

Packages. Pay special attention to any packages that come to your residence or workplace. Ask yourself these questions: Does the package have a return address? Do I know the sender? Was I expecting this package? Does the package have a greasy or oily residue on it, or does it smell like gunpowder? If so, don't open it! Contact your local law enforcement agency. Don't let your curiosity get the better of you! We investigated a case where a package was delivered to a particular residential location. One of the other residents who was living at the home took it upon himself to open the package in the absence of the addressee because he had a burning desire to know its contents. That curiosity cost him his life.

Following the events of September 11, 2001, and the subsequent anthrax mail killings, packages have come to be viewed in a whole different light. Besides explosive devices, it is well within a stalker's ability to place on or in that package other chemical agents that might cause you to become seriously ill or even cause death. We are not saying that any of the stalkers that we have dealt with have been able to manufacture weapons-grade anthrax, but we are saying that they can easily obtain poisonous materials such as pesticides, arsenic, etc.

Safety equipment. You should maintain a supply of basic safety equipment in your residence, such as a good fire extinguisher. Dry-powder (ABC-type) extinguishers will handle most common types of fires, but they leave a heavy powder residue. Halon extinguishers put out many fires, including fires started by electrical equipment, and don't leave behind a residue. Carbon dioxide extinguishers are also effective without leaving a heavy residue. You might want to keep a fire extinguisher in your car as well. Keep a couple of good flashlights around, one or two in your house and another in your car. Have some type of medical kit both in your car and your house. This may sound a lot like being a Boy Scout, but you never know when you are going to need these items.

Strong space. A strong space is basically what the word implies: a secure space devised specifically for safely storing your valuables. A strong space can be a closet that you have modified to hold and secure your valuables. Basically, it is a closet with shelves and a solid-core or metal door with a dead bolt. The hinges on the door should be pinned so that no one can pop the hinge pins and remove the door. Building or modifying a closet for this purpose hopefully discourages an intruder from getting specific personal items. Even though most stalkers/burglars would like to spend a great deal of time in your residence, they usually don't, unless they know exactly where you are and when you are going to be home. The harder you make it on them, the better off you are.

Safe room. The safe room concept has been around for many years, but it was just recently brought to the public's attention by the movie *Panic Room.* When we lecture on home security, we talk about how to construct a simple safe room. Of course, there are contractors that can build a safe room with reinforced concrete walls, two-way radios, case-hardened steel doors that automatically slide shut and lock, closed-circuit television cameras, and a myriad of other security features that cost a bundle. Most people don't have that kind of bank account. The safe room we are going to describe is something that everyone reading this book can develop in his own residence. Now if you live in a rental property, I am not sure your landlord would take kindly to you beefing up one of his rental's rooms. This is how we suggest you set up your safe room:

- If you have the luxury of having a bedroom with an attached bathroom, think about using this room, but only if the primary entry door is a single door, not a double—we have found that a double door is too difficult to secure for our purposes.
- Install a metal-clad solid-core door or a metal door used in an exterior commercial application. Make sure the hinges are installed so that the hinge pins cannot be removed from outside the safe room.
- Install a dead bolt and a rim lock on the door. Some people have also opted to have a security bar installed that goes across the door from the inside. This adds to the strength of the door. Remember, you are not planning on living in the safe room, only waiting in it until help can arrive.
- Make sure all the windows in the room can be locked. Most neighborhoods are not going to take kindly to seeing burglar bars on the outside of your windows, especially if your housing tract has an association that doesn't allow that type of security device. However, if your neighborhood already has a few homes in the area with these types of devices as an everyday deterrent, you might want to consider putting some up. You can always install an interior set of bars. Just be sure to follow the manufacturer's as well as the local fire marshal's rules for safety in case of fire; we want you to be able to get out in this situation.
- Have a phone in the room. Phone lines can be cut, so think about having a cellular phone with you. Having a small, battery-operated citizen's band radio in the room is also a good idea. They are cheap and can be set up or stored in a closet. There is usually someone monitoring channel 9 on the radio so that your request for help can be heard.
- If you feel comfortable with it, have a weapon secured in that room, as well as a flashlight and extra batteries. We need to stress again that you be certain your children cannot gain access to this weapon. Also have a medical kit in the room, just in case you are injured before getting into the room. A small fire extinguisher is not a bad idea, either.

- If you have an alarm system monitored by a central security station, make sure that your safe room has an alarm panel installed in it, or at the very least has a remote panic alarm button for that security system.
- You can incorporate your strong room within your safe room, thus having one room doing double duty. In fact, it is probably wise to store as many of your valuables as you can in your safe room when you plan on being away from your home for a longer period of time, such as when on a vacation. Investing in a bank deposit box for long-term storage is something else that might work for some of your smaller items. We also suggest that if you own a computer, you back up all your files and secure the backup disk in either the safe room or some other place you consider to be safe. There is no way most of us could re-create our computer files if someone took or destroyed our computer.
- Even though you have designed this room as a safe room, don't save it for a rainy day; use it for whatever you normally need to. As long as you have it stocked with the items we have suggested, it should ready at any time. The purpose of the room is to provide you with a temporary place of safety until you or someone else can call the police.

Home safes. Home safes are a good idea. These safes range in price from the very reasonable to the outrageous. As we said previously, you can rent a safe deposit box, but for the most part, there is never enough room for files and other items you might want to keep in the safe deposit boxes we've seen. We have also found that convenience of access is always a problem when dealing with banks. There are two specific types of safes, those that protect against fire and those that protect against theft. A fire-resistant safe is designed to house records and protect them against fire. These should not be confused with data safes, which are specifically designed to store computer diskettes and have a different set of specifications than do many other fire safes. Most fire safes are designed only to protect paper documents and have classifications such as 30P, 60P, 90P, and 120P. The number reflects the number of minutes it can protect, and *P* refers to the paper rating. They also have ratings based on time exposed to fire before their contents will burn. For example, a "one-hour rated safe" is designed to maintain its interior temperature at less than 150 degrees Fahrenheit with an 85 percent humidity rating when exposed to a fire blazing at two thousand degrees Fahrenheit for one hour. Because of the way they are manufactured—with walls designed to repel heat and not an attack—they should not house valuables such as money or jewels. One of the ways we make a burglar-resistant safe act as a fire safe is to set it into a concrete floor. This will usually take care of both problems. There are safes out there that claim to both stand up to a forcible assault and stop fire damage, but they are going to be more expensive, of course.

The not-for-profit Underwriters Laboratories has developed ratings for safes. Each safe that you look at should have a letter rating. For example: a B-rated safe has walls less than $\frac{1}{2}$-inch thick, steel over the lock work less than one inch thick, and a combination lock, whereas a safe rated TRTL-30 will resist attack by an oxyacetylene torch and other burglary tools for up to thirty minutes. Underwriters Laboratories also rates fire safes as to how long that particular safe can withstand a certain amount of heat without failing. By the way, be careful when buying a used fire safe. They can lose structural integrity if they are bounced around, dropped, or struck, or if they have already been in some type of fire.

Property identification. Remember when we discussed evidence collection in a previous chapter? Property identification and evidence collection go hand in hand. If your stalker enters your residence and takes items as a trophy or as a way to threaten you, he then becomes a burglar. Residential burglary is a felony in almost every state we are familiar with, and it usually carries some type of prison sentence upon conviction. (Of course, that doesn't mean the burglar will always be sentenced to prison.) When the law enforcement body that is conducting your stalking investigation conducts a search either in the field or as a result of a search warrant issued against your stalker, they may locate your property. The best way for us to be able to find and collect your property (and then later testify that what we found was your property) is to have you properly identify it. Unfortunately, most people do not take the time to identify or catalog their prized personal property unless required to do so by their insurance company.

(Note: we realize that we have discussed in other chapters of this book that stalkers will often enter your house and take items that have special meaning to you, such as an heirloom pendant or undergarments. They will also rearrange furniture and leave things behind that would cause you to be fearful. However, you must also keep in mind that many of the stalkers we deal with have heavy drug habits and will steal items such as guns, jewelry, money, cameras, and other items of value and portability that they can sell to sustain these addictions. That is why we offer these security measures to you, the reader.)

There are several ways to accomplish the goal of identifying your property. Here are some we've seen that work fairly well:

- Etch your driver's license number into the surfaces of property that would lend itself to this type of identification, such as tools and many electronic devices. You can etch your numbers into the property with an inexpensive etching tool that you can pick up at your local hardware store. Some police departments will lend you the tool along with a log so that you can record the serial numbers and description of your valuables.
- Photograph items such as jewelry, firearms, and pieces of furniture.
- One of the easiest ways we have found to visually catalog your personal property is to videotape these articles. This videotape not only provides a record for proper criminal identification purposes but can also be very helpful in insurance loss documentation in case of fire or other disasters.
- Catalog any items that have serial numbers so that your law enforcement agency can enter them into any loss database they have available to them. This way if officers run across an item

they believe to be stolen, they can run the serial number and get a stolen property hit, thus allowing them to recover the property and/or arrest the person in possession of the item.

Escape routes. If you have a two-story house, set up an escape route in case of either intruder or fire. Also invest in one of the collapsible ladders that can be attached to a windowsill, allowing you and your loved ones to climb down out of the building. If you have children, plan some type of escape drill at least once a year. In this drill, plan a set location where you will meet once you have cleared your residence.

Visitor identification. Demand (that's right, demand!) identification from any repair person who comes to the door. If you are the least bit concerned, call the repair person's employer prior to allowing entry. Even if the subject at your door claims to be a police officer, request to see a badge and identification. We in law enforcement should all be carrying not only a badge but also an identification card issued by the chief of police. Anyone can get a badge, but it is more difficult to forge the identification card. Nonetheless, I had a case where a subject approached residents in an area and claimed to be a police officer from another jurisdiction. He was aware that police do have and use a police identification card, so he made up a simple identification card that included his picture. If you are not convinced after seeing these pieces of identification, make a verification call prior to talking with the officer.

Home inspection. If you have been away from your residence for a good part of the day, either at work or shopping, take a little drive around your neighborhood prior to going home. Look for the stalker, who may be waiting on an adjoining street. As we've already mentioned, try to vary your routes to and from work, school, or other locations you frequent, even the time of day you leave for such places. Of course, don't leave anything around your house, such as ladders or gardening tools, that might assist your potential intruder in gaining entry to your house. If you see something suspicious around your house, don't enter until you or your local law enforcement agency has confirmed it is not a threat. The key here is to be aware and alert. Doing the same things in the same way every day without conscious thought can create problems.

Change of clothes. Think about putting an overnight bag in your vehicle with a change of clothes for you and your children. This should contain any necessary medications as well as some extra cash. Hopefully you won't have to use this emergency bag, but you may find it necessary to go to a friend's house or stay at a motel on an occasion, when you just don't feel comfortable staying at home on a specific day or evening. We have had victims who are so traumatized by their stalker that they move back into their parents' residences for comfort and protection from the stalker.

VEHICLE SECURITY MEASURES

Alarm systems. If you decide to obtain an alarm system for your car, get one that allows you to activate the vehicle's interior lights as you disarm the alarm. This lets you get a look inside as you approach the car rather than after you've already entered. It also tends to startle anyone who might be in the vehicle. Another little item you want to look into is one that has a panic alarm, which starts your headlights flashing as well as your horn blaring. Let's face it: there are so many vehicle alarms going off these days that if you want to attract attention, you need something with a bit more flare.

Of course, if you want a system that has the greatest likelihood of actually getting your vehicle back from any thief, stalker, or whomever, look into a vehicle tracking system such as Lojack, Teletrac, or On Star. These systems track your vehicle via sensors hidden somewhere in your car. Some of these systems, such as Teletrac, can also show exactly where your vehicle is at any time on a computer-generated grid. On Star also allows you to communicate with a service operator for a variety of matters, including emergency problems, which could include your airbags deploying. Obviously, this could greatly assist you if you are stranded or if you were being abducted.

Along with an alarm system, it is a good idea to have a trunk-release mechanism installed within the trunk of your vehicle. Most new vehicles have this already in place. This is an excellent safety feature, in case a child accidentally gets into the trunk or you are forcefully put into that same trunk.

When I was in New York in June of 2002, I saw the usage of a significant number and variety of steering wheel locking mechanisms. In my opinion, anything that slows someone down when they are trying to take your vehicle is a good idea. However, given enough time, even these devices can be defeated.

Vehicle maintenance. Proper vehicle maintenance is a must—you don't want to get stranded out there. If you purchase your car new, you may want to opt for the extended warranty package. If your car is used, find a good mechanic. Buy a quality locking gas cap. As mentioned earlier, we have had victims find sugar in their tanks, which when mixed with gasoline will destroy an engine. We have also had victims find rice in their radiators. When the engine runs, the rice cooks and expands, damaging the cooling system and potentially the engine.

Vehicle inspection. When I taught high school drivers' education, we taught our students to inspect their vehicle as they approached it— once they had left it parked for any period of time. This is a useful habit for any driver. Look under and around the car for anything unusual, such as pools of brake or transmission fluid, radiator coolant, or items that don't look like they should be there, either on the pavement or on your car. Check the rear floorboard area to see that no one is lying down. Check for low or flat tires as well. This brings to mind a tactic that has been used by stalkers, sexual predators, and robbery suspects in the past. The drill goes something like this. Say you go into a bank or a store, even for a short time. Just before you come out, the perpetrator walks up to your vehicle and punctures the sidewall of your tire, usually with an ice pick or a similar device. The perpetrator then follows as you drive off. When you stop to check on the flat, the predator makes his move, usually with disastrous results. What should you do if this takes place? If you find yourself with a tire going flat, keep in mind it may be just that: a natural deflation caused by a faulty tire or something you ran over. Of course, if you know that you are being stalked, it could be the work of the stalker, and you should have a plan. If you feel you are in danger, we suggest you get back into your car and drive on the flat tire until you can get the attention of law enforcement personnel or reach a place of safety. The worst that can probably happen in this situation is that a tire, or maybe a rim, might be ruined. (For your information, there is a product that you can get in most automotive supply stores that has both a sealant and compressed air in a can. You place the nozzle on the tire stem and reinflate the tire. This allows you to drive for a few more miles, getting out of harm's way. However, this will only work on normal tire punctures on the tire tread, not the sidewall.)

If you are still driving around in a car old enough to have an exterior hood latch, think about getting some type of locking latch mechanism. This will slow down anyone trying to get into the engine compartment of your vehicle.

Think defensively. When you walk up to your car, keep your keys in your strong hand. Grip them in such a fashion as to have the car key, which is usually fairly long, sticking out between your middle knuckles. You can then quickly insert the key into the lock. This key grip may also assist you in fending off an attacker. Holding the key this way would also be a good idea when approaching your residence to unlock the front door. Thinking defensively also means checking out your immediate environment. Don't walk with your head down. Walk like you know where you are going and can take care of yourself. Studies have shown that for the most part, women who act and conduct themselves in a manner that exudes confidence are less likely to be targeted by assailants. Those persons who act timid, confused, and less in control are more likely prey. Again, think of humans as members of the animal kingdom, living according to the law of survival of the fittest. The hyena goes after the weak and the lame, not as often the quick and the strong.

Know your route. As patrol cops, we were trained always to visualize the location we were dispatched to. This visualization includes side streets, alleyways, and other landmarks in the general vicinity. This helps us develop a plan in case the call "takes a dump" (goes bad). You should start thinking the same way. Always know where you are going. If you have been to the location before, start visualizing a possible escape route if the need should arise. If you have never been to your destination, make sure you have mapped out how to get there. The Internet has step-by-step directions on how to get to just about anywhere in the United States. (A good Web site is expedia.com.) If you don't have access to the Internet, get a good road atlas and carry it with you. The AAA, as well as your local bookstore, should have good maps. *Have a plan—surprise can cause panic.*

WORKPLACE SECURITY MEASURES

Keep in mind, stalkers don't use a "King's X" (a safe zone) approach when they stalk. The enclosures of your workplace are not necessarily safe havens for you or the people you work with, and they may mean nothing to your stalker. In fact, in some scenarios they represent a good place for stalkers to ply their trade. Over the last couple of years, workplace violence has increased at an alarming rate, and some of that violence is due to the stalker's acting out not only on the victim but on her coworkers as well. You need to take certain measures at your workplace as well as in your personal life to maximize your security.

Employer awareness. Make your employer aware of your situation. When you make an initial contact with the employer regarding a stalking situation, have that contact documented; in fact, insist that documentation be made. In most cases, no documentation usually means there will be little or no recourse for you against the employer when and if any future stalking behavior takes place and is reported.

In other words, a smart employer will initiate a file or refer you to Human Resources if available, so that they can initiate a file.

Stalker description. Get a photo, if available, or a physical description of both the stalker and his vehicle into the hands of the appropriate management and security personnel. In early 2003 we had a case in which a violent stalker was stalking a male who worked for a large aerospace corporation. After conducting a search of the stalker's residence, we located a map in which he had circled the location of the business as well as written notes concerning how to get to that location. Fearing that the stalker would be attempting to contact and/or injure our victim at work, we contacted the head of security for the victim's place of business and gave him photos of the stalker and of the vehicles he drove. This is normal protocol procedure for us.

Employee inquiries. Ask your receptionist or manager to handle any inquiries made about you, including personal visitors, phone calls, or faxes. We know this can be a touchy matter, as we've had stalkers call their victims' place of business as many as fifty to one hundred times a day, as well as tie up fax lines. As noted before, this is a double whammy for the victim—not only does she have to deal with the hassle of a stalker but also an angry employer. Unfortunately, this scenario can result in the victim losing her job.

For those employers who might be reading this portion of the text, keep in mind that there may be a stalking role-reversal going on in your business that you should be aware of. For example, we had a stalker who worked in a small advertising business. Over the course of a year he would get several calls a day from his ex-girlfriend. This led the employer and other employees to believe that she was stalking him, when in truth, he was paging her several times a day stating that he had to talk to her about their young daughter. He was doing this to both harass and keep track of her.

Parking. Get permission to park your vehicle in the most secure and well-lit area you can—hopefully in an area where the vehicle can be monitored. We have had victims' vehicles vandalized on a regular basis at work.

Packages. Opening packages at work should be the same as at home: if you aren't expecting it, be suspicious. Again, make others in your workplace environment aware of your being stalked; advise them not to open packages addressed to you, for their own safety. This can be a real problem for anyone who has a receptionist or a personal assistant. For the most part, their jobs require them to open and disseminate certain mail addressed to their superiors. If you now find that you are a victim of stalking, you must sit down with them and explain the need for more caution when dealing with packages and other correspondence.

Coworker stalkers. If your stalker is a coworker, the burden of protection becomes a big issue for your employer; therefore it is imperative that you notify your boss immediately. Again, keep records of when the stalking behavior takes place—dates and times, as well as the nature of the behavior. Also indicate in those records what transpired after your contact with your supervisor. Was your contact followed up at all? Was the matter handled appropriately by your Human Resources personnel? The bottom line: was the issue handled to your satisfaction?

Keep in mind that employers are like everyone else; they need to be educated on the stalking issue. Be patient, but persistent. Your employer's task of dealing with the situation is doubly difficult: before she can make any kind of a binding decision on the fate of the alleged stalker, she has to first be certain that a stalking is in fact taking place. Your employer can avail herself of a variety of firms involved in the workplace violence issue. Some of these security firms have stalking experts and forensic psychologists on their staff to assist the employer in dealing with these issues. She can also contact a law enforcement professional and inquire about some remedies. The worst thing management can do is nothing, thereby letting the behavior continue.

A MESSAGE FOR EMPLOYERS

This section of the text is as good a place as any to talk to you, the employer, about your responsibility concerning stalking. Unfortunately, in this day and age, stalking is affecting the workplace more and more. Many employers are rising to the occasion by becoming keenly aware of their responsibility in this regard, and are taking some type of action to assist not only the stalking victim but her fellow employees as well. It should also be noted that given the right set of circumstances, one of your employees may in fact stalk you. It's happening more and more frequently: you fire a disgruntled employee, and that employee begins to stalk you. These stalkers can be the worst kind, as they are fueled by one of the most passionate human motives—revenge. Because of real-life scenarios where ex-postal employees have gone on killing sprees, "going postal" is now a common phrase used among law enforcement personnel to describe a situation where an ex-employee comes back to haunt the workplace. Obviously, workplace violence and stalking does not occur only in the postal service. It is an ever-increasing problem in our workplaces across the nation. It affects all businesses, large and small. One study informs us that over one million individuals are victimized annually while working; five hundred thousand victims lose 1.8 million work days and over $55 million in wages each year.[2] A 1996 study tells us that 4 to 6 percent of all homicides in the workplace are committed by coworkers or former coworkers.[3] This same study, put out by the National Institute for Occupational Safety and Health (NIOSH), states that homicide is the leading cause of occupational injury causing death among females in the workplace.[4] We know from studying many of the reviews of these workplace homicides that some of them were a direct result of an intimate partner or DVS showing up at the victim's place of work and committing the murder.

As a recent example, we counseled the service manager of a large auto dealership in Orange County who advised us that he had fired a troublesome employee. After a short time period, the service manager began being followed by this individual. We are now monitoring the continuing behavior of this individual.

Listed below are a few ways of trying to prevent workplace violence or stalking scenarios from plaguing your organization:

- Have a very specific written policy in place that describes what you consider workplace violence. Part of that policy should discuss harassment/stalking. Make sure that each employee is advised of the policy at the time of hiring and signs a form stating that he has read and understood its contents. The policy should be reviewed along with other policies such as sexual harassment at least once a year. Many organizations do this when they conduct an employee's yearly evaluation. Have the employees sign that they have both read and understood the policy review at the time it was presented to them.

- As soon as you become aware you are going to fire an employee, consider taking some of the following threat management steps before taking action: Have a meeting with the employee's immediate supervisor, the company security manager, and the personnel officer, if there is one. This meeting should be designed to gather as much information about the employee's threat potential as you can, in order to determine how the employee may react when faced with the firing. The data you gather on this employee should include a photo of the individual, if possible, as well as a description and the license plate number of her car.

- Once you've obtained the information you want, formulate a plan for the day of the firing. As soon as the employee is fired, have the employee remove all of his belongings from the workplace. Have any final pay or reimbursement checks ready, and collect all keys or entry cards immediately. Cover all the bases, so that there is no reason for that terminated employee to come back onto company property. Advise the employee that there is no reason for him to be back on the workplace grounds for any reason.

- Instruct your security people or other trusted employees to notify you immediately if the ex-employee is seen anywhere on the property. At the first sign of trouble, contact your local police department and have the trespasser removed.

- If you or any of your employees are followed, harassed, or repeatedly contacted by the ex-employee, keep a log and contact the police.
- If it appears that a stalking is beginning to take form, obtain a civil workplace restraining order against the troublesome employee. We will discuss this order in more detail in chapter 7, Legal Remedies.

Of course, we have just glossed over some of the preventive measures one can take concerning workplace violence. Having a consulting forensic psychologist available for your human resource staff, or having a place to conduct a threat assessment employee interview when a potential problem surfaces are other issues that should be addressed.

One other thing we would like to discuss concerning the dismissal of the problem employee, whether he is a stalker or not, is how to soften the dismissal. We are acutely aware that each job termination action is different. Due to safety issues, some must be done swiftly without additional compensation, but many others afford the employer a chance to help the employee's cooling-off temperament. Therefore you might seriously want to think about softening the blow of the termination with a severance package of some type. This may go a long way toward short-circuiting any negative behavior your problem employee was thinking about. We just investigated a case of a forty-year-old female who was beginning to stalk a younger male with whom she had had a torrid love affair. This same female apparently was having problems with work. The employer contacted us because the employer was fearful of the female and also expressed that this female was now stalking her. The employer had already been advised by a security expert in regard to giving the female a severance package; we counseled the employer concerning the stalking issues. After weighing all of her options, the employer opted to offer the severance package, which to this point seems to have eliminated a potential workplace violence issue.

Keep in mind that lawyers are now finding the area of workplace violence to be a very lucrative field of litigation. The attorneys who have spoken to us concerning the litigation aspect of workplace violence have all stressed these key issues: Did the company have a specific workplace violence policy in place? Was this policy made available to individual employees, and was it actively enforced? Again, we feel strongly that these policies should address the stalking issue within the workplace. This area of litigation was once again brought up at a recent threat management conference that I attended. The speaker, who is both an attorney and a well-respected consultant in the area of workplace violence, strongly cautioned that "negligent supervision" is becoming very fertile ground for litigation.*

CHAPTER 6 SUMMARY

- General security measures
  - Family notification
  - Children
  - Trip itinerary and personal information
  - Variation of routine
  - Cellular phones—use for emergencies

- Home security measures
  - Post office boxes
  - Confidentiality
  - Doors—solid-core and metal-clad are the best for security

---

* The workplace violence litigators we talked to said that California's Department of Industrial Relations under Cal OSHA has some of the best models and research for handling workplace violence concerns in the country. Go on-line and search under "Cal OSHA" or "California Department of Industrial Relations," and then type in "workplace security" or "workplace violence." You will get access to several articles and guidelines. Type III is the one type we are referring to, but there are other types of workplace violence perpetrated against employees. This should give you a place to start.

- ○ Garage doors—secure with pins; get an automatic door opener with multiple code entry
- ○ Security lights
- ○ Windows—make sure all windows can be secured
- ○ Home alarm systems—they can usually be cheaply installed and provide good peace of mind
- ○ Telephone security
- ○ Pick-up—mail, newspapers, or flyers left around the outside of your home or apartment
- ○ Weapons—always think before using; use what you know and are comfortable with; *always secure weapons away from children*
- ○ Packages—be aware of what could be inside; if it looks suspicious, it probably is
- ○ Safety equipment
- ○ Strong space
- ○ Safe room
- ○ Home safes
- ○ Property identification
- ○ Escape routes—always have one planned ahead of time
- ○ Visitor identification
- ○ Home inspection—take a look around before you enter your street or house

- • Vehicle security measures
  - ○ Vehicle alarm systems—get one that lights up the interior
  - ○ Vehicle maintenance
  - ○ Vehicle inspection—always check around your car before you get in
  - ○ Think defensively—don't walk with your head down; check out your environment
  - ○ Know your route

- • Workplace Security Measures
  - ○ Employer awareness

- Stalker description
- Employee inquiries—let calls and inquirers be screened by fellow employees
- Parking—park in an area where your car can be monitored
- Packages—be suspicious; alert those who might open them for you
- Coworker stalkers—nip the problem in the bud; document and advise employer

- A message to employers
  - Formulate a workplace violence plan or policy to protect yourself and your employees, as well as lower your exposure to potential legal action
  - Remember that domestic violence, as well as the domestic violence stalker, often follows the victim to the workplace

CHAPTER 7

LEGAL REMEDIES

The purpose of this chapter is to discuss what legal resources you may use against your stalker. As we examine these tools, we assess the pros and cons of each. Bear in mind, however, that we are not lawyers; therefore this information should not be construed as legal advice. Making legal decisions should not be done without first consulting an attorney. Nevertheless, it is useful for you to understand each of these remedies. We should also mention that they may have a different name and/or format in your particular state. Once you understand the concept, you can convey the information to the proper authority, who should be able to point you in the right direction.

RESTRAINING ORDERS

Temporary Restraining Order (TRO). A temporary restraining order is designed to put your stalker on notice immediately that he must stop harassing, contacting, or otherwise communicating with you in any way, shape, or form. To obtain a TRO you must first petition the court in charge of issuing them. For example, in my county, this would be the superior court in the jurisdiction where the stalking occurred. In other states the TRO could be obtained in a municipal court.

When petitioning the court, you are required to fill out a series of legal forms, which are then submitted to the court for approval or denial of the order. These forms usually include pertinent information such as the name and address of the stalker, as well as your own particulars. The form also has a section of facts, or "standards of proof." This is the area where you carefully document (from your diary or log) why you want the TRO issued against your stalker. This standard of proof section would include your stalker's continual contacts, harassing letters and calls, and example of his physical pursuit, as well as any threats made to you. This is also the area where you would want to discuss the stalker's harassment (if any) of any of your family members or significant others. In most situations you must show that you made a reasonable effort to notify the stalker, within a set period of time, that you are filing a TRO against him. This is done so that he will have the opportunity to come to court and express his views on why he feels the TRO should not be issued.

There may be a provision in your TRO requirements that allows for an "ex parte TRO" to be issued. Here "ex parte" means being done for or on behalf of one party without notice to the other party. This order is issued when the victim cannot serve the stalker or notify him about the restraining order procedure, only after the victim has shown good faith in trying to contact the stalker but has not been able to do so. Once obtained, the ex parte TRO is normally in effect for a short period of time, such as twenty days, and the victim must continue to attempt to serve the alleged stalker with his copy during that time. The ex parte TRO usually cannot be enforced until the stalker is legally served.

In most cases, the restraining order is not free.* It will cost both to obtain one and to have a marshal or court server serve the order. Some jurisdictions allow persons over the age of eighteen and not related to the victim to serve the order, but we recommend against that practice

---

* According to Orange County Deputy District Attorney Jane Shade (see appendix A for more information about her), "Many courts allow a person to petition for a 'no cost' order if he or she meets certain low-income standards. . . . Some courts automatically waive all fees if the TRO is related to domestic violence as defined by law." District Attorney Shade strongly advises those who have a problem obtaining a TRO due to limited funds contact their local women's shelter for direction and support.

unless the server is a law enforcement officer. Remember, you are dealing with the stalker mentality; don't place anyone in harm's way unnecessarily. Additionally, when you use a marshal or official process server to conduct your service, there is less likelihood for mistake, or for questions to be raised on the part of the stalker or the stalker's attorney. Once the stalker is served (make sure you get certified copies of the service), then the judge can set a date for a hearing on your permanent restraining order.

Some jurisdictions, such as the Westminster Police Department, have specially trained personnel to assist victims of stalking and other domestic violence-related problems with obtaining a restraining order.

It is always a good idea to keep at least two certified copies of the TRO on your person at all times. If you have to call the police because the stalker violates the order, you have a copy to give the officers when they respond to assist you. When they document the contact in their police report, they can incorporate your order. Once this has been accomplished, the stalker cannot claim to have no knowledge of the order. Having extra copies of the TRO also comes in handy when your stalker has not been served. If the stalker has not yet been served with a copy of the TRO, the officer dispatched to assist you can then serve him when the officer makes contact with him. This service will then be documented in the officer's report. You must also distribute a copy of your served TRO to the law enforcement entities in whose jurisdictions you live and work. The same holds true once you have obtained your permanent restraining or protective order. (A protective order "restrains" the person served with the order from following or contacting, etc., the person being protected by the order. In essence, a restraining order and a protective order are the same.)

In California, for example, restraining and protective orders are placed into a statewide database, so when a record check is run on a subject for wants (i.e., to see if the subject being detained is wanted for any crime) and/or any outstanding warrants, he is also being checked for restraining order information. Even with that, many agencies still want copies of the orders available to them in their record divisions.

Again, each jurisdiction and state is different; follow the guidelines your state has laid down for distribution of a TRO. The National Stalker and Domestic Violence Reduction Act authorizes all states to place civil restraining orders along with abuse-type prevention orders into the National Crime Information Center (NCIC) database.[1]

Permanent restraining order. Once the TRO has been properly served, and all requirements met, the permanent restraining order may then be issued by the magistrate. The duration of the restraining order can vary. In California and other states, such as South Dakota and Hawaii, the length of a restraining order can be up to three years. Some states have a clause in their protective and permanent restraining orders that allows a magistrate to extend or renew the order if he deems that the threat still exists. In criminal cases in California, the victim can be granted a domestic violence restraining order, which affords a ten-year duration. In New Jersey, a victim may be able to obtain an order that has an indefinite time limit unless altered by another court action. The same holds true in Connecticut, when the restraining order stems from domestic violence. There is usually a specific distance that the court assigns to the person on the receiving end of the restraining order: in other words, the distance that person must stay away from the individual filing the order. This distance is often a hundred yards. In the Sandra Potter case, the judge granted a ten-mile radius, which her stalker must observe. There are other restrictions the court can impose. In another of our cases involving a female stalker, the court granted a ten-year restraining order along with a specific order that the stalker not enter the city of Westminster during that restraining period.

Restraining order punishments. Violation of a restraining order or protective order can itself be either a felony or a misdemeanor, or it can qualify as contempt of court. "However, in most states felony treatment is reserved for repeat offenders."[2] A few states require minimum jail time for those who violate an order. In Hawaii, those who violate a domestic violence order are required to spend "at least forty-eight hours in jail for the first violation, and thirty days for any subsequent violations." Illinois mandates seven consecutive days in jail for a violation. Colorado states that any sentence levied on a protective order violation must run "consecutively with the sentence imposed for the crime giving rise to the order" (i.e., run as a separate sentence after the protective order sentence has been served).[3] We like a couple of new additions that other states have adopted concerning protective order violators. Hawaii, Massachusetts, and Rhode Island have included counseling as part of their criminal sanctions, and Washington has a section that allows for the judge to order "electronic monitoring" of a violator as an option.[4] California also includes this under Penal Code section 646.9(j) when probation is granted.

An important point to keep in mind is that once a restraining order is issued, many states now require the person served with an order to relinquish all firearms and not to purchase any additional weapons. For example, in California, even an attempt to purchase a firearm during the restraining order is a misdemeanor penal code violation. Delaware, Hawaii, Illinois, Massachusetts, Montana, and Pennsylvania are just a few of the states that have some type of restrictions on the possession of firearms by an individual served with a restraining/protective order. Additionally, the federal government has a statute regarding this situation:

> It shall be unlawful for any person who is subject to a court order that—
>
> - (A) was issued after a hearing of which such person received actual notice, and at which such person had an opportunity to participate;
> - (B) restrains such person from harassing, stalking, or threatening an intimate partner of such person or child of such intimate partner, or engaging in other conduct that would place an intimate partner in reasonable fear of bodily injury to the partner or child; and
> - (C)
>   - (i) includes a finding that such person represents a credible threat to the physical safety of such intimate partner or child; or

    o (ii) by its terms explicitly prohibits the use, attempted use, or threatened use of physical force against such intimate partner or child that would reasonably be expected to cause bodily injury; or

- (9) who has been convicted in any court of a misdemeanor crime of domestic violence, *to ship or transport in interstate or foreign commerce, or possess in or affecting commerce, any firearm or ammunition; or to receive any firearm or ammunition which has been shipped or transported in interstate or foreign commerce.* (*U.S. Code*, vol. 18, Section 922 [g][8–9])

We quoted this entire federal United States code section as an example of how detailed and at times complicated these sections can be. For the rest of this chapter we will provide a synopses of the other U.S. code sections relevant to our discusstion. For those who are in law enforcement or who are just curious about thumbing through large, heavy law books, you can go to the library or the Internet to conduct further research on the sections we will present.

TRO pros and cons. In our police department's stalking protocol, which deals with stalker evaluation, we don't always recommend obtaining a restraining order, at least not initially. Each stalker is different; there may be times when we want to avoid the possibility of kicking the stalking up to the next level of intensity, at least not until we're ready to use a different tactic, such as mental health intervention, to defuse the stalker's behavior. Depending on what we ascertain in the threat assessment interview, we may feel the stalking is in its early stages, and thus presents a lower level of threat. This gives us additional time to conduct a more in-depth investigation without the worry of a possible escalation. Admittedly, we do not use this tactic very often, but we have used it. There are other times when we feel a stalking is underway, but there is not enough articulable evidence for a restraining order to be issued. Also, some public figures do not want the press (which scans court records regularly) to know they have had a restraining order issued. This is privacy concern for with them.

We recently had an opportunity to talk to John Lane, who, as we noted earlier, is a principal for the Omega Threat Management Group, based in the Los Angeles area. (See our section on stalking resources in appendix A for more information on this organization.) One of the services Lane's company offers is protection and threat management for high-profile public figures, primarily media personalities. Lane told me that when dealing with a threat to one of his clients, his group will assess the level of that threat and then make a determination on how to handle the problem. Lane said if they feel they can manage the situation "behind the scenes" via ongoing assessment oversight—i.e., bodyguards and surveillance protection teams—they will. However, if the threat is such that it requires law enforcement intervention, then they will usually opt for a restraining order. Lane said once that decision has been made, they will make a concerted attempt to keep the client's name concealed by trying to have the judge order the information on the restraining order affidavits be sealed. He admitted, though, that this can be difficult to accomplish. Lane said he feels that restraining orders do have their place but that they often create additional concerns for the clients he deals with. This is a very expensive endeavor, and most of us could not afford these services. Bear in mind, many of the stalkers we encounter couldn't care less about being served with a restraining order, especially the ones with serious mental problems.

One of our male victims complained that he was accosted by his female stalker in the court parking lot just minutes after she was admonished by the judge to stay clear of him. The female stalker told the victim as she attempted to grab and kiss him, "Now I know more than ever that you love me, because you took the time to take me to court!" Another example of this type of behavior was epitomized by a male stalker we recently arrested on a probation violation resulting from our case. The stalker, who lived and worked in a city some forty miles from where the victim worked, was once again showing up during the day at or near her workplace. He told the detectives who arrested him something to the effect of "I know I have a restraining order against me. I know that I have a felony conviction for stalking.

But I am very partial to the iced tea I get at this particular Del Taco."
Obviously, the Del Taco was located very close to where the victim
worked. These same stalkers will often carry their copy of the
restraining order around with them, along with other court papers pertaining to the case. Sometimes they draw pictures and make interesting incriminating comments concerning how they feel about the
victims in the margins; these make excellent courtroom exhibits.

The last example we want to share with you, probably more than
any of the others, shows how little respect many of these individuals
give to the orders and the people who issue them. Not too long ago, I
was in a central superior courtroom waiting to see the judge on an
arrest warrant request I had before him. While I was waiting, the judge
was conducting a hearing on another domestic violence stalking case.
From what I could understand, it was a protracted and violent case.
The defendant/stalker was a very large male in his early thirties. The
victim was a petite young female with two very young children. The
stalker had just spent a period of time in jail for spousal abuse, and the
judge was informing the stalker about the stipulations in the criminal
stay-away order he was being served with. When the judge was finished, the stalker said he understood all the requirements of the order.
As the judge was calling the next case, the stalker walked back to the
rear of the large courtroom, where his estranged wife was, and began
to confront her about the order, and what kind of problems this was
going to cause him. As soon as the bailiff overheard this, he started to
walk back to the stalker, who immediately fled. This is why we continue to tell the people we instruct concerning restraining orders that
stalkers just don't—and probably will never—get it.

We like restraining orders because they give us leverage against
the stalker. Sometimes the stalking will stop with the first TRO; not
often, but it does happen. Generally, we expect the stalker to violate
the restraining order, affording us the opportunity either to file separate criminal cases for violating a court order or to add considerable
depth to our stalking case. Sometimes we like to provide the stalker
with a personal touch by serving the order ourselves. This gives us a

chance to get to know our stalker a little better, while at the same time intruding on his comfort zone. It also makes the stalker painfully aware he is being monitored.

Another benefit of restraining orders is that, as a result of the federal Violence Against Women Act of 1994, TROs and other protective orders are valid and enforceable under the "full faith and credit" provisions of this act in states outside their state of issuance.[5] In other words, if a victim has an order from state A and is stalked or harassed in state B, that order must be treated as if it was issued in state B. When the suspect is prosecuted in state B for violation of the restraining order, then state B's punishments are the ones affixed to the suspect, even if they are different from that of state A.[6] (The actual federal crime of interstate violation of a restraining order is listed under sections 2262[a][1] and [a][2] of the *U.S. Code*, vol. 18. According to this law, it is a federal crime to cross state lines to injure an "intimate partner." The injury must be physical and the defendant must have intended to commit the crime when crossing the state line. The section also goes on to say that it is a federal crime to force or coerce an "intimate partner" to cross state lines if the force or coercion leads to physical harm of the victim [Note: Synopsis—refer to Federal Criminal Code and Rules for details]).

Along those same lines, the federal antistalking law, known as the Interstate Stalking Punishment and Prevention Act, enacted in September 1996, strengthens the enforcement of court restraining and protective orders from one state to another. This bill, which was authored by Congressman Ed Royce of California and sponsored in the Senate by Senator Kay Bailey Hutchison of Texas, also makes it a federal crime to cross state lines with the intent of harassing or injuring someone. These federal laws mandate long punishment—from five to twenty years if the victim is injured, or up to life if the victim dies. Of course, we would like to see long prison sentences for all felony violations of stalking. The longer the stalkers stay in, the better the victim's quality of life. (Section 2261[a] of the *U.S. Code*, vol. 18, states that it is a federal crime to cross state lines with the intent to injure or harass *any person*, if during the course of, or as a result of, the travel, the traveler places the person or a member of the person's immediate family in reasonable fear of death or serious bodily injury [Note: Synopsis—refer to Federal Criminal Code and Rules for complete information].)

Workplace restraining orders. Since stalking violence and a growing number of other violent crimes, such as murder and assault, are becoming more frequent in the workplace, the workplace restraining order was developed. As yet, not all states offer this type of order. However, if you're being stalked in the workplace, you may want to research the availability of one of these orders and bring it to the attention of your employer, if the need arises. If for some reason you can't get the employer to obtain a workplace order, make sure the order you personally obtain specifies in the language of the document that there are to be no workplace contacts.

This restraining order is applied for in the same way as the temporary restraining order. In the case of a place of business, an attorney for the business or the business owner makes the request on behalf of both the employee being stalked and his or her fellow employees. The judge is asked to order the subject to stay away from the job site and make no contact with the victim or other employees. This request usually includes not making any calls, and not sending packages, letters, cybercommunications, or faxes. The order is served and enforced the same way as the TRO. These orders can be modified by the court just about any way the judge feels is necessary. Therefore, if the stalker works in the same building as the victim, he would be restrained from contact or harassment in that particular workspace. That might mean the stalker would have to change locations, hours, or perhaps even have to leave that job site altogether.

Criminal stay-away orders. This order is just what it sounds like—an order is issued in a court of law by a judge demanding that the subject stay away from the victim. The judge can modify the order any way she wishes. In this case, however, violation of the order is a criminal offense, not a civil one, and prosecution will be pursued on that basis. These orders are not usually issued by a judge until after the stalker has been arraigned on other charges in the court that is currently hearing or dealing with his case. According to the legal eagles we talked to, one of the benefits of these orders is that the victim need not take any action to obtain the order. She does not have to be present when the order is issued or petition the court herself to issue an order. The judge can make the order of her own volition or at the request of the prosecutor handling the case.

Stalking Emergency Protective Order (EPO). California, as well as some other states such as Texas and Kentucky, has enacted legislation that allows for emergency protective orders to be issued in domestic violence and stalking cases. In California, officers in the field are able to obtain an EPO—similar to a TRO—whenever they feel a victim is in immediate danger from a stalker. The stalker can then be served immediately in the field by the officer. Most of the orders last only a few days—up to seven days in California and thirty days in Texas—but this allows the victim time to apply for a traditional restraining order and still have the stalker legally restrained during that time period. We have found this order to be very beneficial for our street cops. Instead of trying to get the stalker—who may in fact be an estranged husband or a live-in boyfriend—to find another place to stay, the officer simply applies over the phone to an on-call judge, who issues the order. The potential stalker is then immediately restrained from harassing or being near the victim. This includes making phone calls, sending faxes, or using other electronic devices to contact and harass the victim.

Antistalking protection orders. There are twenty-nine states, such as California, Maryland, Georgia, and Alaska, that have antistalking protection or restraining orders. These orders can be issued by a judge during a pretrial scenario or as part of the sentencing of the stalker. These orders are primarily designed to fit the stalker who is not considered a DVS.

THE STALKING TORT

The California legislature has added a new section to its civil code, section 1708.7, which allows victims of stalking crimes to sue their stalkers in civil court. This law is now being used by civil attorneys to sue the stalker. Oregon, Texas, and Wyoming have similar stalking tort law. We believe the offshoot of this section may be that attorneys also begin suing employers for failure to provide a safe working environment for the person being stalked. You can bet that lawyers are looking for new and fertile fields to plow. Mark our words, litigation against employers who fail to protect their employees is going to be on the increase.

According to Orange County Deputy District Attorney Jane Shade, who teaches seminars at threat assessment venues, "More corporate and business attorneys will advise their business clients that they have a duty to obtain a workplace restraining order on behalf of the victim and/or for the safety of the employees at the workplace."

CHAPTER SEVEN SUMMARY

- A temporary restraining order (TRO) is a common and frequently used tool against a stalker. However, there may be times when it is not wise for a TRO to be issued, especially when the threat assessment plan indicates another plan of attack must be tried first. Thanks to federal legislation, restraining and protective orders issued in one state can be valid in other states.
- There may be other legal procedures to lessen a stalker's ability to stalk, such as workplace violence restraining orders and criminal stay-away orders. Check to see if they are available in your community or state. When having your stalker served with a restraining or protective order, try to use a professional certified in process serving.
- All of the orders listed in this chapter are meant to assist in the fight

against the stalker. They are only as good as the enforcement body that backs them. Sometimes the mere issuance of an order may cause the stalker to stop negative behavior; more often than not, though, the stalker ignores the order, which sets the stage for his arrest and prosecution upon violation of that order.

- Employers have to get on board concerning workplace stalking, or else they may be subject to an employee lawsuit.
- Some states such as California, Texas, and Kentucky have passed legislation that allows primary law enforcement responders to obtain emergency protective orders (EPOs). These orders can be served by the officers at the initial time of field contact with the stalker.

CHAPTER 8

A STALKING TRIAL— WHAT TO EXPECT

The only exposure millions of Americans have to courtroom procedures is through viewing some of the more high-profile televised trials. The circus atmosphere of some of these trials has been quite obvious, especially when the "ringmaster" (the judge) lets the "clowns" (the lawyers) in the center ring get out of hand. This is not to say that many courtrooms are not treated as theatrical stages, but most of the time, the judge has substantial control over the proceedings. Let's just say that after thirty years of involvement in the trial process, we have seen many strange and unusual things take place within those hallowed halls of justice. However, we have worked with some truly fine prosecutors and judges along the way. These are dedicated people who care about the victim.

For those readers who may not be familiar with courtroom procedures, we will discuss some of the basics of a trial, along with information regarding stalking proceedings in particular. Again, keep in mind that each state, and possibly each jurisdiction, may do things somewhat differently from the trial process as described below. For the most part, the procedure should be fairly similar to what we present. I have testified hundreds of times in California courtrooms both in and out of my jurisdiction. I have also testified a few times in other states; each time the proceedings were about the same.

245

ARRAIGNMENT

Once an alleged stalker has been arrested or has turned himself in, he hires or is assigned an attorney. Eventually he will be brought before a judge to make a plea. In most cases, at least initially, this plea will be one of not guilty. This not guilty plea allows the defense counsel time to look over all the facts concerning the case. United States Department of Justice statistics for 2001 show that in over 90 percent of the state prosecutors' offices, stalking cases were prosecuted 61 percent of the time.[1]

DISCOVERY

After the plea of not guilty, a process of "discovery" ensues. This is where the stalker (through his attorney) asks for a showing of the "relevant details" of the investigation, such as reports, photos, video and audio tapes, etc., from the prosecutor. The prosecutor may be a city attorney, district attorney, state attorney, or United States attorney, in the case of a federal trial. We should also note that more and more states (such as California, under Penal Code section 1054.2) will not allow the stalker to have identifying information on the victim and certain witnesses. This information would include phone numbers, addresses, etc.

INDICATED SENTENCE

Once the defense counsel has gathered up the entire discovery information and has made at least a brief review, she may go to the presiding judge and ask for what she feels is a reasonable disposition to resolve the case—in other words, what it will take to close out the case. The judge then reviews the facts of the case and gives the defense attorney an idea as to whether probation will be appropriate in the case, or, if a jail sentence is warranted, the approximate length of the sentence. The defense counsel then discusses this information with the defendant, who can either accept or deny the offered sentence. (That is, what the district attorney and the defense have agreed is a reasonable sentence.) Sometimes, though not often, the defense attorney may push for his client to plead guilty to the charges, but his client may fail to cooperate. This is known in the trade as a "lack of client control." In this situation, the defense counsel is forced to go to trial.

Keep in mind that some states still plea-bargain certain offenses; that is to say, they strike a deal with the prosecution for a lower term or lesser charge in exchange for pleading guilty to that lesser charge. This process sometimes expedites the workings of the trial process, but for detectives, plea bargaining can be frustrating. Of course, there are times that a lesser sentence or outcome on a charge is warranted. For the most part, though, we feel the plea bargain cheats the victim by allowing the suspect to get far less than he deserves. It also can place the victim at risk again soon! When this happens, we sit down with the victim and reaffirm our commitment to her, telling her that we are on her side and will continue to be, as we strive to eliminate her problem.

If you are the victim of a stalking that goes to trial, a prosecutor may contact you beforehand to assess exactly how you feel about the prosecution that is going to take place. The prosecutor should also contact you to get your opinion if some type of plea bargain or sentence offer is on the table. We have had victims contact prosecutors and tell them to go easy on a subject because they have begun to feel sorry for them. As we have discussed in prior chapters, many of the stalkers that we have dealt with have obvious mental and emotional problems; these problems are very evident to our victims as well. Unfortunately, too often the victim's compassion for the suspect comes back and bites them once the case has been adjudicated. For instance, we were assigned a case in which the victim was followed and harassed by a stalker, who unfortunately was also the estranged father of her child. The suspect is a diagnosed paranoid schizophrenic who refused to take his medication. We have also been told that he was a person that we refer to as a "bagger." This means he sprays or pours paint into a paper bag and snorts the fumes. This obviously caused a great deal of brain damage. Over the past two years the stalker has been arrested and convicted on numerous restraining order violations. Because our victim felt sorry for him and did not exhibit fear, we could not charge him with a felony. That all changed when the stalker, who, housed in the jail's mental ward, began writing our victim letters describing how he was going to find and secure her once he got out. The letters went on to discuss in great detail what he wanted to do to her sexually. The stalker said he could not stop thinking about what he "needed" to do to her in order for him to feel better. According to jail personnel, they could not force the stalker to take his medication, and they could not stop him from writing letters without a court order. Obviously, we are going to have to get one.

PRELIMINARY HEARING OR PROBABLE-CAUSE HEARING

In states such as California, the defense attorney often requests that a preliminary hearing take place in front of a judge. (Preliminary and probable-cause hearings are only conducted in felony cases.) This is supposed to be done in order to hear specific witnesses in the case testify and to ascertain if there is enough evidence to have the stalker "bound over" (held to answer) for a formal trial.* Too often, however, it seems to us that the defense counsel uses this hearing as a "fishing expedition" to see how well the victim and/or witnesses hold up on the stand and to develop a defense strategy based on their testimony. This puts undue stress on victims and possibly witnesses, as well as allows the stalker another chance to see the victim and attempt to exert emotional control over her.

---

* Even if the stalker is told by the judge that there is enough information to try him on the charges, the stalker still has a right to bail. This creates another problem for law enforcement, because he still needs to be monitored while he is out of custody, assuming he can make bail.

To expedite this preliminary hearing process, California passed Proposition 115, a law that allows the detective assigned to the case to interview the victim, all the officers involved in the investigation, and any number of witnesses to the case. The detective is then allowed to testify in the preliminary hearing on their behalf. The prosecuting attorney decides for whom the detective will have to testify in the preliminary hearing. Although it creates a tremendous burden on the detective (due to all the memorization and court preparation), it simplifies the hearing and eliminates the additional stress placed on the victim and other witnesses who might have to testify. We find Proposition 115 to be especially beneficial when dealing with stalking, domestic violence, and gang-related cases.

After the preliminary hearing has concluded, the judge makes a ruling on whether the stalker will be sent to superior court for trial. If the stalker is held over for trial, he can still plead guilty before the formal trial. It has been our experience on the cases we have worked and consulted on that either before or after the preliminary hearing, most stalkers plead guilty. In fact, many of these stalkers plead guilty to multiple felony charges. We feel that the reason the stalker decides to plead guilty to the charges he is facing reflects the way we investigate the cases. We do our best not to give the stalker a way out!

In other states, and in certain situations in California, a grand jury proceeding may take place. This process allows the victim and witnesses to testify without cross-examination from the defense counsel. Once the facts are heard, the grand jury either indicts or fails to indict the alleged stalker. If the stalker is indicted, the case usually goes directly to trial without a preliminary hearing. If the grand jury fails to issue an indictment, no arrest warrant is issued. That means we have to go back to the drawing board and work harder to obtain additional case evidence. When I was in Alabama testifying on a case, I found that they used the grand jury process frequently.

THE TRIAL

Pretrial conference. Again, if you are a victim of a stalking testifying in either a preliminary hearing or a trial, you should have a chance to speak directly with the prosecutor who is trying the case. All the prosecutors that we deal with conduct this victim interview as a standard operating procedure. This pretrial conference gives the victim and prosecutor a chance to make sure they are on the same page. This is not to say the prosecutor will coach you, but he will at least discuss what questions will be asked on the stand, so there are no surprises. If it is a stalking trial, the prosecutor hopefully has done his homework and is familiar with the stalking phenomenon. If you reside in a jurisdiction that takes the stalking problem seriously, it should prosecute the stalker vertically, meaning that (as we have discussed previously) a prosecutor is immediately assigned to the victim and the investigator in charge of the case. These individuals will then work with the victim throughout the entire trial process. In the past, I frequently instructed prosecuting attorneys on the why and wherefore of stalking. It is very important that these prosecutors are familiar with the stalking phenomenon before jumping into a case. This instruction also included how to successfully prosecute stalking cases. Over the past few years, with the advent of specialized stalking prosecutors housed in the office of the district attorney, those knowledgeable attorneys have taken on the mantle of being the stalking victim's champion. We cannot overemphasize that stalking cases are unique and need to be prosecuted by persons that understand their uniqueness.

What to wear. Think about what clothing to wear in the courtroom. You are the victim of a frustrating and often emotionally and physically debilitating crime. You must present a positive image to the jury. Dress in a professional manner. This may sound trivial, but the items of clothing you pick should make you feel good about yourself. The better you feel, the more confident and positive you will appear. Don't wear bright, flashy, or revealing clothing; you are not there to be the center of attention. You are there to tell the truth the best way you know how and look dignified when you accomplish that goal.

The courtroom. The layout of each courtroom is different, although there are some basic elements that are standard in most every courtroom. In the back of the room, there is usually a series of benches or chairs where onlookers are allowed to sit. This area is called the gallery. In front of the gallery is a rail with a gate, separating the gallery from the defendant (in this case, the alleged stalker), the defense counsel, the plaintiff (you), the prosecuting attorney, and the judge. You will be either sequestered in a separate room other than the courtroom or asked to sit somewhere outside of the courtroom. This is done so that you cannot hear other witnesses' testimony. The lead investigator in the case or a district attorney investigator will usually be sitting with the prosecutor at one table facing the judge, while the stalker and his attorney will be sitting at another. There will be a uniformed officer in the court, known as the bailiff. The bailiff's function is to maintain order in the court, and to keep an eye on the defendant. The judge will sit in an elevated structure at the head of the court, usually with a court clerk sitting to one side for assistance. The court clerk is there solely to assist the judge with duties such as keeping track of the court calendar or shuffling attorneys or law enforcement personnel back and forth from the judge's chambers. On the other side of the judge is the "witness box," where testimony is given. On the right or left side of the courtroom is the "jury box," where the members of the jury sit. Lastly, there will be an individual in the courtroom who will take notes on every word that is said, called the court reporter or court stenographer. This person may sit close to the witness box.

The swearing in. After the court is brought to order, and after everyone has been seated, either the court clerk or the bailiff will then ask you to stand at a place they indicate.* They will ask you to raise your right hand or place it on a Bible and will ask you to swear an oath to tell the truth. You will then be asked to state your name, spelling

---

* Many witness stands or boxes can be slightly elevated, so if you are called to testify, watch your step getting into one. We don't want you to get flustered from a fall just before you have to testify. I can attest to looking foolish after a slip.

portions of it for the record. The judge (or some other court official) will then tell you to have a seat in the witness box, which may be equipped with a microphone. Some of the newest courtrooms are now equipped with computers used by the court reporter to display testimony on a monitor directly in front of the judge, so he can visually follow your testimony. This will often preclude the judge's having to request a specific line of questioning read back by the court reporter. The court reporter can also quickly obtain a printed copy of what has been said, so, if need be, the copy of the transcript can go with the judge back into chambers for a review.

Direct examination. The prosecutor begins the trial by asking (you) a series of questions concerning the stalking incident(s). The answers given are known as direct testimony. Whenever you are asked a question (either by the prosecutor, the defense, or the judge), you should listen to the question in its entirety, think before speaking, then answer the question as clearly as possible. The hesitation that may ensue from thinking the question through completely ensures that you will give the best answer possible, and it allows the opposing counsel and the judge time to object to the question and make a ruling on the objection, if so desired. This happens frequently but is not an indication that the trial is going poorly. If you don't understand the question, say so. If you don't remember the answer to a question, you should say so and never guess. Guessing will only lead to trouble. Above all, you should always tell the truth. When the prosecutor asks questions, look directly at him, which will assist you in formulating your answers. When you do this, you will be better able to hear and understand what the prosecuter is asking without being distracted by the defendant, jurors, or others in the courtroom. As a point of information, those who are listed as witnesses for the defense and are asked questions by the defense are also giving direct testimony.

Cross-examination. After the prosecuting attorney is finished with his questions, the defense counsel gets a turn. It is the defense counsel's job to make sure none of his client's rights are violated, and to defend the client against the charges, if possible. Unfortunately, it is our opinion that too many defense attorneys attempt to liberate their clients by clouding the issues. This is accomplished by trying to put words in your mouth, back you into a corner, or make you look confused and unsure of yourself. This is usually done in an effort to sway the jury into wondering whether you are sure of the facts of the case. It may not be right, but perception plays a definite role in a trial setting. If the jury thinks you are lying or confused, it will cause problems for the prosecution. In all fairness, we do know defense attorneys who actually do what they are supposed to do, that is, defend their client in a true and just manner, but it has been our experience that these individuals are few and far between.

Rebuttal. After the defense has stopped asking questions, the judge will again ask the prosecutor if he has any additional questions for you. A good prosecutor can sense where you may have struggled under cross-examination, so he will attempt to clear up your responses by asking you additional questions. As we have previously indicated, you may also see a district attorney investigator or the actual detective assigned to your case sitting next to the prosecutor throughout the course of the trial. It is her task to assist the prosecutor in his line of questioning by answering questions and making suggestions via notes throughout the trial. These investigators can help formulate these rebuttal questions. After the prosecutor has taken his final turn, the judge will then ask the defense if she has any additional questions. When they have both stopped asking questions, the judge will dismiss you from the witness stand in one of two ways: either as subject to recall, meaning that you can leave, but need to be available for further testimony, or without being subject to recall. Even if you testify in a trial and have been dismissed without recall, don't be surprised if you get a phone call from the prosecutor or his investigator requesting that you return to court to answer some more questions. This usually occurs because the defense has had a witness testify that needs to be rebutted by your testimony. Once all witnesses have been heard, the attorneys will make closing arguments. Then the judge will explain to the jury their instructions. The case will then be sent to the jury for deliberation and hopefully a just finding, or verdict. The verdict can be one of guilty, not guilty, or in some cases, a hung jury, meaning the jury is hopelessly deadlocked on the issue and cannot make a finding. The judge can opt to send the jury back for further deliberations, but if the jury members still cannot come up with a guilty or not guilty verdict, the case is ruled a mistrial.

The prosecution can then refile the charges and set a date for a new trial. If the defendant is found guilty, his attorney can submit to the court for a hearing for a new trial or appeal the verdict to a higher court. Once the stalker is found guilty, two things can happen. If he is out of custody at the time of trial and is charged only with a misdemeanor crime, the judge can order that he post bail, or he can give him an OR (i.e., release him on his own recognizance), giving him a date to return for sentencing. (We prefer that the stalker not be allowed out of custody, but the law concerning bail is very strict. A person has the right to bail unless we can prove to a judge that he is a flight risk or a danger to society. It is difficult to get most judges to revoke bail on misdemeanor cases.) On the day the stalker returns to court for sentencing, a few events can take place. If jail is part of his sentence, the judge can order that he be taken into custody immediately, or he can give him a date in which the stalker is to report to the jail for incarceration. If the stalker is to be placed on probation, he is given a set period of time in which to report to his probation officer. If the stalker is convicted of felony stalking, he would remain in custody until such time he is to be sentenced. Now we have seen stalkers convicted of felony stalking remain in custody until they the day of sentencing, get credit for time served (CTS), and walk out of the courtroom on formal probation, without doing any additional time. If he is sentenced to state prison, he will remain in jail until transported to prison for the duration of his sentence. Once the stalker completes a prescribed portion of his sentence, he is eligible for parole. Should the parole board grant the stalker parole, then he would be released from prison and assigned to a parole officer. Some prison inmates, including some stalkers, opt to serve all their required time in prison and walk out on their day of release without any more time to be served or any parole agent to contend with.

If the defendant is found not guilty, he is free and not subject to being tried on the same charges again. However, if he *reoffends*, even against the same victim, the stalker is subject to arrest and prosecution on these new charges.

Courtroom etiquette. Obviously, if you yourself are the victim of a stalking crime, you are under a great deal of stress. Therefore it is understandable that during a trial, it may be impossible to keep those emotions bottled up. If you display some outburst of emotion (usually tears), the court will either take a break or wait a few moments for you to regain composure. Our only suggestion is to try not to let these emotions get the better of you. Find ways to keep them under control. That may mean not looking at the defendant or anyone else in the courtroom, for that matter, except the one asking the questions. By all means, we do recommend that you not glare at or otherwise gesture toward the suspect at any time. This includes not reacting (if at all possible) to the defendant if he decides to throw a fit or says something loud enough to his attorney that it causes you to become angered or hurt.

It is okay to look at the jury. During any sidebars (where the judge talks to both the prosecutor and the defense attorney) or any in-chamber meetings (where the judge and attorneys retire to the judge's chambers for a sometimes-heated discussion, possibly leaving you in the witness stand) you may look at the jury. However, you should not try to engage the bailiff or defendant in conversation. It is absolutely *forbidden* for you to talk to the jury (even outside the courtroom), unless otherwise instructed to do so by the judge or prosecutor. Whenever discussing the case with the prosecutor or investigator, you should make sure no jurors are within earshot; such conduct could easily result in a mistrial. Also, you should not talk to any other witnesses or other victims in the case while the trial is ongoing.

Mental competence hearing. Sometimes in a stalking trial or other trials involving defendants with questionable mental capabilities, the defense counsel will ask the judge for a hearing to determine if the defendant is mentally competent to stand trial. (Some of us in the business refer to this as "candling" the suspect. Candling means holding a candle up to one side of the subject's head and seeing if the light shines through on the other side.) If the subject is believed by the judge to be unfit to stand trial, the judge can send the suspect away for a mental evaluation. Once the evaluation is completed, the suspect may or may not be brought back for trial. This process can take several months. If the subject is not found to be fit for trial, then he is remanded to one of the state's psychiatric treatment facilities for a prescribed period of time (depending on the courts and statute laws pertaining to the crimes charged), for further evaluation and treatment. It has been our experience that most offenders that have been evaluated have returned some months later for trial. It is our opinion that for the state to keep an individual for a prolonged period of time, they would have to be severely mentally incapacitated. That is not to say, however, that the ones that are returned to stand trial, once convicted, would not go back into some type of treatment program.

This brings to mind one afternoon when we responded to a call by a young woman who was being followed by a man. When we contacted the woman, we found that this man had been following her from a Los Angeles County city for several blocks and had jumped onto a bus that took her to the east end of our city, where it dropped her off in her residential area. The woman had been able to flee the bus without incident but said the male had been staring at her as he sat somewhat hunched over in his seat. She said he was breathing hard and appeared to have his hands down in his lap throughout the bus ride. We canvassed the area of the bus stop and found the suspect, who had just broken into a residence in the area. There he had armed himself with a knife and had taken some items, which he had stuffed into his pockets. We arrested him for residential burglary, and transported him to our police department, placing him in a holding cell. The suspect acted strangely before being placed into the cell. When we went back to interview him, we found our boy masturbating and licking the jail house walls. We felt this was probably a fair indication that our suspect might have a few problems. The judge in the case sent him off for evaluation. Ninety days later, he came back certified as able to stand trial and was convicted on first-degree burglary. His prior arrest record showed that he was probably a sexual predator as well. I am always amazed at how the doctors in our state's criminal mental institutions can find these people fit to stand trial so quickly.

Periphery family court proceedings. We need to discuss family court proceedings for those stalking victims who have children and issues concerning custody. Again, each state is different in how its family courts operate. We have found the family court—the court that handles child custody and visitation issues—to have a direct bearing on DVS cases. A situation often arises where the left hand does not know what the right hand is doing. As we discussed in chapter 2 in the section dealing with the DVS, we have had many aggravated cases in which the male stalker continually grills his young children during visitation on what mommy is doing, where she goes, and whom she sees. The list of mental abuses on the children for the purpose of controlling the victim is often endless.

The family court policy may be to appoint an attorney for the children involved to protect their rights. The judge will many times appoint a psychologist to evaluate your children, you, and the stalker/father of the child.

We start having problems when the judge or commissioner begins granting some visitation rights to the stalker/father. This directly conflicts with what we in law enforcement are trying to stop. In one case the judge advised our female victim that she could not monitor or tape the children's phone calls with the stalker. The stalker had been using these phone opportunities to gather more information on the mother as well as to bash and degrade her while on the phone to his kids. We had been having her tape these conversations, but then had to tell her that she could tape only the conversations the stalker had directly with her. If you are a victim, you should be aware that this may occur. We suggest that you ask your district attorney or law enforcement professional to try to coordinate with the family court. We open a direct line of communication with the victim's custody attorney, who then keeps us up to date on all the family court issues. When she gives us a heads-up, we can then contact our prosecutor so that he may be able to intervene with the presiding family court judge. Still, at times we have found this to be a very difficult process.

CHAPTER 8 SUMMARY

- Arraignment—defendant pleads guilty or not guilty
- Discovery—defense gets all copies of evidence given to the district attorney; defense is also supposed to provide to the prosecution all information they have on the case as well; both defense and prosecution are supposed to provide any witness lists they might be using at trial
- Indicated sentence—a sentence a judge feels fits the facts of the case; presented to both defense and prosecution upon request prior to trial
- Preliminary hearing—held so that a judge can decide if there are enough facts to have the case sent over to superior court for trial
- The trial
  - Pretrial conference—meeting between victim, prosecutor, and sometimes detective prior to trial in order to go over facts of the case
  - What to wear—dress should be in a dignified manner
  - Courtroom
  - Swearing in
  - Direct examination—testimony given by the plaintiff to questions asked by the prosecutor if witness for the defense, testimony in response to questions asked by defense counsel
  - Cross-examination—usually questions asked of the plaintiff by defense counsel
  - Rebuttal—testimony given to questions after a cross-examination has been completed
  - Courtroom etiquette—conduct should be in a professional manner

CHAPTER 9

A REVIEW OF STALKING

N ow that we have this book, let's take some time to reflect on what we have covered. Prior to 1990, stalking existed but hadn't been labeled as such, and it wasn't considered a crime until California enacted the first stalking statute. The California legislature passed the law in 1990, and it went on the books in January 1991.

We now know that under the legal definition of stalking, which is a "course of conduct" crime, certain elements must be present. These include a period of the following of, and/or some type of harassment or threatening behavior toward, the victim. These types of behavior have to amount to a "credible threat." There also has to be some type of damage or injury to the victim in the form of either physical or emotional trauma. All fifty states have antistalking statutes. Many of these statutes are similar in definition but not in the penalty that is meted out. A growing number of these states' statutes include the stalking of significant others or immediate family members of the victim as persons who can also be victims of the harassment.

We now know that over one million women and at least 370,000 men are stalked annually in the United States. We know that the authors of the study that calculated these figures also estimated that about 1 out of every 12 women and 1 out of every 45 men will be stalked at some point in their lives. Over half the women stalked are stalked by an intimate partner, spouse, or boyfriend. Most men are stalked by acquaintances rather than by previous intimate partners.

Stalking has become so prevalent that experts have begun to classify stalkers into categories or typologies. For our purposes, we have learned that there are maybe as many as twelve different typologies that have been developed to classify stalkers. We classify them as domestic violence stalkers (DVS), acquaintance stalkers (AS), and stranger stalkers (SS). The largest category of stalkers is born out of domestic violence situations. Studies have shown that about 90 percent of all women killed in a domestic violence situation are stalked first. The most dangerous time for a woman in a domestic violence situation is when they leave or attempt to leave the batterer, who then becomes the stalker.

Most stalkers have stalked multiple victims, or "targets." Our experience with the stalker has shown us that there is usually one specific victim that the male stalker and sometimes the female stalker seems to return to after he or she has finished stalking another victim. We have referred to this victim as the genesis victim (GV).

The majority of stalkers suffer from personality disorders such as histrionic, borderline, or antisocial disorders. Even though these stalkers have disorders that can be diagnosed, they are still perfectly aware of what they are doing when they are doing it. They are also culpable for their acts. Some others have mental conditions such as paranoid schizophrenia, and they can suffer from psychotic episodes. It may be debated in court whether those in this latter group were cognizant of their actions at the time the stalking behavior took place. After profiling the populations of stalkers we have investigated or conferred on, our findings have shown that many of these stalkers were either physically or psychologically abused while growing up. Still, this by no means justifies or excuses their behavior.

Stalkers utilize specific tools while plying their trade. They may start out with greeting cards and gifts, but when those fail, they revert to harassment techniques such as vandalism, burglary or trophy collection, and/or surveillance, as well as constant and unwanted communication.

You can take measures to avoid the stalker and his overtures. These include saying "no" emphatically; pumping up your "sixth sense," or perceptive powers; and monitoring what you and your children do or say on the Internet. Common sense is the foundation of any of the strategies one uses when dealing with a potential stalker.

Being stalked is not the end of the world. We have shown that overcoming the difficulty of being stalked requires a step-by-step process. First comes documentation of everything the stalker gives or leaves behind; without detailed documentation, no successful prosecution will take place. Next comes law enforcement notification and cooperation. If you don't get it initially, keep on trying—you can't be timid, and you have to make your presence known. Finally, prosecution for anything the stalker does, no matter how minuscule, is a must for building that wall of separation between you and your stalker. Remember, many stalkers are serial in nature, and you need to nail them every chance you get.

Reducing your security risks is a good idea even if you don't believe you are being stalked. However, if you are being stalked, you can take some special measures to reduce your risk. These include family notification, special child security options, and the use of private mail boxes, not to mention, as we discussed, an entire array of security devices that you can easily install in both your home and vehicle. We've touched upon procedures such as varying your route home, vehicle inspection, and what you should do to reduce problems in your workplace environment. We also covered the types of safes you can buy and how to build a safe room in your house or apartment.

Another group of tools that we described are those classified as legal remedies. Restraining orders, emergency protective orders, and criminal stay-away orders are all weapons in your state's legal arsenal that you may want to or have to use when dealing with a stalker. These remedies also include federal legislation found in the "full faith and credit" portion of the 1994 Violence Against Women Act, which allows you to have your protective order enforced from state to state. This legislation covers you even if that order was not issued in the state in which the subject is currently following, harassing, or stalking you.

Because of many victims' fears and misunderstandings of the judicial system, we have taken the reader through a step-by-step outline of what to expect in a stalking trial, in which the trial process is covered from the arraignment of the stalker to the final disposition. How to act, where you might sit, and who cross-examines whom are all covered. This hopefully will reduce the stress if and when anyone who reads this book actually has to go to trial as a victim, witness, or juror.

It has been our intention from the very start to inform and enlighten you, as well as to show you that there really are people like that out there. In short, we hope we have described the stalking phenomenon well enough for you, the reader, to make informed decisions, should you ever have the misfortune of being stalked.

AFTERWORD

We hope you have learned enough to get started dealing with whatever caused you to be interested in this particular subject. If you are one of those who are in fact being stalked, we especially hope this tool has given you a handle on the steps necessary to begin alleviating your problem. We in law enforcement would all like to give these predators an overdose of "Preparation P"—Prison. But until that happens, good luck, and don't despair—we are currently writing a text for law enforcement personnel on how to identify and case-manage these creatures. We believe that the more men and women in uniform who get on board the "S.S. Antistalker," the greater your chance of not becoming a victim of one of these insidious criminals. You've heard the old saying "seek and ye shall find." So if you don't find assistance on the first go around, keep on seeking, and you'll eventually find that person in law enforcement who will help you. I have met a lot of good cops, district attorneys, judges, and social workers in my travels; they are all there to help the victim, so hang onto hope, and start applying the information this book has given you.

LAW ENFORCEMENT AND LEGAL PROFESSIONALS

CONTACTS INVOLVED IN THE ISSUES OF STALKING

The following individuals have been on the forefront of the stalking issue. We worked with these individuals when the investigation and prosecution of stalking crimes was still in its infancy stages. They have agreed to be listed in this text as a resource.

Gregory S. Boles retired in September of 2000 after years of being the investigator in charge of the Los Angeles Police Department's Threat Management Unit. (This unit handles high-profile cases such as media personalities and well-positioned public figures.) Boles is now the director of global threat management for one of the largest international private threat management and risk consulting firms in the world, Kroll, Inc. Boles is not only a very knowledgeable individual in the field of stalking and threat management but extremely conscientious as well. He is currently the national president of the Association of Threat Assessment Professionals (ATAP). He has appeared on shows such as *Good Morning America* to promote stalking and threat assessment issues and has testified as an expert on stalking cases both inside and outside of his jurisdiction. He is the global director of

Kroll's threat management practice (more information available on-line at www.krollworldwide.com).

Ray Bray, M.P.A., is a bureau chief with the California Commission on Peace Officer Standards and Training. He manages the Training Program Services Bureau, the research and development arm of this commission. Bray served with the Concord and El Cerrito Police Departments prior to his current position. He has had lengthy experience in law enforcement management training, having developed over three hundred training courses including the Violence Against Women Act (VAWA) grant program for California law enforcement. He has lectured at the FBI academy as well as numerous colleges and universities. He has held an associate professorship at Sacramento State University and the University of Kentucky at Louisville. Bray directed the California Crime Prevention Institute, the California Institute of Criminal Investigation, and the Department of Justice Advanced Training center. He holds a Bachelor of Arts in criminal justice and a master's degree in political science as well as one in public administration. Bray was responsible for assembling consultants to design a two-hour stalking telecourse designed to train law enforcement personnel on how to investigate stalking cases. The resulting video has assisted law enforcement personnel and prosecutors in better understanding the stalking phenomenon. His team completed a revised stalking training telecourse in 2001. Bray can be contacted at:

> Commission on POST
> 1601 Alhambra Blvd.
> Sacramento, CA 95863

John C. Lane Jr., M.P.A., developed, as a lieutenant, the Los Angeles Police Department's Threat Management Unit (TMU). This unit was the first of its kind and was designed to vertically manage high-risk offenders that stalked high-profile media and public figures in addition to ordinary citizens. It has been the model for many other units created to do the same in other agencies throughout the nation. Lane is the founder the Association of Threat Assessment Professionals (ATAP) and remains an expert in stalking, workplace violence, and corporate security. In 1997 he retired from the LAPD and is now one of the principals of the Omega Threat Management Group, Inc., which can be contacted at:

> 1801 Avenue of the Stars, Ste 1101
> Los Angeles, CA 90067
> (310) 551-0007
> Fax: (310) 551-2671
> E-mail: omegatmg@aol.com

The Omega Threat Management Group is involved in managing workplace violence issues, stalking in the private sector, and protection and threat management for individuals involved in the media spotlight.

Another resource we feel is crucial in the fight against terror, threats, and stalking, is ATAP, an organization mentioned above. If you are a threat assessment professional in the private sector or law enforcement, or are a mental health professional, this is an organization that you should consider joining. We have found the annual conference, held at the Disneyland Hotel in Anaheim, California, to be extremely informative and helpful for all those professions previously listed. This conference, and the networking that results as a by-product, is an invaluable tool in better understanding the elements of threat assessment, thus allowing you to do a better job. You can get further information on the conference and membership by going to the Omega Threat Management Group's Web site, available on-line at www.omegatmg.com.

This is the portion of the book where I give out the information on my shingle:

Detective Mike Proctor
Westminster Police Department, Family Protection Unit
8200 Westminster Blvd.
Westminster, CA 92683

Mailing under:

> Duck Works Criminal Consulting (PMB)
> 31441 Santa Margarita Pkwy, Ste A-347
> Rancho Santa Margarita, CA 92688

(Detective Proctor's literary agents are Ashley and Carolyn Grayson of the Ashley Grayson Literary Agency, (310) 514-0267.)

Los Angeles County Deputy District Attorney Rhonda B. Saunders is in charge of the Stalking Threat Assessment Team (STAT), which she established in 1997. She has greatly assisted the California legislature in amending the antistalking law for the positive on several occasions. Saunders is an internationally recognized consultant and lecturer in the areas of stalking, workplace violence, and criminal threats. She is currently a member of the training faculty of the United States Secret Service National Threat Assessment Center in Washington, DC. Saunders has appeared on many programs to promote issues in regard to stalking. Rhonda has handled several high-profile celebrity stalking cases including the stalkers of Madonna, producer/director Steven Spielberg, and Gwyneth Paltrow. Saunders is currently the president of the Los Angeles chapter of ATAP and can be contacted at:

> Los Angeles County District Attorney's Office
> 6230 Sylmar Ave., Room 201
> Van Nuys, CA 91401

Orange County Deputy District Attorney Jane Shade is currently the assistant department counsel for the Department of Child Support Services of Orange County. She has also served as the senior deputy district attorney assigned to the Orange County Family Support Division; the supervisor of the felony and misdemeanor operations of the North Justice Center, housed in Fullerton, California; and the supervising deputy district attorney for the Orange County Family Violence Unit, which she was instrumental in creating.

Besides having her Juris Doctor, Shade has a master's degree in political science and is responsible for published cases, primarily *People* v. *Carter*, 60 Cal. App. 4th 752 (1998), concerning the enhancement of great bodily injury in a domestic violence-related case. Shade's other professional activities and achievements include serving on the Orange County Bar Association Judiciary Committee, the State Bar of California Resolutions Committee, and the Orange County Court Referral Committee, as well as being named Attorney of the Year for the Orange County Women Lawyers Association. She also formed the Domestic Violence Investigator's Group for Orange County prosecutors and law enforcement personnel and served as the chairperson for the California District Attorney's Association Committee on Domestic Violence. Shade has taught numerous classes and seminars on both domestic violence and stalking prosecution, and is one of the leaders in the prosecution of elder abuse cases. She developed one of the first general instructional videos on stalking and was one of the subject matter experts on the most current (2000) POST training video on the crime of stalking. Shade currently serves on the board of directors for the Orange County Women's Transitional Living Center. She is an excellent prosecutor and has a wealth of information on how to prosecute and manage stalking cases. She can be reached at:

> Department of Child Support Services
> 1055 N. Main St.
> Santa Ana, CA 92701

San Diego Assistant City Attorney Gael B. Strack is another long-term pioneer involved in the prosecution of child abuse, domestic violence, and stalking for the City of San Diego. She is currently the assistant city attorney for the criminal division handling domestic violence and special projects. Her previous positions have been as head deputy attorney for the Child Abuse and Domestic Violence Unit, head appellate attorney for the criminal division, and the supervising attorney in the Child Abuse and Domestic Violence Unit. Strack has published articles on the prosecutions of manual strangulation cases in which she is a well-known expert. She has received numerous honors and awards in her work in the field of domestic violence. Since 1994 she has instructed at over 175 venues throughout the United States, lecturing on workplace violence, domestic violence, and stalking. Gael has been involved in the development of both of the California POST stalking investigation telecourses. We have had the pleasure of lecturing at some of the same conferences with Ms. Strack, and we have found her to have a wealth of information on any topic she is presenting. She can be reached at:

> San Diego City Attorney's Office
> 1200 Third Ave., Ste 700
> San Diego, CA 92101
> E-mail: gbs@cityatty.sonnet.gov

San Diego Deputy District Attorney Kerry Wells has been a prosecutor in San Diego for the past twenty years after graduating magna cum laude from the Whittier College School of Law. She was one of the original attorneys assigned to prosecute child abuse cases when the district attorney's office first established a Child Abuse Unit in 1985. In 1989 Wells was chosen to become the first chief of the newly established Domestic Violence Unit. Under her direction this unit became the largest specialized domestic violence unit in the state and developed pioneering protocols for the prosecution of domestic violence that have been nationally recognized.

Ms. Wells has lectured extensively throughout the state and the nation on the subjects of domestic violence, child abuse, stalking, and trial tactics. She is probably best known for the prosecution of Elizabeth Broderick, who murdered her ex-husband and his wife after stalking them for several years. The Broderick case received international attention and was one of the first cases to be covered live, gavel to gavel, by Court TV. It was the Broderick case that led to Ms. Wells's interest in the much-neglected and misunderstood crime of stalking.

In 1994 Wells established the Stalking Strike Force of San Diego County, the first such task force of its kind in the country. The Strike

Force has as its goals increased education and awareness of the crime of stalking and an improved multidisciplinary response to stalking behavior. San Diego's unique and aggressive approach to handling stalking cases under Wells's leadership has received international attention and has been recognized as a national model in a report by the National Institute of Justice. The Stalking Case Assessment Team, which targets particularly difficult and dangerous cases, has been featured in numerous news articles both here and abroad, and it recently won the Governor's Victims Services Award for "outstanding services in advancing victims' rights." Wells has had the honor of lecturing on stalking at Scotland Yard to law enforcement officers from throughout the United Kingdom and recently was the featured lecturer to Mongolian prosecutors and judges in Ulaanbaatar, Mongolia.

Wells is also recognized as an expert in cyberstalking and has consulted with the United States Department of Justice and former Vice President Al Gore on the first federal report on the subject. She has written numerous articles on the investigation and prosecution of stalking and threat cases, teaches at the San Diego Police Academy on the subject, and wrote the first law enforcement training manual on stalking. Until recently, she was the chief of the San Diego District Attorney's Office, South Bay Division, but has since been appointed superior court judge.

FORENSIC PSYCHOLOGISTS

Since there is a growing need in both law enforcement and the private sector for good forensic psychologists, we decided to include a couple of contact names. We know these individuals and feel they have a great deal of expertise in both the threat assessment and stalking fields.

Michael A. Zona, M.D., is a threat management expert who recently completed a two-year fellowship at the University of California's Institute of Psychiatry, Law, and Behavioral Science in the capacity of

Senior Fellow and clinical instructor. Dr. Zona has a done a great deal of research in the threat management field, especially in the area of stalking and obsessional behaviors. He worked for several years with the Los Angeles Police Department's Threat Management Unit, assisting both in the training of the unit's investigators as well as consulting on many of their cases. His stalker typology has been recognized and adopted by various state, federal, and corporate entities. Dr. Zona is a nationally recognized speaker who is board certified in psychiatry and neurology as well as geriatric psychiatry and forensic psychiatry. He is currently a principal in the Omega Threat Management Group, where he can be contacted at:

> 1801 Avenue of the Stars, Ste 1101
> Los Angeles, CA 90067
> (310) 551-0007
> Fax: (310) 551-2671

J. Reid Meloy, Ph.D., is a diplomate in forensic psychology of the American Board of Professional Psychology. He is the former chief of the Forensic Mental Health Division for San Diego County and now devotes his time to a private civil and criminal forensic practice, as well as research, writing, and teaching. He is an associate clinical professor of psychiatry at the University of California San Diego School of Medicine and an adjunct professor at the University of San Diego School of Law. He is also a Fellow of the American Academy of Forensic Sciences, and is past president of the American Academy of Forensic Psychology. In 1992 he received the Distinguished Contribution to Psychology as a Profession Award from the California Psychological Association; in 1998 he received the first National Achievement Award from the Association of Threat Assessment Professionals; and in 2000 his stalking book received honorable mention for the Manfred Guttmacher Award, given by the American Psychiatric Association. He is also president of Forensis, Inc., a nonprofit, public-benefit corporation devoted to forensic psychiatric and psychological research (available on-line at www.forensics.org). Dr. Meloy has authored or co-authored over 140 papers published in peer-reviewed psychiatric and psychological journals, and he has written or edited seven books: *The Psychopathic Mind* (1988), *Violent Attachments* (1992), *Rorschach Assessment of Aggressive and Psychopathic Personalities* with Dr. Carl Gacono (1994), *Contemporary Rorschach Interpretation* (1997), *The Psychology of Stalking: Clinical and Forensic Perspectives* (1998), *Violence Risk and Threat Assessment* (2000), and *The Mark of Cain* (2001). He is a sought-after speaker and psychological consultant on various civil and criminal cases throughout the United States, including the Madonna, Gwyneth Paltrow, and Martina Hingis stalking cases, the Polly Klaas murder case, and the Oklahoma City bombing cases. He is also a consultant to various law enforcement and intelligence agencies. He can be reached by e-mail at jrmeloy@san.rr.com or at the following mailing address:

> J. Reid Meloy, Ph.D., A.B.P.P.
> Forensic Psychology
> P.O. Box 90699
> San Diego, CA 92109

Kris Mohandie, Ph.D., is a police psychologist with over a dozen years of experience in the assessment and management of violent behavior. He has worked in field responses and case investigations for local, state, and federal law enforcement organizations including the Los Angeles Police Department's Threat Management Unit. He responded on-scene to the O. J. Simpson barricade in 1994 and the North Hollywood bank robber shootout in 1997. Dr. Mohandie assisted in the Los Angeles County District Attorney's prosecution of Steven Spielberg's stalker as well in 1997. He regularly consults on stalking and threat cases in both the private and public sector. Dr. Mohandie has conducted extensive trial-pending and prison interviews of violent offenders, including those of a number of notorious stalkers. Most recently, he developed and implemented a model school violence threat management training program for the Los Angeles City and County School Districts, a program being taught throughout the United States as well as Canada. His new book, *School Violence Threat Management: A Practical Guide for Educators, Law Enforcement, and Mental Health Professionals,* was released in November 2000 and is now in its second printing. Dr. Mohandie's work has been featured in the *Los Angeles Times, USA Today,* on the entertainment network *E!,* and in various network news programs. He can be reached by e-mail at mohandie@mail.earthlink.net.

As we have alluded to before, we are quite aware that since the inception of California's stalking law, several other law enforcement agencies have begun to take stalking and threat management much more seriously. We are also aware that more and more professionals from the fields of medicine and psychology have taken up the banner of stalking and threat management. Many have formed consulting companies and are performing a needed service throughout law enforcement and the private sector as well. Our hats go off to those individuals. The people listed in this appendix are some of the people that have we have associated with over the years. They represent a tremendous amount of expertise in the areas of stalking and threat assessment. Their contributions to the pool of knowledge in both of these areas has been significant.

APPENDIX B

SUGGESTED OTHER READINGS AND WEB SITES ON STALKING

W hen we first started investigating stalkers in the early 1990s, there was not a great deal of information written on the stalking phenomenon. In the past five years there has been a great deal of forensic research being done on this issue. A quick search of the Internet will reveal a growing number of journal articles and papers on the subject of stalking, primarily in the United States, Great Britain, Australia, and now Canada. There is also a growing number of books dealing with the various aspects of stalking. We have listed a few Web sites and books in this section. If you are as interested in the topic of stalking as we are, then it is imperative that you get out and gather as much information on the subject as you can. These listings should get you started in the right direction.

Douglas, John et al. *Obsession.* Pocket Books, 1998. Douglas is one of the founders of the FBI's Behavioral Science Unit. This work profiles stalkers, killers, rapists, and their victims.

Meloy, J. Reid, ed. *The Psychology of Stalking: Clinical and Forensic Perspectives.* San Diego, Calif.: Academic Press, 1998. We feel this is one of the better-edited books on the scientific approach to stalking. Dr. Meloy has written a great deal on the "obsessional follower" and other topics that are associated with stalking. His works can be found listed on the Internet and are well worth reading.

Mullen, Paul, Michele Pathe, and Rosemary Purcell. *Stalkers and Their Victims*. Cambridge: Cambridge University Press, 2000. This is another well-written book developed by researchers in the area of stalking and its associated behavior.

Sullivan, Mike. *Safety Monitor: How to Protect Your Kids Online*. Chicago: Bonus Books, 2002. This is a book on Internet safety tips. Detective Sullivan has appeared on *The Oprah Winfrey Show* to discuss cyberstalking, including many of the tips and techniques presented in his book.

We feel that one of the best Web sites on stalking as well as other victim topics belongs to the National Center for Victims of Crime, available at www.ncvc.org. There are many other Web sites relevant to the topic of stalking. Here are just a few more:

- National Domestic Violence Hotline: www.ndvh.org. Additionally, they have a toll-free number—1-800-799-7233—which should get you in touch with a domestic violence group in your area.
- National Coalition Against Domestic Violence: www. ncadv.org.
- National Violence Against Women Prevention Research Center: www.wcwonline.org/violenceprev/index.html.
- Victims For Justice Coalition Stalker Information Page: www.wincom.net/vfj/vfjstalk.htm. This group is housed in Canada and handles not only stalking but a variety of other criminal justice information. Phone/fax: (519) 972-0836.
- If you want a copy of the Violence Against Women Act you can call the Department of Justice Information Center at 1-800-421-6770.
- Office of Violence Against Women: www.ojp.usdoj.gov/vawo/.
- Specialized Training Services: www.specializedtraining.com. Additionally, they have a toll-free number, 1-800-848-1226. This company has several books as well as video- and audio-

tapes available on stalking, workplace violence, threat assessment, sexual offenders, and other related topics. Most of their offerings are by authors in the field of psychology. They also arrange for speakers on the various topics just listed.

NOTES

CHAPTER 2: TYPES OF STALKERS AND WHY THEY STALK

1. Patricia Tjaden and Nancy Thoennes, *Stalking in America: Findings from the National Violence Against Women Survey* (Washington, D.C.: U.S. Department of Justice, National Institute of Justice, and Centers for Disease Control and Prevention, 1998).

2. Bonnie S. Fisher, Francis T. Cullen, and Michael G. Turner, *The Sexual Victimization of College Women*, NCJ 182369 (Washington, D.C.: U.S. Department of Justice, 2000).

3. Tracey Budd, facsimile to author, October 24, 2002. The *BLS* itself is listed in the bibliography.

4. Michael A. Zona, Russell E. Palarea, and John C. Lane Jr., "Psychiatric Diagnosis and the Offender-Victim Typology of Stalking," chap. 4 in *The Psychology of Stalking: Clinical and Forensic Perspectives* (San Diego, Calif.: Academic Press, 1998), p. 76.

5. Ibid., p. 77.

6. Ibid., p. 78.

7. Ibid., p. 79.

8. J. Reid Meloy, Beth Davis, and John L. Lovette, "Risk Factors for Violence among Stalkers," *Journal of Threat Assessment* 1, no. 1 (2001):11. I discussed this research with Dr. Meloy before the study was published.

9. James Alan Fox, *Trends in Juvenile Violence: A Report to the United*

States Attorney General on Current and Future Rates of Juvenile Offending. U.S. Department of Justice, Office of Justice Programs [on-line], www.ojp.usdoj.gov/bjs/pub/pdf/tjvfox.pdf [March 1996].

10. Craig A. Perkins, *Age Patterns of Victims of Serious Violent Crime: A Bureau of Justice Statistics Special Report*, NCJ 162031, U.S. Department of Justice, Office of Justice Programs [on-line], www.ojp.usdoj.gov/bjs/pub/pdf/apvsvc.pdf. [July 1997].

11. Raymond J. Corisini, *The Dictionary of Psychology* (Philadephia: Brunner/Mazel, 1999), pp. 788–89.

12. Ibid., p. 865.

13. Ibid., p. 857.

14. Otto F. Kernberg, *Aggression in Personality Disorders and Perversions* (New Haven and London: Yale University Press, 1992), p. 39.

15. Ibid., p. 38.

16. Ibid., p. 41.

17. *Diagnostic and Statistical Manual of Mental Disorders (Text Revision)*, 4th ed. [*DSM-IV-TR*] (Washington, D.C.: American Psychiatric Assocition, 2000), p. 457.

18. Corisini, *The Dictionary of Psychology*, p. 57.

19. *DSM-IV-TR*, p. 714.

20. Ibid., p. 717.

21. Ibid., p. 710.

CHAPTER 4: LIMITING YOUR STALKING EXPOSURE

1. Mike Sullivan, information provided on an airing of *The Oprah Winfrey Show* titled "Child Stalkers Online," television broadcast, April 17, 2002.

2. David Finkelhor, Kimberly Mitchell, and Janis Wolak, *Online Victimization: A Report on the Nation's Youth*, National Center for Missing and Exploited Children [on-line], www.ncmec.org/en_US/publications/NC62.pdf [June 2000].

CHAPTER 5: WHAT TO DO IF YOU BELIEVE YOU ARE BEING STALKED

1. Michele Pathe and Paul Mullen, "The Impact of Stalkers on Their Victims," *British Journal of Psychiatry* 170 (1997):12–17.

2. Michael Proctor, "Stalking: A Behavioral Overview with Case Management Suggestions," *Journal of California Law Enforcement* 29, no. 3 (1995):63–69.

CHAPTER 6: REDUCING SECURITY RISKS

1. Kenneth A. Hanfland, Robert D. Keppel, and Joseph G. Weis, *Case Management for Missing Children Homicide Investigation* (Olympia, Wash.: Office of the Attorney General, State of Washington, and U.S. Department of Justice, Office of Justice Programs, Office of Juvenile Justice and Delinquency Prevention, 1997).

2. Ronet Bachman, *Violence and Theft in the Workplace* (Washington, D.C.: U.S. Department of Justice, Bureau of Justice Statistics, 1994).

3. *Violence in the Workplace: Risk Factors and Prevention Strategies*, Department of Health and Human Services, National Institute for Occupational Safety and Health publication 96-100 (1997), p. 7.

4. Ibid., p. 4.

CHAPTER 7: LEGAL REMEDIES

1. *Enforcement of Protective Orders*, U.S. Dept. of Justice, Office of Justice Programs, Office for Victims of Crime, Legal Series Bulletin 4 [on-line], www.ojp.usdoj.gov/ovc/publications/bulletins/legalseries/bulletin4 [2002].

2. Ibid., p. 4.

3. Laws mentioned cited in *Enforcement of Protective Orders*, pp. 2–3.

4. *Enforcement of Protective Orders*, p. 2.

5. Ibid., p. 3.

6. Ibid., p. 8.

CHAPTER 8: A STALKING TRIAL—WHAT TO EXPECT

1. *Prosecutors in State Courts 2001*, NCJ 193441, U.S. Department of Justice, Office of Justice Programs, Bureau of Justice Statistics Bulletin [online], www.ojp.usdoj.gov/bjs/pub/pdf/psc01.pdf [May 2002].

BIBLIOGRAPHY

Bachman, Ronet. *Violence and Theft in the Workplace*. Washington, D.C.: U.S. Department of Justice, Bureau of Justice Statistics, 1994.

Budd, Tracey, and Joanna Mattinson. *Stalking: Findings from the 1998 British Crime Survey*. Home Office Research, Development and Statistics Directorate Research Findings 129. London: Home Office, 2000.

Corisini, Raymond J. *The Dictionary of Psychology*. Philadelphia: Brunner/Mazel, 1999.

Diagnostic and Statistical Manual of Mental Disorders (Text Revision). 4th ed. [*DSM-IV-TR*]. Washington, D.C.: American Psychiatric Association, 1994.

Enforcement of Protective Orders. U.S. Department of Justice, Office of Justice Programs, Office for Victims of Crime, Legal Series Bulletin 4 [on-line]. www.ojp.usdoj.gov/ovc/publications/bulletins/legalseries/bulletin4 [2002].

Finkelhor, David, Kimberly Mitchell, and Janis Wolak. *Online Victimization: A Report on the Nation's Youth*. National Center for Missing and Exploited Children [on-line]. www.ncmec.org/en_US/publications/NC62.pdf [June 2000].

Fisher, Bonnie S., Francis T. Cullen, and Michael G. Turner. *The Sexual Victimization of College Women*. NCJ 182369. Washington, D.C.: U.S.

Department of Justice, Office of Justice Programs, National Institute of Justice, 2000.

Fox, James Alan. *Trends in Juvenile Violence: A Report to the United States Attorney General on Current and Future Rates of Juvenile Offending.* U.S. Department of Justice, Office of Justice Programs [on-line]. www.ojp.usdoj.gov/bjs/pub/pdf/tjvfox.pdf [March 1996].

Hanfland, Kenneth A., Robert D. Keppel, and Joseph G. Weis. *Case Management for Missing Children Homicide Investigation.* Olympia, Wash.: Office of the Attorney General, State of Washington, and U.S. Department of Justice, Office of Justice Programs, Office of Juvenile Justice and Delinquency Prevention, 1997.

Kernberg, Otto F. *Aggression in Personality Disorders and Perversions.* New Haven and London: Yale University Press, 1992.

Meloy, J. Reid, Beth David, and John L. Lovette. "Risk Factors for Violence among Stalkers." *Journal of Threat Assessment* 1, no. 1 (2001):3–16.

Pathe, Michele, and Paul Mullen. "The Impact of Stalkers on Their Victims." *British Journal of Psychiatry* 170 (1997):12–17.

Proctor, Michael G. "Stalking: A Behavioral Overview with Case Management Suggestions." *Journal of California Law Enforcement* 29, no. 3 (1995):63–69.

Prosecutors in State Courts, 2001. NCJ 193441. U.S. Department of Justice, Office of Justice Programs, Bureau of Justice Statistics [on-line]. www.ojp.usdoj.gov/bjs/pub/pdf/psc01.pdf [May 2002].

Sullivan, Mike. Information provided on an airing of *The Oprah Winfrey Show* titled "Child Stalkers Online." Television broadcast, April 17, 2002.

Tjaden, Patricia, and Nancy Thoennes. *Stalking in America: Findings from the National Violence against Women Survey.* Washington, D.C.: U.S. Department of Justice, National Institute of Justice, and Centers for Disease Control and Prevention, 1998.

Violence in the Workplace: Risk Factors and Prevention Strategies. Department of Health and Human Services, National Institute for Occupational Safety and Health Publication 96-100, 1997.

INDEX